CHARLES WECHSLER

LAND OF THE INLAND SEAS

These pages:

*Early morning sunlight bathes these rocky
sentinels at Sinclair Cove, Lake Superior,
a part of Provincial Park, Ontario, Canada.*
TOM ALGIRE

Pages 4 and 5:
*Goat Island separates the American from
Horseshoe Fall, main attractions of the mighty
Niagara, greatest wonder of the Great Lakes.*
ED COOPER

Pages 6 and 7:
*An autumn cathedral: Hardwood forests sequester
this country lane in Lincoln County, Wisconsin.*
TOM ALGIRE

Pages 8 and 9:
*Built over a century ago, the Eagle Harbor
lighthouse in Michigan remains as a warning
of danger along the south shore of Lake Superior.*
TOM ALGIRE

LAND OF THE INLAND SEAS

The Historic and Beautiful Great Lakes Country

by William Donohue Ellis

GREAT WEST SERIES

AMERICAN WEST PUBLISHING COMPANY
PALO ALTO · CALIFORNIA

RONALD MORREIM

A crystalline spray diffuses the winter sun near Grand Marais, Minnesota.

Special Consultants

Frank F. Hooper
Chairman, Resource Ecology Program
University of Michigan

Jack L. Hough, Ph.D.
Department of Oceanic & Atmospheric Science
University of Michigan

Richard J. Wright, Ph.D.
Director of Archives
Northwest Ohio–Great Lakes Research Center
Bowling Green State University

Other Books in the GREAT WEST SERIES

FIRST EDITION

Library of Congress Card Number 73-90798   ISBN #0-910118-47-7

CONTENTS

PREFACE

Lake effect is the meteorologist's phrase for the special violence of Great Lakes fall storms. Ninety-five thousand square miles of water slowly build up and store heat energy all summer, then when fall polar air drifts in and absorbs that heat, it explodes upward, replaced by a cold, driving wind. A lake effect similarly characterizes the history, environment, economics, and culture of Great Lakes America. Rich resources built up slowly for ages until viewed by the cold eye of European mercantilism which triggered a kinetic reaction.

Gunpowder mixed with melted snow was the ink for that first regional record, which, unlike most other stories in the world, began being recorded very near its beginning. The Jesuit priests—on the cutting edge of white exploration—painfully but regularly scrawled the daily westward record in reports that were published in France as the seventy-two annual volumes of *Jesuit Relations*.

That record was one of young men aging fast in a cold country where white-water rapids dumped priests, Indians, and fur men against rocks; where a thick blanket of snow drove men to eat their moccasins; where aroused Indians tracked and tortured intruders.

The Jesuits wrote of beauty, too, amid the resinous fragrance of forests so thick they held a piece of the night all day. But violence dominated the record as the Europeans pressed inland for the beaver in an aggressive fur trade. The French fur men pushed their forts and posts west so fast that they were at Sault Ste. Marie before the English to the south had established Philadelphia. The English woke to the French advantage in strategy and in fur, and the wars began in earnest.

The fur exploitation was followed by territorial wars. Then, as much of the region came under the flag of the new United States, it saw in rapid succession assault on the forests, the settlement of the plains, and the development of the wheat navy. Ensuing waves of settlement came for iron ore, railroad rights-of-way, labor, profit, and glory, and a more benign violence set in—that competitive vigor sponsored by cold climate, rich resources, and progress. Great Lakes country became America's industrial-commercial heartland. This great weight of population and concrete stressed the sweet inland seas and forests to the point that the great-grandson of a forester may now have to send fifty miles for a tree for his yard and water for his table.

Today, with the shrewdness of an aging fighter, the embattled region is husbanding its advantages, moderating its demands on the waters, restoring them, and preserving vast tracts of the wild. The Herriott map of 1650 shows Lakes Superior and Michigan open-ended, indicating their final bounds were unknown. This book also is open-ended, because a new era of exploration and settlement has begun. Some of the new explorers are moving into the remote areas of Minnesota, Wisconsin, Upper Michigan, and Ontario, putting commercial opportunity second to living in the wild. Other thousands, on the other hand, are moving from exurban areas back to the central city. Canadians are moving to the United States. Specific groups of Great Lakes Americans are moving to Canada, for the same kinds of ideological motives that brought the waves from Europe here.

The destiny of the Great Lakes is so far from molded at this writing that while Minnesota plans a great decentralization, leading off with an experimental community for 50,000 people in the northern forest, mighty Chicago is planning a giant 15-year, $15-billion development for 120,000 settlers in the Loop, involving moving some forest right downtown.

Discovery and settlement are resuming in Great Lakes America.

WILLIAM DONOHUE ELLIS

Part One
THE LAND AND THE WATERS

The Great Lakes as we know them today are young, dating from the last retreat of the Wisconsin Glacier some fifteen thousand years ago.

However, the layers of bedrock forming the lake basins are ancient. As the center of the region depressed, the outside edges of the rock layers turned upward, forming a set of nested stone bowls. Some of those turned-up, curved edges were soft, some hard Niagaran dolomite. The soft ones eroded, becoming arc-shaped beds for the waters, like Lake Michigan, Lake Huron, and Georgian Bay. Where the edges were hard, the walls contained the waters and partitions developed, like the Door and the Bruce peninsulas, the Niagara escarpment, and the Lake Superior shores.

The sharp, perpendicular cliffs of Shovel Point rise specterlike from the fog along the Lake Superior coast.

TOM ALGIRE

15

CHAPTER 1

A GULL'S-EYE VIEW

A perspective of the vast watery heart of a continent—
an area of pulsating commerce and serene wilderness

FROM THE MOON, they are visible to the naked eye. By satellite camera they dominate interior North America, photographing stark black among the soft earth hues of the continent. They are the largest area of inland sea on the planet—the Great Lakes.

A satellite view verifies in seconds a concept not wholly grasped when one studies geography: the picture of the vast watery heart of the continent flowing in three drainages, north, east, and south. Thousands of long, narrow lakes in Canada aim their lengths at Hudson Bay like lines of force; other thousands are drawn into the southbound Mississippi; thousands more, lined up nearly parallel, pour into the Great Lakes–St. Lawrence outflow. Yet, the headwaters of these three massive concourses are separated by only a short day's portage.

The Great Lakes watershed appears more sharply defined, less sprawling than the other two. Its tributaries do not meander but dump abruptly in short, parallel lines off the steep Canadian shield and the Allegheny foothills into the Great Lakes flow.

The uncluttered satellite view uncovers another insight no map quite conveys—the Great Lakes as a continental hub with the Lower Peninsula of Michigan as its center. The sharp definition of the satellite view emphasizes this Great Lakes circle, Lakes Michigan and Huron forming two halves of it. Concentrically, the Bruce Peninsula arc between Lake Huron and Georgian Bay is clearly part of the fragmented semicircle of rock opposite it, the Door Peninsula arching between Lake Michigan and Green Bay. Looking more closely we see that circle filled in by a

dotted line of islands—Manitoulin, Cockburn, Drummond, Rock, and Washington.

A satellite view of the bowl shaped center of the continent highlights a ring of hard Niagara dolomite reinforcing the lakes' shapes, resisting erosion by these powerful seas, and keeping them separated—the same rock lode that defies the thrashing pressure of the waters of four lakes pouring over the brink of Niagara Falls and lashing at the walls of the Niagara Gorge, which holds Lakes Erie and Ontario apart.

The lens reveals this narrow Niagara River, which takes the downhill pressure of the waters as they sweep down the stairway from Lake Superior's surface 600 feet above sea level through the lower levels of Michigan, Huron, and Erie, to Lake Ontario's 245 feet.

The lakes decrease in size, too, compressing the waters through constricting channels over the major stepdowns. The drop from Superior to Huron at Sault Ste. Marie is 22 feet. The Niagara River descends 60 feet before the brink at the falls, where it plunges 167 feet, then down another 98 on its way to Ontario, which finally discharges 233,900 cubic feet per second into the St. Lawrence River.

Except for Lake Erie, which is in a sense a wide connecting river, these vast storage lakes that blacken the satellite photograph are deep: the maximum depth of Superior is 1,333 feet; Michigan, 923; Huron, 750; Ontario, 802; Erie, 210, though its average depth is only 58 feet.

One wonders, how much water *is* that, in the earth's largest freshwater body? But what answer has meaning? "Sixty-seven trillion gallons" leaves us with the same

A rare color photograph taken from Skylab Four. Georgian Bay is at left, Lake Erie at right, Lake Ontario at top center.

Seen by moonlight from a satellite, the Great Lakes are the dominant feature of the continent's interior; the circular central basin outlined by Lakes Michigan and Huron is easily traced.

question. So does "ninety-five thousand square miles." Natural history writer, Robert Allen answers that it is "enough water to cover all Canada twelve feet deep"— and Canada is the earth's second-largest nation!

D ROPPING DOWN to a pilot's-eye view, we lose scope, but we gain color. The waters turn blue. At the head of the lakes in large breaks in the forest cover are county-sized patches of red over the iron-ore ranges—the Vermilion, Mesabi, Gogebic, Menominee, and Marquette.

Michigan's Upper Peninsula is green with huge national forests, except around the iron-mine openings. Over the eastern end of the peninsula one looks down on a com-

plex of channels where the three largest lakes meet. White-water rapids of St. Mary's River boil seaward. The Sault Ste. Marie locks skirt these rapids to lower ships twenty-two feet from Superior into Huron. Just to the south the Straits of Mackinac connect Lakes Michigan and Huron. These two key constrictions today govern a ponderous bulk of marine traffic of iron ore, coal, and wheat. However, they were once strategic fort locations governing wars of empire.

Flying south over Lake Huron, the boundary between the United States and Canada seems actually visible in two parallel lines of ore boats—upbound ships to the east, downbound to the west.

Over sprawling Detroit, or Chicago if that is the route,

one looks down on a vast humanscape—a reminder that the Great Lakes region supports 40 million of us, about 1 percent of the world population.

The contrast is stark if the flight is over the plains of western Ohio, Indiana, or Illinois, a precise checkerboard of sparsely settled 360-acre squares, ruled on the land by order of the Ordinance of 1787—demarked now by county, township, and field roads.

The contrast is abrupt again as the plane comes over the eastern end of Lake Erie and the checkerboard breaks up into a picture-puzzle landscape of meandering, random road patterns—presurvey New York.

Over the junction of Lakes Erie and Ontario, one looks down on another strategic site on the continent. Ships are bypassing Niagara Falls through the Welland Canal with cargoes for Europe. Networks of electric cables carry Niagara hydroelectric power to the eastern United States and Canada.

Across Lakes Erie and Ontario one flies parallel to Canada's corridor of power: Windsor-Hamilton-Toronto-Ottawa-Montreal-Quebec, a narrow, straight-line stretch containing 20 percent of Canada's people. The south shores of Erie and Ontario can be navigated at dusk just by the lights, which make a resplendent map of contiguous cities.

At the outlet of Lake Ontario, where it pours the waters of five lakes into the St. Lawrence, one looks down on the Thousand Islands. These are the tops of ancient hills in a rock bridge, the Frontenac Axis, which connects New York's Adirondack Mountains to the Canadian shield,

	THE WORLD'S FOURTEEN LARGEST LAKES		
	(In Order of Size)		
	LAKE	SURFACE AREA (Square Miles)	LOCATION
1.	Caspian Sea	152,239	Europe-Asia
2.	**Lake Superior**	31,820	North America
3.	Lake Victoria	26,820	Africa
4.	Aral Sea	25,659	Asia
5.	**Lake Huron**	23,000	North America
6.	**Lake Michigan**	22,400	North America
7.	Lake Tanganyika	12,700	Africa
8.	Great Bear Lake	12,275	North America
9.	Lake Baikal	12,162	Asia
10.	Lake Nyasa	11,600	Africa
11.	Great Slave Lake	10,980	North America
12.	**Lake Erie**	9,930	North America
13.	Lake Winnipeg	9,094	North America
14.	**Lake Ontario**	7,600	North America

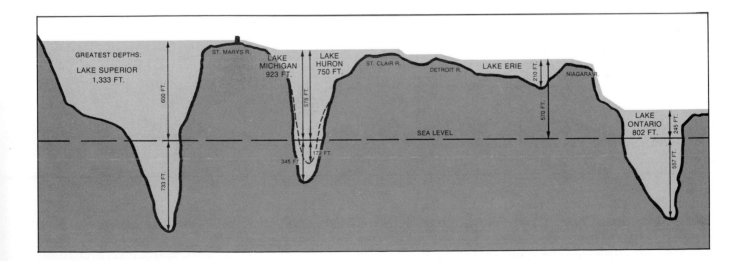

Duluth, at the very head of the lakes, is the region's largest iron ore and wheat port. One bulk carrier like this can haul the harvest of twenty-five thousand acres—thirty 65-car trainloads.

creating one of the most graceful regions in this continental watershed.

While the Great Lakes form a single, vast watershed as seen from the air, each has a distinct personality when one comes down to earth. The largest lake in the world, Superior, is deep, cold, and brutal—still very much Hiawatha's Gitche Gumee, "shining Big-Sea-Water." Still surrounded by road-scarce wilderness, Superior has summer winds flavored evergreen, winter winds opaque with fine-flake snow that piles up deep enough to bury trucks. The rocky shores still successfully lock out all but the adventurous. The land mass north of Superior is riddled by so many lakes that mapmakers are still registering new names. In this remote void, where the sky is God-high and

pale, animals still outnumber men. Yet close by, at the west end, rise the ore docks and grain elevators of Port Arthur, Two Harbors, Beaver Bay, Duluth-Superior, and smaller ports, shipping the grain from the Great Plains hinterland and iron ore and taconite from the ranges.

There are interruptions in the Minnesota forest, where surface mining has dug terraced holes big enough to engulf towns. Inland of the forests wheat plains march west over flat yellow miles of the U.S. and Canada.

Superior's western coasts are pronouncedly peopled by descendents of Norwegian, Swedish, and Scottish people, who thrive on a climate that builds character, "We have nine months of cold weather and three months of winter." Some residents' cars are equipped with radiator heaters to

Grand Traverse Peninsula stabs a dozen miles into Grand Traverse Bay, Michigan. The many scenic peninsulas and bays give the lakes ten thousand miles of coast, nearly a third in Michigan, washed by four lakes.

be plugged into the 110-volt garage circuit at night.

Lake Superior water is cold and clear with visibility down thirty-six feet. Its north shore is Canadian and totally wild. Its south shore is the Michigan Upper Peninsula, almost totally covered by state and national forests, the two largest being the Hiawatha and the Ottawa national forests, watered by wild and scenic rivers.

Superior's outflow is through the white-water rapids of St. Mary's River. The construction of the Soo locks in 1856 to bring shipping around these rapids was a major event in the economic history of both nations, unlocking the vast iron and wheat lands.

In sharp contrast to cold, lonely Superior is Lake Michigan, which pierces three hundred miles south into the Midwest heartland. Lake Michigan maintains a dual personality. Its northern waters are a playground, with all the sight-seeing wonders around historic Mackinac Straits, a strategic zone in the fur trade, Indian wars, and Jesuit missionary work among the Indians. These historic sites draw thousands of visitors, while the northern waters draw fishermen. The Door Peninsula, demarking Green Bay, is a national resort area leaning toward the sedate; families return year after year after year to the same oft-painted wooden hotels.

The southern two-thirds of Lake Michigan is a working lake. The west-coast industrial shore—Sheboygan, Milwaukee, Racine, Kenosha, Waukegan—supplies the world with flour, beer, cars, machine tools, cheese, engines,

Chicago, giant hub of the lakes embracing eight counties in two states, is constantly tearing down and rebuilding. The Chicago River has been uniquely engineered to flow out of, not into, the lakes.

tractors, and a catalog of allied products. The south loop of the lake—the high-density Chicago complex, including Hammond and Gary, Indiana—works the lakes hard. This industrial loop extends up the east shore intermittently to Grand Rapids, Michigan.

On the Lower Peninsula of the state of Michigan, the northern third again is sports country, primarily for skiing, fishing, and hunting. Like the Upper Peninsula, it is largely national and state forests. The southern two-thirds is shore-to-shore middle-sized industrial cities: Bay City, Midland, Grand Rapids, Lansing, Kalamazoo, Battle Creek, Jackson, Benton Harbor, Pontiac. On the eastern rim, of course, spreads the vast auto city and its satellites.

Illinois and Indiana both have a proprietary interest in

Lake Michigan but differ dramatically from the state of Michigan in personality. Ohio, Indiana, and Illinois are true sister states in development: Their top tiers of counties are heavily industrialized, with emphasis on automotive and steel-related work. Their middle counties are corn-hog farm country, with some wheat and general farming. Their capitals—Columbus, Indianapolis, and Springfield—are centered in each state, lined up as major stops on the old National Road along the 40th parallel. Their southern tiers of counties contain their founding history and have a southern accent, with proud old queen cities on the Ohio River—Cincinnati, Evansville, Cairo— long antedating the buildup of their northern cities. These three states are kin in history, economics, and character.

LAKE HURON also has a pronounced split in personality. It, too, is a sporting and wildlife lake along its broken northern shoreline, the crescent formed by Bruce Peninsula and Manitoulin, Cockburn, and Drummond islands, which guard the entrance to Georgian Bay. The entire Georgian Bay complex with its bastions and islands is the Midwest's summer playground and a trip backward in time. Jesuit and Indian history whispers at every island and stream mouth. Plants and animals from between glacial advances survive here on Bruce Peninsula and Manitoulin Island. Indians named Jones and Smith live on Georgian Bay's shores. Huron's western waterfront has some industry.

Shallow Lake Erie is hardworking water, heavily industrialized from Toledo to Lorain to Cleveland to Buffalo and deep inland—to Akron, Youngstown and Canton to the south. On its north shore, the Ontario Peninsula is a high-density area containing hardworking cities like London, Kitchener, Guelph, and Port Colborne. This arrowhead of Canada, stabbing southwest to split the water into Lakes Huron and Erie, is one of Canada's heavy population zones. Although the arrowhead is industrialized, it is crowded with historic shrines. The Jesuits and fur men were active here because this was the stronghold of the Hurons, whom the priests judged the easiest to convert to Christianity.

The eastern loop of Lake Ontario is the Golden Horseshoe. On the Canadian side is that nation's most intensive industrial area, unusual in its freedom from smoky factories. Using clean natural gas and hydroelectric power from Niagara, the factories are architecturally splendid and landscaped like parks.

Niagara Falls is, of course, the scenic wonder of the Great Lakes and a whole tourist industry of its own. The Welland Canal, which takes shipping past the falls, is pivotal, raising inbound ocean vessels 326 feet into Lake Erie. Construction of the Welland parallels or surpasses the Soo locks in continental commercial importance.

The most spectacular feature of the Golden Horseshoe is Toronto. Canada's industrial giant of 2.5 million people is ultramodern and ultraprosperous. The queenly citadels of Quebec, Montreal, and Ottawa lament sometimes Toronto's flamboyance and Americanism, but they value its financial strength.

Lake Ontario, on both its shores, remains genteel vacation country, with a population that sports white slacks for cocktail hours on the fantails of old, lovingly varnished boats. Inland are other vacation-type waters, including New York's storied Finger Lakes along old U.S. 20, which cuts through the Iroquois country—Batavia, Canandaigua, Geneva, Seneca Falls, Auburn.

At the outlet of Ontario one enters the fabulous St. Lawrence concourse, dropping down 1,200 miles and 232 feet to the sea. The personality changes abruptly here. Midwestern industrial bustle, Canadian and American, is shed like a sweaty work shirt. Grandeur sets in.

It begins with the magnificent Thousand Islands, actually numbering over 1,700 if you count the two-tree islands. The Canadian Islands are mostly farming islands; the American, recreational and residential. On both sides,

	PHYSICAL CHARACTERISTICS OF THE GREAT LAKES					
LAKE	SURFACE AREA (Square Miles)	DRAINAGE BASIN EXCLUDING LAKE (Square Miles)	MAXIMUM LENGTH (Miles)	MAXIMUM WIDTH (Miles)	HEIGHT ABOVE SEA LEVEL (Feet)	MAXIMUM DEPTH (Feet)
SUPERIOR	31,820	48,200	383	160	600	1,333
MICHIGAN	22,400	45,460	321	118	578	923
HURON	23,000	49,600	247	101	578	750
ERIE	9,930	22,750	241	57	570	210
ONTARIO	7,600	34,800	193	53	245	802

The camera looks west from the U.S. at Horseshoe Falls, the Canadian half of Niagara, just beyond the divider, Goat Island. Five miles west, in Canada, the Welland Canal takes ships around the falls.

however, the islands wear no yellow neon or any urban hairnet of utility-pole wiring. The scene is green and serene—as the St. Lawrence must have been when white men first saw it four and a half centuries ago.

GREAT LAKES HISTORY moved upstream. Five years after Columbus's landfall, John Cabot and twenty-eight men sailed out of Bristol, England, on the *Matthew*, landing near the mouth of the St. Lawrence in the late afternoon of Saturday, June 24, 1497. Stupefying today is the apparently slight importance of this vast continent to early European arrivals. Cabot lingered only to plant Henry VII's flag. Then he returned for ten pounds reward.

For a third of a century North America and her Indians were allowed their vast silence. Then, chartered to look for a short route to China, the Frenchman Jacques Cartier came three times (1534, 1541, 1544), successively nosing his vessel farther up the St. Lawrence on each voyage, finding the great Saguenay River mouth, then the Indian settlement, Stadacona, at Quebec, and then another, Hochelaga, under the great mountain at the mouth of the Ottawa. The red men took him up the mountain, which he named Mount Royal (Montreal). It is not his fault that, as he looked to the west, he did not see a continent twice the size of Europe; he was a young contract-vessel master on a specific commission. What he did see was a boiling rapids blocking his route to China (*La Chine*). Naming them Lachine rapids, he returned to France. For sixty years more the Indians had their vast forest to themselves.

The decades rolled down to 1604 and the arrival of a young French military man with cavalier locks flowing down over steel corselet and lofty ideas of settlement, development, and empire. By 1608, the French king's soldier, Samuel de Champlain, had pushed up the St. Lawrence to Stadacona, below the rock at the place the Indians called *Kebec* ("the narrowing of the waters"). With a heavy sense of destiny, Champlain built three two-story cabins to house his sixty French people and to become capital of New France. The Algonquins sensed that this man had come to stay.

In the 1600s, in-wading Frenchmen were accompanied by a rare corps of tough, dedicated men—the Jesuit priests—come to bring Christianity to the Indians. These black-robes moved inland to set up jack-pine altars in sheltered groves. They begged rides westward into the interior in the long canoes of Indians returning home after bringing furs to the French boats, which could not get upstream of Lachine rapids. Thus the Jesuits moved out into the wilderness in front of the fur traders.

The Jesuits wrote down several variants of the Algonquian and Iroquois languages. Then they translated Christianity into Huron, Chippewa, and Sioux. The language factor would later be important when the Indians took sides between Frenchmen and Englishmen. Nearly as important, the Jesuits sketched and sent back maps tracing their routes of travel and the shapes of rivers. Frenchmen following could then make faster progress.

The Indians' route west from Montreal was not via Lakes Ontario and Erie, which pointed southwest. They paddled due west up the Ottawa to the Mattawa, and up that stream to Lake Nipissing, and then down French River or any one of several others into Georgian Bay and Lake Huron. Thus, the early French left Lakes Ontario and Erie undiscovered.

FAR SOUTH OF THE LAKES but east of the mountains on the Atlantic seaboard, Englishmen were forming New England, New York, and Virginia. While the French faced ever inland, the English looked seaward and concentrated on building a narrow shelf of towns along salt water, locked off from the interior by the mountains.

To the north the Jesuits, shadowed by the fur traders,

paddled constantly deeper into the Great Lakes country along the north shores, planting Catholic missions, the fleur-de-lis, and French fur-trading posts. In 1672, Louis Jolliet and Father Jacques Marquette worked their way into Green Bay and up the Fox River, seeking the Father of Waters. Paddling up the Fox to near present-day Wisconsin Dells, they portaged to the Wisconsin River and floated downstream to discover the Mississippi.

In 1679, Sieur Dulhut built a sturdy fur post at the head of Superior. The French thus staked out a vast territory encompassing the Great Lakes and part of the Mississippi —while English colonists were hardly venturing into the upper Hudson River.

On an August morning in 1679 men sweating for the young Robert Cavelier, Sieur de la Salle, commandant of Fort Frontenac and white hope for French fur trade, launched a miracle. Pulling on ropes, his men towed the first real ship built on the Great Lakes up the Niagara River, above the falls, into Lake Erie—the *Griffon*, forty-five tons. La Salle sailed the *Griffon* to Green Bay; then by canoe he explored down the Mississippi to claim the south for France.

He extended the French crescent empire from the Gulf of St. Lawrence through the Great Lakes and down the Mississippi to the Gulf of Mexico a century before the English colonies united as states.

When the English colonists along the Atlantic coast finally looked up from their road building and town building, they found they had become encircled on the north and west by outposts of Frenchmen, who were shutting them out of the Great Lakes fur trade. Making alliance with the fiercest North American Indian confederation, the Iroquois Five Nations of New York, the English lashed out against the French in a series of wars, which were extensions of simultaneous English-French wars in Europe.

The English outflanked the French by installing a fur-trading post far to the north on St. James Bay, the Hudson's Bay Company. They paid Indians more for furs and attracted the best pelts northward, transshipping over a rapids-free route to England.

The English supported the Iroquois in a long, bloody war against French fur posts and French Indians in the Ontario Peninsula between Lakes Huron and Erie, and extending west to Michigan, Mackinac, and beyond.

It would mean a delay of decades, however, to continue attacking individual, isolated French fur posts lost in the vast forest on a maze of waterways. Victory swiftly would be theirs, the English felt, if they struck at Quebec, which they felt was the key to the entire crescent-shaped watery French empire. They sent James Wolfe with an armada and eighty-five hundred men to do the job.

Quebec fell in 1759, and with it, New France.

England came into an empire with place names like Frontenac, Pontchartrain, St. Ignace, St. Louis, Fond du Lac, De Tour, Point aux Barques.

WHEN THE ENGLISH COLONIES south of the lakes opted for revolution, the Canadian-English colonies declined their invitation to join. This warned the American colonies that they might have a hostile Canada to the north, loyal to England. They therefore took steps to strengthen fortifications on Lake Ontario's south shore.

Following the exploration by fur traders came a long era of discovery by lumbermen; there was no important settlement, because when timber near the logging streams was gone, the loggers tended to move west, leaving behind with the stumps only a few trapped by large families or a love of the cutover land. But the abandoned camps became inchoate towns like Spruce, Maple Ridge, and Bad Axe in Michigan's Lower Peninsula.

The lumber waves gave impetus to sailors, who moved their lumber boats ever upstream to inland ports. Clippers did not quickly give way to steamers but advanced in size and design alongside the sidewheelers. The vessels carried west lumbermen imported by lumber companies from Sweden and Germany to level stands in Wisconsin and Minnesota forests.

Later the boats carried west waves of farm-settlers. Vessels enabled a settler to get to his land faster and carry more farm equipment. More important, vessels made a western farm viable by providing transport for a man's future crops back to eastern markets.

Plodding slowly behind the mariners, the canal men and railroaders dug their way west, laying down towns along their rights-of-way. Inching west along these routes came thousands of Irishmen doing the construction. Unlike other nationals, who would settle in groups and retain strong ethnic characteristics for generations, the Irish would drop off the canal or railroad at a thousand places and blend swiftly.

The wave of iron men came next. Opening the iron-ore veins of Michigan's Upper Peninsula and Minnesota required thousands of men. The ore companies sent recruiters to Sweden, Germany, and Wales.

Civilization moved upstream. Not until 1858 would

In 1678, La Salle's expedition left Fort Frontenac to go upstream of Niagara, build the first real ship for the fur trade, and secure the west for France.

Minnesota become a state. Intense Canadian development was not yet this far west, and Canadian authorities in Quebec and Ottawa nervously listened to reports of American railroad construction plans aimed north at the Minnesota-Canada border. They watched even more nervously the War Between the States, leaving the North with a powerful army and a roster of victorious generals looking for some place to fight. Canada was only a collection of seven quarrelsome British colonies. But they could agree on one thing: America was a dangerous neighbor. The colonies confederated in 1867, forming the Dominion of Canada.

WHILE FUR OPENED THE REGION, lumber developed it, and canals and railroads and farming settled it, the iron mines would become a hundred-year focus at the center of its way of life. They would launch a pervasive metallurgical industry with mills from Oswego to Milwaukee. They would give rise to an iron navy of enormous ships, now reaching a thousand feet from bow to flag. They would create a huge rail net for coal and the diapason of metal-using, metal-supporting industries, from machine tools to automobiles. What made it work so well was the broad highway of water.

One-fifth of all Americans and two-thirds of all Canadians live in Great Lakes country. Most would be surprised to know that—if traced back—they live here *be cause* of the lakes which, midnight to midnight, supply three trillion gallons to the workshops that furnish livelihood to this great weight of population. Indirectly, it requires 40,000 gallons of water to build a car, and this is automotive country. It requires 180 gallons of water to manufacture one copy of a Sunday newspaper, and the northern part of the Great Lakes region is paper-pulp country. It takes 27 feet of water to float most ships, and the 2,300-mile stairstepped waterway freights over 100 billion ton-miles of shipping to and from its 110 U.S. and Canadian ports; the Soo canal stairway up to Lake Superior lifts more tonnage than the Panama, despite the winter freeze.

Hydroelectric power needs a great weight of downhill water, and the massive Canadian snowmelt falling off the high, hard ridges in the Canadian shield sends rivers like the Saguenay hurtling down through turbines to power the industries. Canning, mining, lumbering, fishing, food processing, steelmaking, and general manufacturing are big water-using concerns, and the region's yearly manufacturing output is above $50 billion worth—which is a lot of water through the mills.

For a hundred years the English found allies in the Iroquois, the French in Algonquian peoples. Here twentieth-century artist Rex Woods depicts Champlain and Brûlé among the Hurons.

27

CHAPTER 2

BIRTH OF THE LAKES

The retreats and advances that over the eons have scooped out lake basins and sculptured stairsteps across the land

To DECODE MOST of this continent's geological story, we are dependent upon subtle clues planted empty eons before the evolution of erect walking, history-recording beings. The Great Lakes region, on the contrary, is so young that we actually have human eye-witness observations of the formation *as it was happening*.

One such witness is as recent as metal-using, tool-making man. His message is decipherable and preserved for us by another human who had a two-part name, Agis Salpukas. The observer, as described by Salpukas, was very calm for a being with keen territorial imperative instincts who was actually witnessing violent geological evolution. He said, simply, "I expected it." He was watching gale-driven waters tear away two feet of land to form a new Lake Erie shoreline. The first level of his not-so-crude shelter was flooded, and he was watching from his second level while pouring a liquid into drinking vessels for other shore-dwelling humans from flooded shelters.

This host also had a two-part name—Alex Steve, swimming coach, Monroe High School, Bolles Harbor, Michigan. While it took a million years to form the Lake Erie Basin, the Bolles Harbor shore had just been reshaped by two feet in eight hours. Mr. Steve was probably calm because as a teacher he knows the Great Lakes country is still in a dynamically formative stage. He had earlier watched Lake Erie tear out his $10,000 concrete retaining wall, implanted to hold the geological status quo. The date of this drama was April 10, 1973; the narrator, reporter Agis Salpukas of the *New York Times*.

On the same night, in Ohio, one full lane of Port Clin-

ton's highway dropped into gale-whipped seas. That same month, Lake Michigan's eight thousand-mile shoreline was radically altered. A rise of one foot in Lake Michigan brings the water twenty-five feet farther inland. Chicago's luxurious Thorndale Beach condominium, which was thirty feet from the lake five years ago, is now on the lake; on April 15, 1973, twenty-five-foot waves put Lake Michigan inside the Thorndale.

Lake Erie's southern shoreline moved inland that year enough to damage 450 houses and gently lower 50 of them into the lake, lap them apart, and float them silently away. South-shore property owners expect to lose six inches of land each year, and in some years as much as two feet, and they move their fences back several times as the landscape continues forming.

In a region of such dynamic geology, vessel skippers threading the Great Lakes' channels, rivers, harbors, and straits dare not use three-year-old charts. Sportsmen see the tributary lakes and streams change to meadows between their boyhood catches of sunfish and their adult search for trout. Shorelines are being straightened into smooth curves as waves and currents build bars, hooks, and spits across shore indentations, creating lagoons that turn into swamps, then muck lands. The lake floors are building deep muds. Marshes are solidifying. Niagara Falls moves upstream 125 feet between a couple's honeymoon and silver anniversary. Thus, topographic maps of the region go out of date while they're being printed.

The bedrock foundation of the Great Lakes region evolved over eons. A vast structure of rock called the

In the steeply tilted formations of graywacke that channel the St. Louis River in Minnesota, one can almost see geological change in action.

GRANT HEILMAN

Great Lakes geology is dynamic. New shorelines form with storms and changing water levels, regardless of man's plans. This Chicago apartment complex was once thirty feet from Lake Michigan.

"Canadian shield" loops down from the north into the Great Lakes region. Formed during thousands of millions of years, it contains records of emplacement of huge amounts of granite and other igneous rocks erupting molten from deep in the earth. This was followed by cooling and hardening, erosion of the landscape on a grand scale, deposition of great layers of various sediments, outpouring of more lava, and erosion again—all repeated many times. Finally, a half billion years ago, the long process left the shield a stable, gently-rolling surface.

Onto this base the Paleozoic seas flooded, laying down marine sediments of sandstone, shale, and limestone. Some areas sank but were kept nearly filled by the flood of sediment. One of these areas is the Michigan structural basin, centered near Midland in the Lower Peninsula and extending outward to the circle seen on a common road map almost fully outlined by Lakes Michigan and Huron. Twelve thousand feet of different layers of marine sediment underlie the center of this basin.

The Great Lakes basins bear no resemblance to the shapes of their predecessor Paleozoic seas; but after the waters drained away, about 200 million years ago, the shaping of the Great Lakes region as we know it began. Mighty river systems and slow erosion of the land etched the softer rocks where they surfaced, carving broad valleys that would become the lake basins.

Only a million years ago the region was invaded again. The continental glaciers of the Pleistocene epoch moved down from the north through the lowlands and spread out of them, gouging the bedrock deeper and dumping most of the debris far to the south. After several episodes of glaciation the final northward retreat of the ice margin began.

Only about fifteen thousand years ago the ice margin retreated north, and lake water ponded between to the divides, forming the first known Great Lakes. One of these, called Early Lake Chicago, spilled over a low spot and drained southward to the Illinois and Mississippi rivers. Another, Lake Maumee, at the southwestern corner of the Erie basin, flowed through a gap at what is now Fort Wayne, Indiana, and drained down the Wabash River to the Ohio, and thence to the Mississippi.

Many retreats and minor advances of the ice margin then made a complicated series of lake stages with different surface levels and different exits. In the Michigan basin, major lakes existed whose surfaces were 60 feet, then 40 feet, then 25 feet above the present Lake Michigan. In the Erie basin Lake Maumee at one time stood 227 feet above present Lake Erie, and there were many other stages at lower levels, during each of which beaches were cut and built. These are easily visible today as shelves on the land.

While ice still formed a dam to the east in the Ontario basin, the glacier's edge retreated northward in the Huron basin and allowed the waters of Erie and Huron to flow westward across central Michigan in the Grand River Valley. Grand River, emptying into the Michigan basin, built a hundred-square-mile delta.

Retreating still farther, the ice margin then uncovered the Little Traverse Bay lowland in the north end of Michigan's Lower Peninsula, allowing Huron to drain westward and bringing its surface down to that in the Michigan basin, 60 feet above the present lake. Two epi-

sodes of downcutting of the Chicago outlet lowered the lakes to 25 feet above present level. This brought into existence Early Lake Algonquin at 605 feet above sea level in both the Michigan and Huron basins.

Meanwhile, in the Superior basin west of the shrinking glacier, there was a Lake Keweenaw, draining to the upper Mississippi.

Ice retreat in the Ontario basin then allowed the Erie basin to drain eastward. It discharged at Rome, New York, down the Mohawk River to the Hudson and on to the Atlantic. (This outflow helped shape the future route of the New York State Barge Canal.) The drainage lowered Lake Erie to below its present level and gave Early Lake Algonquin (in the Huron and Michigan basins) a second outlet so that it drained east to the Erie basin as well as south to the Illinois River.

Further retreat of the ice margin then opened an exit at Kirkfield, Ontario (east of Georgian Bay), and surface level in the Huron and Michigan basins fell to 555 feet above sea level (25 feet below present level). The southern outlets went dry.

By this time the ice front had retreated north of the St. Lawrence Valley. That broad valley was still depressed be-

As the last glacier receded, lakes formed from the melt in low places; at higher levels the melt ran off as streams, converging into rivers that changed course as the retreat uncovered still lower channels.

Through the ages lake levels have dropped. After a light snow even the untrained eye can in many places observe a terraced progression of ancient shorelines, as here on Lake Michigan's north shore.

cause of the tremendous weight of ice that had only recently withdrawn; therefore it was flooded by seawater, which extended inland nearly to the Ontario basin and northwest up the Ottawa River Valley to beyond Ottawa. Erie drained over the rocky Niagara escarpment and began cutting the Niagara Gorge. Ontario emptied almost directly into St. Lawrence waters.

THEN IN A VIGOROUS but short-lived advance, the glacier moved down again toward the southwestern end of the Superior basin; its lobes covered part of the Michigan and Huron basins and closed the Kirkfield outlet east of Georgian Bay. Lake Superior still drained to the Mississippi. Huron and Michigan rose to discharge again at Chicago and Port Huron, and reoccupied the Algonquin shores at 605 feet above sea level. This initiated what is called the main Algonquin stage. In the east the ice did not recross the St. Lawrence Valley.

The margin of the ice soon retreated northward in the Huron and Michigan basins, and the shore of Lake Algonquin followed it. At the maximum extent of Lake Algonquin, the ice margin extended from the Ontario basin through a point just south of Kirkfield, Ontario, across the northern edge of the Upper Peninsula of Michigan, and across Lake Superior from the Keweenaw Peninsula to the Canadian shore on the northwestern rim of the Superior basin. The western end of Superior contained Lake Duluth, which drained down the St. Croix River to the upper Mississippi. Lake Duluth's surface stood at levels of 830, 800, 770, and then 750 feet above sea level during pauses in the downcutting of the outlet to the St. Croix River.

Soon vigorous melting of the ice began. The glacial margin was in full retreat across a terrain still depressed from the years of heavy ice. When the ice left the vicinity of North Bay, Ontario, the waters of three upper lakes drained out there, down the Mattawa River to the Ottawa arm of the St. Lawrence Seaway. Lake Superior, flowing eastward down the St. Mary's River, dropped to a level 70 feet below its present elevation; water in the Michigan basin fell to its Lake Chippewa stage, 350 feet below the present lake level; the main body of Lake Huron dropped to its Stanley stage, 415 feet below present lake level; and Georgian Bay lowered to the Lake Hough stage, 455 feet below its present level. This was the situation just ten thousand years ago—only yesterday.

The land to the north and east was rising rapidly at this time, rebounding from the ice. This raised all the steps in the upper chain of lakes. When the North Bay sill came as high as the old southern outlets, five thousand years later, Huron, Michigan, and Superior were at the same elevation, forming Lake Nipissing, 605 feet above sea level. This largest of all the postglacial lakes at first had three outlets: the still-rising North Bay exit and the old, stable ones to the south (at Port Huron, Michigan, and at Chicago). Lake Nipissing may have endured for a thousand years, it made some of the strongest shore features of the region—wave-cut bluffs and broad beaches bordered by massive sand dunes. After the North Bay outlet rose too high to carry any of the discharge, increased flow to the south started cutting down the bed of the St. Clair River, and the lake level was lowered.

There was a halt in the downcutting of the outlet of Lake Huron, however, which held Huron and Michigan for a time at the Algoma stage, 595 feet above sea level. Then, probably because of a shift in river channel, downcutting resumed until Huron and Michigan came to their present levels—580 feet above sea level—about three thousand years ago. Meanwhile, the sill of the Superior basin at Sault Ste. Marie had risen above the level of the southern outlets and Superior became independent, rising above Huron, where it has been ever since.

What is the Great Lakes' future? The land to the north of Lakes Superior and Huron is still rising at a rate of one foot per hundred years. The outlet of Ontario, on hard rock, will be worn very slowly by the clear lake water flowing over it. However, it is rising faster than it wears down, and the resulting slight rise in lake level is felt on its southern shores. The future for Superior is the same—a natural hard rock sill at the Sault, reinforced by man's construction of the Soo locks system, is rising slowly.

Lake Erie will be the first to experience a major change. Niagara Falls, wearing away the brink, is retreating headward at about five feet per year; the Niagara Gorge will

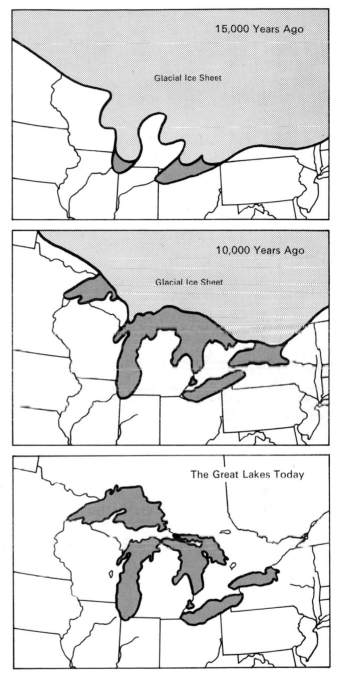

The lakes had many previous shapes. As the Wisconsin glacier retreated in periods of warming climate, lakes formed at its melting edge in the Great Lakes basin, becoming larger as the glacier melted more and withdrew farther. In colder periods the glacier would readvance, pushing the waters out of the new lakes and diminishing them. Ensuing withdrawals re-created them, at the same time rearranging the divides that shaped them.

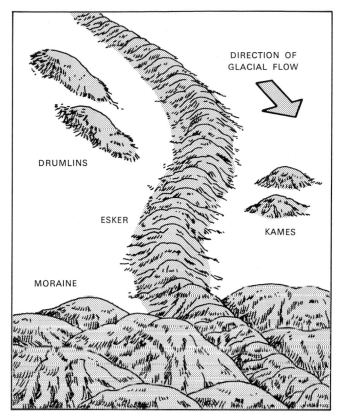

Glacial debris, in variously shaped deposits, forms the skeleton of much Great Lakes topography.

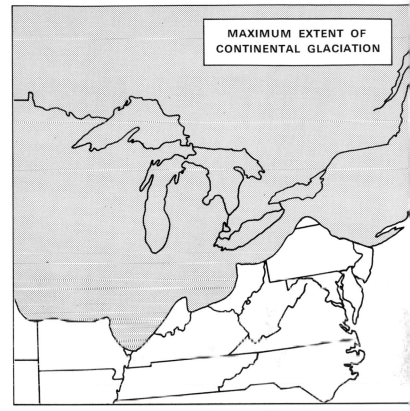

MAXIMUM EXTENT OF CONTINENTAL GLACIATION

Although the last ice sheet advanced only through Wisconsin, earlier glaciers extended farther south.

ultimately eat its way into Lake Erie and drain it completely. When Erie is drained, Huron and Michigan will be lowered.

Though the Great Lakes came to approximately their present average levels three thousand years ago, wave action on the shores continues its work—especially during the years of high levels, which come and go in response to variations in precipitation.

WHILE GLACIERS WERE SHAPING the immediate lake basins, they also sculpted the plains. When a glacier resumed its retreat after a halt, it left behind a moraine, a low hill made up of glacial debris dropped in much the same way as a melting snowdrift beside the highway drops an elongated pile of gravel thrown into it by snowplows. These moraines are positioned not only at the rims of the lakes but also far to the south—anywhere the glacier began a halting retreat during a melting climate. Hence to the

south we have lines of long, low hills like those running east from Shelbyville, Illinois, into southern Ohio and bending northerly to Pennsylvania, then southerly to Long Island, New York. The substance of these ranges is highly miscellaneous rock and soil collected by the glacier in its grinding trip down over North America.

The same kinds of materials were also deposited in different patterns important to midcontinental ways of life. When rising temperature forced a more rapid and steady retreat, this accumulated detritus, instead of forming ranges of hills, was spread evenly in broad till plains. This collection of soil, debris, and rock—scraped off Canada and spread over New York, Ohio, Michigan, and Illinois—would overlay the bedrock with a deep, fertile mantle, which in turn sponsored thick vegetation and forests. This overburden kept preglacial rock outcroppings scarce, thus concealing for many years much of the deeper, mineral-rich rock.

Another type of land feature, found particularly in

While the hard dolomite layers of the lake basin form sheer cliffs on some shores, softer layers, pulverized by waves, turn others into sandy beaches, as at Presque Isle, Pennsylvania.

Michigan, is the conical hill, or *kame*, formed by streams flowing in tunnels on or through the ice and carrying along gravel and sand. When such a stream came to the edge of the glacier or to an outlet hole in the bottom, it would surge out, piling up water-sorted pebbles, rocks, and debris in a cone.

The composition of these kames differs somewhat from the moraines. In forming a moraine, the melting glacier edge merely eased its mixed load straight down, and the

components retained their relative and random positions. However, the kame has more definition. Fast-running streams separated the fine from the coarse, the sand from the boulders. Coming off the rim of the glacier, the fine materials would arc out with the water, while a boulder reaching the lip would plunge straight down. Therefore a kame will often have a south slope of fine sand and a north slope of boulders.

Another set of glacial footprints over the region are

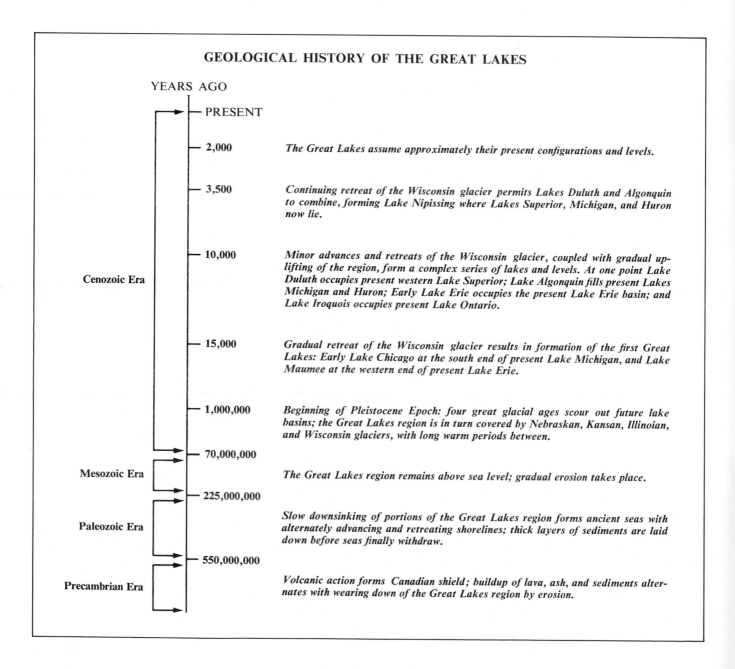

GEOLOGICAL HISTORY OF THE GREAT LAKES

YEARS AGO

PRESENT	
2,000	The Great Lakes assume approximately their present configurations and levels.
3,500	Continuing retreat of the Wisconsin glacier permits Lakes Duluth and Algonquin to combine, forming Lake Nipissing where Lakes Superior, Michigan, and Huron now lie.
10,000	Minor advances and retreats of the Wisconsin glacier, coupled with gradual uplifting of the region, form a complex series of lakes and levels. At one point Lake Duluth occupies present western Lake Superior; Lake Algonquin fills present Lakes Michigan and Huron; Early Lake Erie occupies the present Lake Erie basin; and Lake Iroquois occupies present Lake Ontario.
15,000	Gradual retreat of the Wisconsin glacier results in formation of the first Great Lakes: Early Lake Chicago at the south end of present Lake Michigan, and Lake Maumee at the western end of present Lake Erie.
1,000,000	Beginning of Pleistocene Epoch: four great glacial ages scour out future lake basins; the Great Lakes region is in turn covered by Nebraskan, Kansan, Illinoian, and Wisconsin glaciers, with long warm periods between.
70,000,000	
225,000,000	The Great Lakes region remains above sea level; gradual erosion takes place.
550,000,000	Slow downsinking of portions of the Great Lakes region forms ancient seas with alternately advancing and retreating shorelines; thick layers of sediments are laid down before seas finally withdraw.
	Volcanic action forms Canadian shield; buildup of lava, ash, and sediments alternates with wearing down of the Great Lakes region by erosion.

Cenozoic Era · Mesozoic Era · Paleozoic Era · Precambrian Era

Grooves cut by glaciers are so crisp they look man-made; this example is on Kelley's Island, Lake Erie.

granite, gneiss, copper, iron ore, and gravel collected during the glacier's course.

During centuries of warmer weather, the thickness of the ice decreased, relaxing the pressure and retracting the glacier. As it retreated, plant and animal life followed its face north at a respectful distance. During darker centuries, the glacier advanced again, fossilizing mammoths, mastodons, and marine life.

The weight of the thickest part of the glacier pressed the edge outward and southward in lobe-shaped salients. These lobes were driven not only south but east and west as well. Each lobe became a smaller version of the total ice field.

Man has used everything this evolution built. Abandoned lake outlets became beds for canals and highways. Ancient beach lines, now high above water, became footpaths, then trails, then railroad shelves, and were always chosen as the level for military forts. Glacial spillways, till plains, and lake beds became meadows in Wisconsin, orchards in New York, forest and wheat fields in lower Canada and Michigan, and the great rent-payer in the corn and hog latitudes of Illinois, Indiana, and Ohio.

eskers—long, narrow ridges ranging from a quarter mile to many miles in length. They were formed by streams, flowing on, in, or under the ice, which became choked with debris like a clogged pipe. When the ice pipe melted, this material would settle down right where it was in a steep, elongated pile, 20 feet to 200 feet high, depending on the diameter of the pipe.

Drumlins are hills, shaped like overturned kayaks, that point in the direction of the ice movement. These piles of till or outwash were smeared by the ice floes into streamlined shapes.

A *nunatak* is a high, hard point around which the glacier flowed. The very tip of the arrowhead of land pointing southwest dividing Lakes Huron and Erie is a nunatak. It separated the glacial front into two lobes, the Erie and the Huron. Today it holds these lakes apart—for awhile.

The kames, moraines, eskers, drumlins, and outwash plains were mixed accumulations of limestone, sandstone,

UNAWARE OF THESE MASSIVE natural earth movements, Frank DeVries climbs onto his bulldozer at 7:00 A.M. and shatters the air north of Toledo, cranking his puny twin 400-horsepower diesels to life. He is specially trained to operate this new twin-engine bulldozer with the highest daily cubic-yard capacity in the earth-moving world. His assignment is restoring the Lake Erie beach line. A sign on the side of his machine says, "We Move the Earth," and DeVries carries himself with that belief.

DeVries is still amazed at the power of his bulldozer. But he might be staggered to know that as he teaspoons earth in three-cubic-yard cuts, nature is tilting up the whole northern part of the continent—an inch every ten years for each hundred miles north of the great continental hinge under the lakes—tending to pile the waters up against the southern and eastern shores.

Meanwhile, we humans must plan in shorter term. Frank DeVries runs an hour overtime because the radio forecasts rain tomorrow, and the governors of the Great Lakes states meet to plan a break-wall system bigger and tougher than the one behind Alex Steve's dwelling, to hold the shape of the lakes . . . for awhile.

CHAPTER 3

THE RESTLESS SKIES

*Capricious extremes of a climate spawned in local clouds
and in oceans and mountains thousands of miles away*

ATTENTION WESTERN LAKE ERIE and surrounds: dark mammatus cumulus forming off Port Clinton, with billowing cumulonimbus above. Alert for possible violent thunderstorms, high winds. Tornadoes possible. Small craft warnings are up." His report given, Coastguardsman J. C. Richards released the electronic button, and the special continuous weather signal on 162.55 megahertz reverted to inaudible in hundreds of schools, police stations, vessels, farm kitchens, and commercial radio stations. Richards knew that captains crossing Lake Erie would immediately order deck gear lashed down and would move up from their sea cabins to bridges. Farm wives would drive out into fields and tell their husbands. Police would ready emergency gear.

After the Fourth of July Great Lakes storm disaster in 1969, Congress established five VHF continuous-broadcast systems for the protection of lower lakes people. The weathercaster gives cloud information so the listener can further localize the report by looking to his own local sky and using his judgment—Great Lakes country has a large population of cloud readers. The region lives on weather, which is important to a half thousand commercial vessels, about a million and a half small craft, several counties of orchards, and several thousand square miles of Central Plains corn and wheat. One-fourth of all Canadians and one-seventh of U.S. citizens live and work in the fractious Great Lakes climate.

It is not a hostile climate, because the extremes are needed for the work that goes on here; 50°-below-zero weather thickens the beaver pelt, and 50-inch snows keep the lake levels up to float 50,000-ton cargoes out of shallow ports, and 95° heat ripens corn in a short season. However, the keynote *is* extremes.

What is the general climate? The region straddles too much latitude and longitude to have a uniform climate. In late May and early June, farmers in the corn-hog plains across northern Ohio, Indiana, and Illinois are already squinting through visible heat vibrations off hard-packed field roads; but in Wisconsin a Holstein is still nuzzling aside lingering snow in a fence corner to reach the pale sprouts. On Michigan's Upper Peninsula an iron-ore dispatcher turns on the electric thawing switch so frozen ore will pour from hopper cars to vessels. High-fashion secretaries in Montreal still wear deerskin boots to their high-rise offices in Ville Ste. Marie, and fishermen in the Maritime Provinces squint into cold fogs.

The cold country begins along an imaginary horizontal drawn through the sac of Saginaw Bay. Hopper cars are equipped with electric heaters to thaw the iron ore so that it will dump into the docks and flow through the chutes to the vessels for spring shipment.

Yet in mid-August lockmasters on the upper Rideau Canal in Ottawa warn northbound boaters navigating from as far south as New York City or Toledo to cover their heads against severe sunburn. In August the entire Great Lakes region burns about equally hot but differs in comfort. Ninety degrees on the south shores of the lower lakes is swelteringly humid, while 110° is comfortable in dry Minnesota.

While the intensity of the summer heat is about the

When black water meets pewter sky and camp smoke rises straight, cloud readers know Gitche Gumee is about to make weather. Heat energy stored in these vast waters creates climate—both benign and violent.

39

GRANT HEILMAN

REGIONAL CLIMATES

MINNESOTA. Probably the fairest climate in the Great Lakes, along with Wisconsin. Relatively storm-free over the land. Enough rain for farming. One of the most healthful climates, good drainage, dry atmosphere.

Dramatic temperature variations ranging 169°, from 59° below zero to 110° above. Minnesota is the source of three of the continent's great water systems: the Great Lakes, the Red River to Hudson Bay, and the Mississippi watershed, which begins at Itasca in the Willow River, flowing via the Crow Wing, the Prairie, the Platte, the Elk Run, and the Minnesota to the Mississippi.

WISCONSIN. Nine thousand lakes. The eastern and northern climate is moderated by the Great Lakes. Generally fair and cool. Northern Wisconsin averages 55 to 60 inches of snowfall per year; southern Wisconsin, 30 inches.

ILLINOIS AND INDIANA. These states include both the northern and southern temperature belts. The mean annual temperature in northern Illinois is 48.4°; in the center, 52.4°; in the south, 59.8°. Precipitation in the north is 33 inches; in the south, 48. Some years snow at Chicago is as deep as 66 inches. Both states are affected by most of the storm systems moving east or northeast across the U.S.

MICHIGAN. The Great Lakes moderate the climate on the western side of the Lower Peninsula. In the Upper Peninsula the prevailing winds, being northwest, are not moderated by the lakes, and winter climate is severe. Rainfall is rather even over the state, but snowfall is much heavier in the north. In 1968–69, 298 inches of snow fell on L'Anse-Barega near Keweenaw Bay.

OHIO AND PENNSYLVANIA. Very similar to Indiana, but moderated by Lake Erie. The pronounced characteristic is the changeability of climate. The northern belt has an average temperature of 49°; summer temperatures average 71.6°, winter, 29.8°. Precipitation averages 38 inches per year; snowfall, 45 inches. Farmers close to the lake expect 200 frost-free days.

NEW YORK. The part of New York drained by the Great Lakes experiences very heavy snow, averaging 87 inches in the Oswego latitude and 126 up near Massena. Lying in the eastern cloud belt, New York receives less sun than Ohio, Indiana, Illinois, and Michigan. Summers are cool, winters cold.

ONTARIO. Huge Ontario has a vast range in climate, but in the Great Lakes watershed there is commonality. At the southern arrowhead, its climate is comparable to Michigan's Lower Peninsula and New York State, with a good, long 175-day frost-free season. Near Georgian Bay and east of it, 120 days of snowfall are average. West of Lake Superior, Ontario's climate is similar to that of Minnesota.

same, the length of the hot season is not. Northern Wisconsin, for example, will typically have 110 to 130 frost-free days; middle Wisconsin, 135 to 160 days; and southern Wisconsin along Lake Michigan, 175 days.

Minnesota's snow-squeaking 50° below in January seems less chillingly piercing than Chicago's damp wind at 32° above.

Despite this variety, these separate climates generally have a common birth in the 95,000 square miles of Great Lakes surface, which causes a reaction between the fair winds from the Southwest and the foul ones from the Arctic region.

The Great Lakes are climate makers—and climate *receivers.*

Since climate is global, the Great Lakes region receives winter weather largely born in the Southwest—Arizona, New Mexico, Colorado, and Utah—which moves to the Great Lakes generally on two tracks. Winds and storms

ROHN ENGH

North of Milwaukee, one digs down to meet the mailman.

forming in the Southwest frequently follow a path northeast through the plains of Nebraska and Oklahoma, tracking up across Lake Superior, and sometimes farther east across Lakes Huron and Erie. Developing as they travel, these fronts become more intense and generate more weather en route. The other track, the East Coast storm path, brings the southwest wind east along the Gulf of Mexico to be deflected north along the Appalachian chain and hit the eastern Great Lakes.

Summer weather is modified locally by heat buildup from the sun; but much of it also comes from cold fronts off the Pacific swinging east, usually without many low centers, generally bringing showers and light thunderstorms. Heavy storms from the Pacific generally go north to Canada, missing the Great Lakes. However, this imported mild weather is augmented by some homemade local storms that curl the hair.

Lakes Erie and Michigan have unique weather patterns. Winds from the west and southwest pick up moisture, then cool and drop their moisture as snow or rain on the leeward side of the lakes. Sometimes as much as seven inches of rain will suddenly be dumped over Gary, Indiana, lower Michigan, and upper Michigan across Lake Superior; in winter it will be a snow blitz. Where Erie is concerned, this is compounded by the sudden high rise of land, which forces the moisture-laden air currents abruptly upward.

Some cold outbreaks move south from Canada with massive waves of arctic air. These do not usually result in major storms, although occasionally a road-closer comes out of Canada.

Fall weather is a legacy from summer. Having stored up summer's heat, the Great Lakes give it back to the atmosphere in the fall. The air, becoming colder than the water, takes heat from the water. When this transfer takes place gradually, it gives fair weather, tempers the chill, and extends the growing season alongshore.

Fall storms begin to hit the lakes by September. Decreasing energy from the sun creates cold dense air over the Canadian plains, which is sucked slowly southward by storms moving into the Gulf states. The battle between cold polar air and warm, moist air over the lakes makes intense low-pressure storm centers.

Why do these storms hover over the lakes? Why don't they move on? And why do they bedevil the leeward side of the lower lakes more than Minnesota and Canada? The

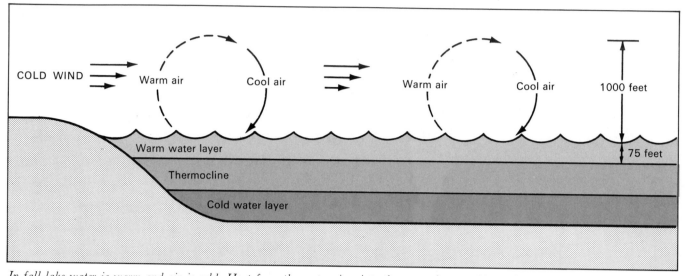

In fall lake water is warm and air is cold. Heat from the water rises into the atmosphere, sucking cold air down to the water, where it in turn becomes warmer. This rotary action stirs up autumn wind and waves.

lake-effect snow squall, especially on Lakes Michigan and Erie, and somewhat on Ontario, is a collision of water temperature and land temperature. Open-water temperature does not go below 32°, whereas land can get much colder. When an eastbound low-pressure center passes the lakes and hangs over Ontario, a vast counterclockwise swirl develops around it, sending a northwesterly arc across the top of the lakes. On their southeasterly return, these winds pass close to the water, pick up moisture, and at the same time are warmed by the water. This warm, moist air immediately condenses as snow (cold air will not hold as much moisture as warm). Hence, a northwest wind makes heavy snow squalls on the southeast shores of the lakes—intensified where there's a sharp uplift to the land, as on the east side of Cleveland, causing the snowburst type storm that can add eight inches to the landscape in a single hour.

These storms are so capricious that one of them embarrassed a national association of meteorologists, who were meeting in Oswego, New York, in 1972. The professionals looked out the window to see that a surprise storm had dumped five feet of snow in three hours, marooning them for three days and making them a front-page news item.

The reverse effect in the summer, however, is pleasant. Since water temperature rises more slowly than land temperature, the water will reach only 65° to 70° in the lower lakes and 60° in the upper lakes, while the land will be in the eighties. Off-lake breezes develop about 11 A.M. and fan the land.

F AIR WEATHER is largely supplied to the Great Lakes by continental patterns from the Southwest. However, this is modified locally by some explosive homemade weather.

There is a time in spring's fair weather when a lake is about the same temperature at all depths—about 39° Fahrenheit. At that time, therefore, the density of water is the same from top to bottom, and currents started by wind stress on the surface churn the waters from top to bottom. This is called the *spring overturn*.

As summer comes on, stratification sets in. Surface waters heat, and they therefore become lighter and can no longer sink, creating a warm-water layer which floats on the cold. This top layer circulates only vertically within itself by convection. The cold, heavy layer below is left stagnant all summer.

In fall surface water loses heat to the atmosphere until it becomes as cold as the bottom water and the entire volume of water will again mix, as it did in the spring. This is the *fall overturn*.

Later, as surface water approaches freezing, it passes through the maximum-density temperature point (39.2°)

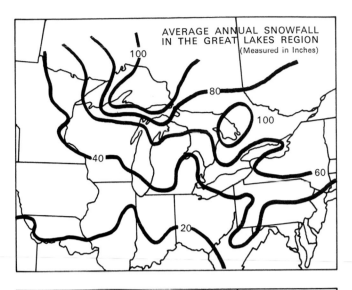

AVERAGE ANNUAL SNOWFALL
IN THE GREAT LAKES REGION
(Measured in Inches)

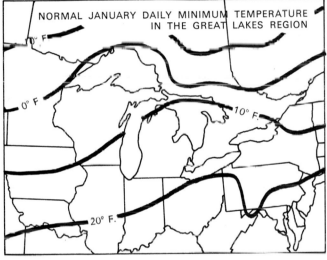

NORMAL JANUARY DAILY MINIMUM TEMPERATURE
IN THE GREAT LAKES REGION

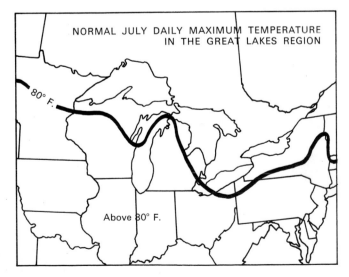

NORMAL JULY DAILY MAXIMUM TEMPERATURE
IN THE GREAT LAKES REGION

and then starts becoming lighter. It will not sink below any dense water still below it. Once again a layered condition exists, enduring all winter. Top water circulates, bottom water at the temperature of maximum density stagnates. In summer there is a middle layer, the *thermocline*, a zone of rapidly cooling water located between the warm and cold layers. It would typically be a layer 30 feet thick, extending from the 60-to-90 foot depth and ranging in temperature from 65° down to 39°.

This thermal sandwich has important effects on the chemistry of lake waters and thus on the plants and animals living there, but here we can only consider it as a weathermaker.

The summer buildup of stored heat over a 95,000-square-mile water surface reaches down about seventy-five feet when the air is 65°. As the fall air temperature drops below that of the water surface, heat rises out of the water into the air. Low-pressure centers moving east across the huge water surface become intensified by this heat, and the rising warm air is replaced by cold air rushing down to the lake surface as wind. The wind creates waves and finally cools the surface water, which sinks, to be replaced by warmer, lighter water rising from below (but still from above the thermocline, the filling in the water sandwich).

These convection fluxes, or transfers of heat, are massive movements. When they happen fast, they are storms. Conversely, warm air over cold water prevents this vertical mixing, giving fair weather.

When cold fall air covers the lakes, a dense, low stratus cloud cover with attendant rain persists over the water. The rising moist heat from the warm water condenses in the colder air, releasing torrents. Until temperatures equalize, the cycle repeats itself, temporarily causing a stationary weather system.

If the lakes have a high percentage of ice cover, the winter may be mild, since the energy transfer diminishes. But generally, near-freezing water is still warmer than the air above, continuing the unstable storm-producing weather.

The most extreme thermal transfers take place from September through December. Dr. Alan E. Strong, who has spent five years observing these phenomena aboard the research vessel *Inland Seas*, explains that when the lakes release most of the heat from above the thermocline into the atmosphere, 100 quintillion calories are loosed.

In summer pleasant onshore winds developing in midmorning cool south-shore cities like Chicago.

In winter slowly cooling Great Lakes waters tend to moderate the climate of these same cities along the shore.

He equates this energy release on such fall days to that of thirty thousand atomic bomb explosions—per day. *If we could capture it, the heat release from the Great Lakes on one fall day could furnish the total U.S. power requirements for a year.*

Spring is entirely different. The Great Lakes are usually placid. Warm air flows across the lakes, but the lower part of the air mass is chilled by the cold lake water, becomes stationary and stagnates as huge, shallow strata; the fast-moving warm air flows over the layer of still-cold air, and the winds do not reach the surface of the water. Thus cumulus formations prevailing over land are absent over the water.

In outwitting this locally made weather, the cloud readers do not read the nature of the clouds so much as the *changes* in them. When aircraft vapor trails suddenly stop dissipating and remain taut, looking like ten-pound lines on trout flies in the sky, southern air is probably spiraling in around a low. Watch out. When loose, frayed cumulus clouds start hardening at the edges, get ready. Harmless when cottony, the hardening edges tell that fresh clouds are forming and puffing upwards—a rain or thunderstorm is coming. If change is rapid, the storm will be soon. Clouds that hang like the bottoms of black eggs (mammatus cumulus) hatch thunderstorms with sudden high, wild winds—and tornadoes. Loose, light, high clouds floating down gently from the north mean good weather. If they're thickening and turning slate blue, however,

there is a buildup going on *above* them and brewing trouble. Puffy cumulus cauliflowers promise fair weather. Cirrus above with altocumulus below them warn, watch the lower clouds; if they thicken, head for shelter or the shore. Mammatus under cumulonimbus warn that a violent storm is coming. Lake Erie, being shallow and lying wholly along the axis of southwest winds, seems to catch such storms most abruptly.

Attention Western Lake Erie Area: possible severe weather alert. Cold front moving east, despite temperatures holding in mid-90's. Altocumulus forming. Barometer falling."

A typical Great Lakes squall commands respect. It begins with altocumulus clouds that develop out of nowhere, looking like a tray of biscuits on a blazing hot day and presaging the kind of hot-weather squall everyone should go through for his diary—once.

July 15 was a tour-folder day, but out on the lake sailors stowed loose objects, and captains automatically noted ports of refuge on charts.

Small sport-fishing boats not warned by radio nevertheless hauled in lines and bait cages in the increasing chop whipped up by a 20-knot wind. Men who sniffed a freshening aquatic richness put south and opened throttles and lifejacket lockers. Diehards who still had not caught the right fish rode their bucking boats, resetting anchors on longer lines. Gulls held closer to shore. The temperature dropped to 90.

Toledo Bureau re-bulletined severe weather—expecting a cold front by 4 P.M. with gusts to 45 miles per hour; tornadoes possible. Coastguardsmen, sighting boats which appeared outbound or unaware, signaled them ashore.

At about 3 P.M. altocumulus clouds lowered the house lights for weather's drama. The water turned slate, blurring horizons except when silent lightning flickered. There was a standstill of wave and wind. Curtain time.

A percussive crash of thunder struck, then rolled toward Canada followed by a lashing rain that made new power-boaters religious. Old ones simply cursed their own pig-headedness. Ahead of them now, they knew, was a fight

for shore. Squirming into storm gear, which companions tried to wrap around them while they kept hands on helms, they stared into walls of water. Coast Guard radio cut into the incessant channel 51 weekend chatter: "Severe storm gusting up to 45 knots. . . ."

The storm moved east, bouncing moored boats in a dozen marinas, snapping lines, tossing heavy dock lockers into the water. As boats came into harbors, bystanders helped them with their lines and marveled that they had made it. Safely moored skippers swore they'd never get caught again.

Up to this point it was a standard hot-weather line of squalls across land and water. But now the wind cut the tops off waves and sprayed them forward in a false surface of solid white that concealed the troughs. Power lines

The Chicago shoreline in another mood—hit by the kind of winter squall that hurls the full fury of wind and water against the frozen land.

Each spring interest focuses on how early the ice will thaw to release ore-hauling monsters from winter berths. This one is laid up in Lake Superior, where navigation resumes late.

ashore went down. Many small boats desperately called the Coast Guard. Cruisers that had made it to port bucked against their lines and occasionally smashed into concrete docks. They rode up and down among heavy wooden dock lockers that had been swept into the water. At Catawba the wind was clocked at 85 m.p.h., a fact that would later be cited to climax the stories of many a marine raconteur and insurance claimant.

Thunder squalls like that one give some warning. There is a similar type of squall that defies even good cloud readers—the *hidden haze squall.* It results from a sudden wind shift. The steady river of moist warm air from the south is the gunpowder waiting to be ignited by cold dry air from the northwest.

Lake Erie can be sunny with a southwest breeze at 1:30 P.M., with a mile of visibility in a smoky golden haze. Then comes a sudden chill. The lights go out. The smoky gold turns greenish-gray. The wind shifts to the northwest. That's the moment: a screeching haze squall blitzes in.

A haze squall is a line thunderstorm or a sharp thermal thundershower, but you never see it coming behind the haze. If a cumulus thundercloud has built up to 50,000 feet and the sun is at a 45-degree angle at 4 P.M., that cloud throws a long warning shadow to the east—maybe a twenty-minute warning. But if the sun is 2 P.M. high—a short shadow—there is no warning.

Wind is not confined to summer. In 1972 gale-force winds of over 34 knots were logged on ninety separate

The icebreaker U.S.C.G.C. Mackinaw *cuts a path for an ore carrier in late January. With a porpoiselike action it can smash through four feet of solid "blue ice" or thirty-seven feet of windrowed broken ice.*

days, more in October than any other month. January and December tied for second.

ICE FORMED THE LAKES and ice governs them. When the waters turn slate gray with twelve- to fifteen-foot seas in mid-November, most ships steam for winter lay-up berths, ending the season. Some continue navigation awhile longer in protected waters. At Thanksgiving marine insurance premiums double. Three days later they triple; three more and they quadruple. That sends many more ships to home ports and puts shore captains with vessels still afloat on ulcer diets, sleeping nights on their Coast Guard radio channel. One bad sea in narrow waters

with high wind or fog can crinkle up enough of a $10 million ship to wipe out a good season. And many a November has bent enough marine iron to keep Great Lakes shipyards on overtime through the winter. Still, if mills are short of ore or there is a strike threatened, some ships operate into December's expensive water.

The beginning of the great freeze in Lake Superior and the St. Lawrence starts a game of high-stakes "chicken." Which vessels will dare to continue sailing the latest, risking ice damage or getting frozen in solid, or frozen out of their home ports? What foreign ocean vessel will tarry latest, picking up cargoes among Great Lakes ports and daring the hazard of getting locked in for the winter by the freezing of the St. Lawrence or the Welland Canal?

Some captains win the race against the ice by a whisker; others lose. In the winter of 1972 alone the ten-thousand-ton British *Manchester Quest* put into St. Johns on February 13 with hull damage from ice and one hold flooded. The Finnish MV *Kostis Prois* took heavy ice damage. The Canadian *Otter Cliffe Hall*, trapped in pack ice in Beauharnois Canal on December 20, was damaged. The *Henry Ford II* was stuck in two-foot ice in Livingston Canal.

The Great Lakes do not freeze all the way across, but the channels, rivers, and harbors freeze, as well as a shelf alongshore that may extend out from two hundred yards to two miles. The narrowing ends of a lake may be iced solid all the way across, sometimes as thick as twenty feet.

Engineers have gradually made small inroads against the ice, lengthening the shipping season by a day or a week in certain parts of certain lakes. Air-bubbler systems placed on the lake bottom have kept shallow channels open. U.S. Coast Guard icebreakers duck-walk back and forth, holding other channels open as lanes of drift ice.

In 1971, however, an addition to the Rivers and Harbors Act launched a major new attack against ice. A conglomerate of U.S. and Canadian governmental agencies and industries backed a task-force effort to keep certain lanes open during the winter, starting with four major operations named Oil Can, Taconite, Open Buffalo, and Coal Shovel. These operations use a fleet of twelve icebreakers ranging in size from the thousand-horsepower cutter *Kaw* to the ten-thousand-horsepower *Southwind*.

Fifty-six Coast Guard stations and their aircraft observe and report ice conditions and other navigation data. The Ice Navigation Center, at the Ninth Coast District Office in Cleveland, operates from mid-December to mid-June with the primary mission of collecting, evaluating, and disseminating ice information to the merchant fleet and to all Coast Guard stations and vessels, the Welland Canal Traffic Control Center, and to fifty-five private enterprises.

At the center Daron E. Boyce, a Great Lakes ice forecaster who is employed by National Weather Service, interprets incoming reports as the ice center creates charts to be broadcast by radio fascimile to ships under way.

After the regular navigation buoys are removed in the fall, the Coast Guard installs a shore-based laser station on Neebish Island in the St. Mary's River to project a blue-green line in the sky over the channel five miles to Nine-Mile Point. The captains can follow the line with safety in this tricky channel. In certain waters an underwater cable will be energized so it can be tracked by shipboard communications.

But the main weapons are icebreakers. Besides the large polar-class *Edisto* and the *Kaw*, ten smaller cutters are at work, plus five 180-foot buoy tenders and five 110-foot harbor tugs. These vessels are extending the season for coal operations into the Toledo-Detroit and Chicago-Milwaukee areas. They're keeping oil moving on Lake Michigan and holding Buffalo harbor open longer. In the first year of the three-year test, they kept several bulk vessels operating until February 1—a spectacular improvement. In the second year, they kept eight ore carriers moving until February 8. If the program is extended, the next step will be to try to keep the St. Lawrence open.

Electric-power interests view the ice breaking with alarm because small chunks can flow into the water intakes of power-generation stations. To avoid this problem the stations emplace ice booms—logs stretched across the rivers. Ice will form *behind* these booms in neat, unbroken patterns, which will stay all winter without entering the intakes to damage equipment.

Power people also fear that ice breaking could cut off water from the plant. An ice dam occurs when large, loose slabs of ice are washed up onto the solid shelf of ice. When enough of these pile up to tilt the ice, the thrust of the Great Lakes slams them up against the nearest shore or dam, or against other ice and continues adding more slabs, which stand slanted on edge. This process can form a mile of pressure ridges—welded slabs standing on edge—which nothing will ever break but summer sun.

Meanwhile, shippers are optimistic for year-round navigation. Sailing until February 8 has already been demonstrated. With ice breaking, accurate ice reports, and a mild winter, the season could resume in a very few weeks.

GREAT LAKES ICE OUTLOOK AT STRAITS MAC 10:30 AM EST THURSDAY MARCH 15 1973 ICE DETERIORATING STEADILY. STRAITS OF MACKINAC NOW REPORTING ONLY SCATTERED FLOES. OPEN WATER SHOWING IN GREEN BAY . . . ST. MARYS RIVER AND WHITEFISH BAY. ICE IN LAKE SUPERIOR MAINLY ONLY NORTHERN SHORES AND WEST END.

NAVIGATION WAS OPENED THROUGH SOUTHERN LAKE HURON AND ALPENA WITH THE ARRIVAL OF THE J. B. FORD AT ALPENA THIS AM.

END. . . .

The chalklike limestone cliffs of the Door Peninsula
rise sharply from Lake Michigan.

After 600 million years of forming the layers of rock that chart
the walls of the Niagara Gorge—capped finally with dolomite
or limestone or shale—came a million years of glacial advances
and retreats. During the retreats a cold pine-swamp ecology of
plants and animals grew up in the wake of the ice.

Thousands of smooth-sided boulders—memorabilia of the retreating Wisconsin Glacier—clutter the landscape on Grand Traverse Peninsula, Michigan, some as small as golf balls and others weighing half a ton.

Stalking through the lush pine swamps was the enormous mastodon, eight or nine feet high at the shoulders, with tusks often exceeding seven feet in length.

BY CHARLES R. KNIGHT, AMERICAN MUSEUM OF NATURAL HISTORY

*A February truce between Superior waters and the north shore
in the cold country—Grand Marais, Minnesota.*

*Derelicts of the forest, these weathered trunks
are bleak evidence of the struggle between the
waters of Lake Erie and its tree-lined shore.*

52

*Wisconsin's thousands of lakes are dotted with islands.
Katinka Lake is typical of the idyllic setting.*

There are 1,702 small worlds of the St. Lawrence: the Thousand Islands,
treasured jointly by the United States and Canada.

Hardy green plants play the protagonist in this struggle for survival on the Grand Sable Dunes, Grand Marais, Michigan, on Lake Superior.

RON & DON BRONDZ

Echo Trail in Superior National Forest, Minnesota, is a paradise for the child who wishes to be a swinger of birches.

JOSEPH FIRE

A shower of sun-made diamonds envelops the wild islands of Georgian Bay, most remaining uninhabited.

ROBERT PERRON

The pine and golden-leaved birches seem to be defying nature as they apparently rise from the solid rock of Lake Superior's Devil's Island.

J. J. MOLLITT

*The landscape of Great Lakes country is accented
by Canada's symbol—the maple leaf.*

Nature's bone structure is revealed in the St. Louis River Gorge, Minnesota.

An autumn setting enhances the beauty of Bond Falls
on the Middle Branch of the Ontonagon, Michigan.

Like a sheer bridal veil, water cascades over a fall on the Genesee River,
Letchworth State Park, New York.

Lynx.

Coyote.

Porcupine.

White-tailed buck deer.

Black bear.

Raccoon family.

Bull moose.

THESE TWO PAGES: GRANT HEILMAN, STEPHEN J. KRASEMANN, BRIAN MILNE, ALLAN ROBERTS, LEONARD LEE RUE III, LEONARD LEE RUE IV, & CHARLES WECHSLER.

Muskellunge.

River otter.

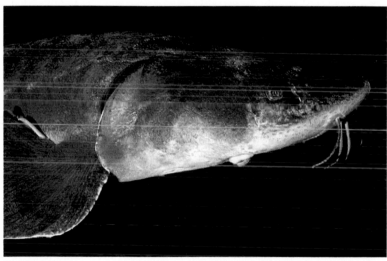

Lake sturgeon.

Sunfish, female and male.

Beaver.

Eastern box turtle.

Cardinal.

Mother screech owl with young.

Male ring-necked pheasant.

Mallard drake.

Great blue heron.

Young herring gulls.

Common loon.

Orange hawkweed.

Wild black-eyed Susan.

Mushroom (fly agaric). Poisonous.

Wood lily.

Water lily.

Spiderwort.

CHAPTER 4

PLANTS OF WATER AND SHORE

*The rich vegetation of a green land, from towering pines
to tiny pads of floating duckweed*

As THE FISHERMEN'S CAR speeds over narrow macadam across Michigan's Upper Peninsula, the guide points to the hemlock–yellow birch forest racing by in the opposite direction and says, "This stand is in tension."

The statement compels attention to the battle for control of the forest being waged between the hemlocks and the yellow birch, and suddenly one is conscious that the whole population of Great Lakes plants is in action.

THE LAKES BEGAN sterile—cold and clear. Silt carried into the stone bowls by tributaries built deltas enriched with phosphorus and nitrogen from plants and animals on land. Siltation, settling, bar-building, and spit-building created quiet coves of shallow water, warmed by the sun and hospitable to tiny plants, which selected different depth zones.

The natural deaths of plants developing a foothold at different depths enriched the bottom, building a marshy environment in which still larger plants took root, creating communities of compatible plants at different well-defined depth zones.

A few Great Lakes shores still have the nearly sterile stony bank or sandy beach, particularly deep, cold Superior, where one looks down into seltzer-clear water and sees the escarpment drop abruptly into thirty-foot water with no beach shelf.

Along the lowlands, however, as on Ontario's north coast, a Great Lakes shore will have a broad marsh zone; some very shallow shorelines are softened by a half-mile buffer of marsh. These marshes are the Great Lakes' incubators, teeming with tiny marine plants or animals, or the infants of larger species. Endless formations of minnows dart through the gentle habitat. It is clear enough for those organisms needing light; it has shaded zones for those needing dark. Parts of it have gentle currents for those needing movement.

The cattails wade out from shore into two or three inches of water. As their dead bodies create a new shore supporting more root fabric, they march still farther out. The bulrushes go beyond into six inches of water. In deeper waters, but not in the same plant communities, we find wild celery, water milfoil, cow lily, white water buttercup, cowwheat, buckbean, leatherleaf, water parsnip, marsh cinquefoil, pitcher plant, pickerelweed.

The Great Lakes country is laced with thousands of small lakes and ponds that are rich in plant life. In these, out beyond the reeds, march deeper-water plants, such as pond lilies, which root on the bottom and send up long stems to the surface on which they unfold flat, floating leaves rafting large blossoms, sometimes sending up long lifelines approaching garden-hose diameter. Beyond the rooted communities, one finds free-floating plants, such as duckweed, which sends down a tiny, quarter-inch root. Bladderwort is a tiny floating carnivore whose bladder traps float below the surface, sending above water a yellow-flower periscope.

The various species of algae are very important contributors to the food chain that lately have gained a bad

Maple, pine, and birch flourish in the humid climate along the shores of the rivers and lakes. Typical is this scene on North River, Quebec.

The cattail, which has twelve different common names, busily converts marshes to meadows.

Plants choose their homes carefully: acres of May apple thrive on the shady floor of an oak woodland.

name. Overfertilized by man's municipal wastes, which are heavy with phosphates and nitrates, algae leap into prodigious growth that the environment cannot employ, and so they multiply.

Moving inland, if one is fortunate enough to walk the Great Lakes terrain with a natural scientist, one may hear the history of the region read from the plants—that there once must have been a pioneer wagon road here, or a devastating fire on that hillside, or over there a cataclysmic storm.

The naturalist is reading a story of plant succession, those normal sequences by which one community of plants replaces another until a stable community develops in equilibrium, the ultimate or *climax* condition. Different factors, including substrate, climate, and human activity, favor different plant communities and their accompanying animals, insects, and microbes. These in turn produce a different type of habitat—which in turn may favor a still different community.

While this action is often obscured from easy view, the sand-dune country of eastern Michigan is a region where the phenomenon is especially visible to the interested lay-

man. As Lake Michigan shrank to its present size, it left successively younger sand dunes ashore. Since plant succession is slow on sandy land, a series of plant communities of varying ages are visible within a few miles of each other, those nearest the water being youngest (pioneer or primary seral stage), those inland increasingly older.

The pioneer plant communities on the dunes are beach grasses and willow, cherry, and cottonwood trees, along with their accompanying fauna.

The next range of dunes inland, probably separated by a pond, will show cottonwood trees giving way to jack pine forestation, with corresponding animal and insect changes. Inland once more, the jack pine gives way to black oak dry forest. Farther inland the dunes wear a moist oak and hickory forest. Although the shoreline dunes begin as dry, sandy soil, the plants on inland dunes are already creating a deep, humus soil with earthworms and snails. In the farthest inland reaches the dune forest climaxes in beech and maple.

The succession can be aborted if winds move the dunes or bury the plants in sand. Then succession begins again in that area, because the sand substrate is nearly the same as when succession first began. However, in Great Lakes areas not built up on sand, a cataclysmic event of wind, fire, flood, or human intervention is unlikely to throw the area all the way back to its original substrate. A new soil base will have been created. In such a case not primary but secondary succession will begin, leading through *different* seral progressions.

Little of the Great Lakes region today presents the stabilized stage of grass and forest that greeted the white man's arrival. Lumbering, town building, farming, railroad building, and natural events such as floods, storms, and vast fires have put most of the region back into motion through secondary seral stages, which gives it a profusion of species of sedges, herbs, grasses, shrubs, and flowers.

The flowers as individuals are less flamboyant than in the tropics, less exotic than in the desert; their impressiveness rather comes from mass effect. Visitors at the right time of year stare in silence at mile after mile of mountain laurel in Canada, a forty-acre blanket of goldenrod in Indiana, or a berm-side strip of bachelor's buttons in Ohio that at highway speeds blurs solid blue.

MOST INSPIRING TO MANY are the Great Lakes forests. In fantasy we treasure the forests for tranquility. In fact, however, a forest is in incessant turmoil. Trees compete for sun, moisture, and minerals in the ground. A typical reforestation in lower Ontario goes through a series of battles, which occur on burned-over tracts. Goldenrod and bracken spring up quickly. Then young trees move in—birch and aspen. They make the ground friendly for spruce. Foxes come to prey upon the small mammals scurrying around under the low spruce cover and upon the moles and voles that burrow.

The birch grow tall; the young spruce upstarts at their feet do not bother them yet. However, the spruce and pine keep growing. This gives enough cover to attract deer or moose, who chomp the buds.

Depending upon terrain, drainage, weather, and other factors, a given community may stabilize at any seral stage where it becomes self-perpetuating and in equilibrium with the physical habitat. Until then, however, the succession continues as the community changes its own environment. For example, as the spruce and pine grow larger, the birch can still reach high above them to get the sun. But these larger evergreens are now dropping prodigious quantities of needles, totally changing the floor, building a thick, puffy mat. It is hard for birch and other seeds to get through this layer down to the soil.

The maple seed, however, has a way of drilling through the mat. Rather quickly young maples are pushing up under the evergreens, and they like shade. They cut off sunlight from struggling young birch that may have gained root. The spruce or pine overtake the birch; a mature stand of pine or spruce shows dying birch, and a pine-forest floor shows dead birch trunks being covered with needles.

Meanwhile, the maples are growing up under the evergreens, dropping more and more maple leaves until the forest floor is changed again. The maple leaves on the floor strand the evergreen seeds above ground and make the maples' takeover of the forest inevitable.

If one drives very rapidly through an area where reforestation of progressively cutover or burned-over land is in different seral stages, the succession of species becomes vivid as the forest changes before one's eyes, particularly in the fall. Then a two-hundred-year battle of the trees appears to be speeded up like an old-time newsreel.

Today the Great Lakes forest picture is divided into three rather distinct bands, running east-to-west, as shown on the map. The boreal forest region is spruce, jack pine, balsam, and tamarack; it runs north out of our story toward the Arctic Circle. Far to the south of that is the beech-maple forest region. Beech is usually the most abundant canopy, with sugar maple dominating the understory. The region contains islands of relic oak-hickory forest on gravelly morainal ridges too dry for beech-maple. Local hemlock communities are present on steep slopes and the edges of plateaus, and some southern and western slopes support white-oak forests. In depressions, we find red maple–white elm communities; in swamps, elm, ash, and maple grow; and throughout the region are inclusions of white oak–red oak–hickory communities. Accessory species are tulip trees 150 feet high, with leaf clusters that look like orchids; basswood; and on drained slopes, chestnut and cherry. The third and largest Great Lakes forest band is known as the hemlock–white pine–northern hardwoods region. It alternates deciduous, coniferous, and mixed forests.

In primary deciduous communities sugar maple, beech, and basswood dominate with yellow birch, white elm, and red maple associated. In secondary deciduous communities aspen, balsam, poplar, paper birch, and gray birch are populous.

This picture captures the plant successions as nature eutrophies a pond. When marsh turns to meadow, buttercups colonize first; later shrubs move in, and finally a full-fledged forest (background).

Coniferous communities sprinkled throughout the region differ according to drainage. On dry sandy ridges, we find white pine, red or Norway pine, and jack pine dominating; in the bogs, black spruce, northern white cedar, and larch. An exception to that brief description is the westernmost part of the band, where hemlock is not present and white pine is dominant.

Boundaries between different types of communities are not crisp because this is a great tension area, a battle zone in which more southerly species are pushing into the receding northern ranks. As one moves north the deciduous communities grow smaller until near the northern limits of the belt only isolated stands exist among the conifers. Patches of conifers in the southern part of the belt are relic communities giving up grudgingly. Accessory to the dominant species named, not necessarily growing together, is a rich variety: white ash, black cherry, white elm, northern red oak, basswood, red spruce, aspen, and jack pine.

Huge areas of Michigan's Lower and Upper peninsulas were once pure white pine. After the intense nineteenth-century lumbering, during which we built a nation with white pine, this tree became rare. Hartwick Pines State Park in Crawford County, Michigan, was established to preserve a piece of the original pine forest, but we cannot hold on even to this sanctuary; it is already changing by natural succession. However, barring outside influence, the conversion should require well over a century.

Spectacular is the word for the aspen communities. They are secondary growth that move into any part of the hemlock–pine–northern hardwoods region where virgin growth has been burned, cut over, or destroyed. Paper birch occurs in all the region's soils, though it is seldom dominant. Few of the individuals are large. A Chippewa Indian recently commissioned to build a replica of the famous Chippewa canoe had to travel over a thousand miles to find a tree large enough for his needs.

In the northwest part of the hemlock–pine–northern hardwood belt, the pines emerge especially strong: white pine, Norway pine, red pine, and jack pine. The period of dominance of jack pine can be 100 years; Norway, over 300; white pine, 250. The combined period of influence on a forest of white-, red- or Norway pine may endure for 600 years.

THE BROAD REGIONS we have just scanned speak of the present and the future. However, there is in the Great Lakes country a remarkable and beautiful peninsula that shows us the past. On the map you will see that Bruce Peninsula, with its matching counterpart, Door Peninsula, 100 miles west, is a surviving, unchipped fragment of the Niagara dolomite bowl, which forms the great circular rim containing Lakes Huron and Michigan. Bruce Peninsula separates Georgian Bay from Lake Huron.

Lumbermen did invade the Bruce in the late nineteenth century, but it was a hard harvest and therefore has been spared enough so that a good reforesting of spruce, red and white pine, and jack pine exists along with hardwoods. Tough white cedar thrives in the bogs and even digs into the windswept limestone cliffs, stunted and twisted, but holding because of its compatibility with limestone chemistry. The peninsula contains a nearly virgin forest of beech, maple, birch, and hemlock—Walker's Woods. Since this stand's evolution is reacting to only natural forces, botanists come here from the man-managed forest areas of the world to study it.

Another set of botanists come to the Bruce because of startling reruns of ancient plant life, which apparently went underground during the glacial wars and survived. The Alaska orchid, a small, delicate species, has been reported in only four places in the world, and Bruce Peninsula is one. In the crack at the foot of the escarpment grows an ancient fern, hart's-tongue, reported also in only three other regions. One fern reported only on Bruce Peninsula and in northern Michigan is the holly fern. The peninsula also offers a great demonstration of the walking fern, which seeds itself from a long, bending leaf, and in this way walks right up mossy rock cliffs and marches across damp forest floors and into caves at the base of the escarpment.

The dwarf iris is about two inches high and escapes our attempts to grow it from seed. New plants sprout from a sprawling parent root web, which has been traveling along the high-water line on the west shore of the Bruce for thousands of years. Botanists worry that nonlocal home builders and commercial developers on this west coast may not realize this.

The cedar swamps on the low west coast of the Bruce provide shelter for rare plants. Sundew is a ground cover that catches insects on the fine hairs of its sticky leaves, which then roll up around the prey to digest it. Pitcher plants are also carnivores, but the meanest flower is the deceptively pretty bladderwort blossom, with a lidded trap for capturing unwary admirers.

On the Bruce's west coast drainage a broad, slow-moving sheet of moisture seeps in just under surface soil, creating cool ground apparently akin to postglacial conditions and friendly to orchids. Thirty-five rare and ancient orchids prosper here. One, the *Habenaria leucophaea*, called by its admirers "*the* orchid," is seldom seen on this continent. Another, called "the rattlesnake" because of the markings on its leaves, may have had a camouflage partnership with endemic serpents.

These beautiful orchids are among nature's most amorous creations in the mating game. Some have a translucent Japanese-lantern pod, lit inside by bright colors that attract pollinating insects in the forest gloom. Some send out perfume to attract insects, then display cosmetic color lines to guide the carrier home. Some grow a leaf balcony for the matchmaker to land on, putting him in precise position to be daubed with pollen on the exact spot on his back where it can be picked up by the lady in his next port. Some siren orchids schedule their fragrance to coincide with the flight time of the desired insect messenger.

FOR TWO CENTURIES Great Lakes vegetation was viewed as man's enemy. Pioneer land prospectors and surveyors wrote east that an area was well watered, flat, and promising, "but unimproved." "Unimproved" meant the land was encumbered by a beautiful stand of trees or grass. "Improving" land meant getting rid of the trees and opening grassland sod, cutting through its tough root net. Hence, energetic and wasteful destruction began in the name of land improvement and later in the name of "best land use." Both were economic concepts.

Today a humanistic concept of land has led to buying back and fencing off forests for public use. Cities are buying land to retrieve green belts around their centers as planners learn that vegetation and standing trees in urbanized areas supply beauty and oxygen, hold ground moisture, cut down noise, moisten the air, and help convert ghettos to "neighborhoods." County agents in northern Ohio, Indiana, and Illinois are recommending that even in farm areas 40 percent of the land be kept in forest for the health of the farms.

Realization is coming, perhaps not too late, that Great Lakes plant life is a dynamic force—a fact long understood by the Indian but only lately appreciated by the white man who controls its destiny.

CHAPTER 5

WILDLIFE IN TRANSITION

A variety of animals, large and small, whose natural habitats provide a living laboratory for the study of past, present, future

IN A SMALL TENT on Isle Royale in Lake Superior, Dr. Durwood Allen pulls off his double mitten only long enough for some fast arithmetic on his clipboard. His breath defrosts part of his white beard as he reads the tally to two young colleagues. Their work shows a three-year average of 530 moose on the island, with a birthrate of 225 calves per year. They are probing for reasons why the herd has stabilized so precisely.

Over on Bruce Peninsula, the wildlife showcase that separates Georgian Bay from Lake Huron, a game warden asks a cooperative crowd not to scare off the exhausted and rare elk trying to swim in to the north shore.

At Point Pelee on Lake Erie, two mammalogists photograph their best find, a seldom-seen female river otter. They decide to request one more week's leave of absence to search for a male.

These men—all studying changes in the dynamic wildlife picture of the Great Lakes region—are part of an army of nature detectives observing wildlife patterns in response to the recent awareness that our ignorance could destroy the animal kingdom.

The Great Lakes basin is a transition area in the continent for mammals. Of 74 endemic species, 28 range the whole basin, 17 are southerners for which the Great Lakes are the northern limit, and 16 are northerners, with the Great Lakes as their southern limit. Eight have their eastern boundary in the Great Lakes region, five their western limit.

For some, the lakes themselves are the barrier, for others the ecology is. For example, the northerners usually do not venture south of the great conifer forests, while southerners stop traveling north when they run out of deciduous woods and smell evergreen. The plant life of the region slightly favors the northern (boreal) species—creatures of pine lands, cold swamps, and bogs.

Fossils show that Great Lakes country once pastured elephants, mastodons, giant beaver, and musk-ox, species that were wiped out by natural forces; but man has since leveled the forests county by county, driving many modern mammals to near extinction—the marten, cougar, fisher, wolverine, bison, elk. (Elk have been reintroduced and may regain a hoofhold.) The gray wolf and moose have fled to the wild northwestern extremes of the region and even there are disappearing. Farming has driven back the black bear, river otter, beaver, and bobcat. In the southern part of the Great Lakes country, the porcupine and some rabbits are losing ground to urban planners and exurban hunters.

The clearing of land, which drives out these larger species, coincidentally admits a host of little invaders from the south, such as the opossum, eastern mole, striped squirrel, and fox squirrel. Today dozens of species of moles, voles, shrews, bats, and rabbits inhabit different parts of the Great Lakes area.

One native that has persisted despite all changes is the raccoon, which night-prowls the entire area amphibiously. While raccoons prefer hollow-tree dens in natural forest, they will accept a suburban attic, preferably with a warm chimney. Therefore, youngsters who will never glimpse a cougar or a moose may well see this cocky

White-tailed deer still flourish in much of the Great Lakes region, particularly the unspoiled northlands along the St. Croix River.

masked bandit. He is driven by incessant appetite, curiosity, and determination not to give ground. This resistance was evident when the construction of a deluxe new lakeside summer colony in Wisconsin demolished natural raccoon dens: when the owners went home for the winter, over a thousand raccoons "subleased" split-levels for the season. There are thirty-one subspecies of raccoons, and an optimism surrounds their durability. They have even become accustomed to man-made noise. West Bluemound Road in Milwaukee is a commuter speedway, yet the trees alongside are homes for raccoons.

Throughout the Great Lakes region roam many other cousins of the weasel family: martens, mink, skunks, badgers, and various otters. Gnawing mammals also remain populous: woodchucks, gophers, beavers, and ten species of squirrels.

The cats have almost all gone to the Canadian side. The lynx, even where extant, is hardly seen at all because of his wariness. His cousin the bobcat, looking similar but smaller with bolder spots, is sighted more often, but a sighting still makes the newspapers.

As recently as four hundred years ago, French soldiers reluctantly working their way upstream from the Gulf of St. Lawrence wrote home about seeing large bobcats and cougars on both shores. They also described caribou browsing on the north shore of Lake Huron and buffalo on the south shore of Erie, and magnificent long-haired, barrel-chested elk charging through the forests.

WHILE POPULOUS WILDLIFE of the Great Lakes region spreads from the Gulf of St. Lawrence to Lake Superior country, there are two long, narrow points of land and one island where nearly the whole drama plays out in three acts: the old, the change, and the new.

For studying disappearing wildlife, Bruce Peninsula is ideal. It is a thin remnant of the Niagara escarpment separating Georgian Bay from Lake Huron. Its three-hundred-foot layered ridge, a showcase of fossil-filled Niagara dolomite, has remained hostile enough toward mankind that ancient wildlife species have been able to survive there.

A place evolving its own wildlife patterns is Isle Royale, a forty-five-mile American island located fifteen miles off Canada in Lake Superior, known to hunters for centuries. The government protects it, but nature is changing it.

To view the present total wildlife population, Point Pelee is ideal. It is Canada's Florida, a nine-mile spear in Lake Erie on the same warm latitude as Spain. It says nothing of the past because it is so delicate that wind and waves change its shape every year. But it is quite a complete catalog of the present because its lush marsh ecology is friendly to nearly every present-day regional species.

The Bruce Peninsula is fifty miles of rocky escarpment that separates Lake Huron from the "sixth Great Lake," Georgian Bay. It forms a huge arc with its counterpart, the Door Peninsula in Wisconsin, which separates Green Bay from Lake Michigan. It is part of the same tough Niagara dolomite slope that separates Lakes Erie and Ontario, and withstands the incessant wear of Niagara Falls. In fact, the Bruce Hiking Trail (480 miles) goes from Niagara Falls along the top of the Niagara Escarpment, across southern Ontario, and right out the length of Bruce Peninsula to Tobermory at its tip.

This rock structure of Bruce Peninsula has also been tough enough to resist most farming and civilization. Wearing a very thin coat of soil, it presents a cliff face to Georgian Bay and slopes southwest under Lake Huron in a marshy coast.

The Bruce has friends all over the U.S. and Canada who want to protect it because it shelters so many forms of ancient life. Ferns descended from dinosaur times shelter massasauga rattlesnakes, while enclaves of hidden flowers here date to the pauses between glaciers. Along the hiking trail on the three-hundred-foot ridge, a man can look down on eagles. If he gets off trail and lets himself halfway down the escarpment, where the surfs of ancient, higher seas cut caves, he may meet a black bear. Turkey vultures, nature's homeliest bird on the roost and most beautiful in the air, nest in caves, while the bald eagle builds a lash-up of sticks on overhanging ledges of the ridge or in trees.

Blue herons stand stock-still in the marshes on the west side of the peninsula, waiting with cocked heads for frogs and fish. Also numerous here is the Caspian tern, with its red bill, black cap, and a screech in the dusk that sends tourists back to their Winnebagos.

Ornithologists were thrilled to discover a single surviving Kirtland warbler. The world population of these birds, believed now to be less than one thousand, commutes between Michigan and the Bahamas. Since the Kirtland nests only in second-growth jack pine, Michigan bird lovers burn off small stands to make sure some area

The osprey has a wingspread of nearly six feet. Often called the "fishing eagle," it nests in tall trees by the shore; spotting its quarry, it dives feet first.

will always be favorable to the rare feathered species.

Now and then a surviving elk may be seen. On one occasion, a great buck elk swam toward shore from one of the islands. Seeing a curious crowd on shore, he veered away until a game warden asked them to move. Then the elk came in and dropped to the beach panting. After resting for five minutes, he rose and moved inland. At a discreet distance, wardens posted the area he chose and sent word to zoologists that a female was wanted.

Beaver have not only survived here but are coming back so strong and are so busily damming the creeks that they are flooding the one-lane roads.

Absence of insecticides, smoke, noise, and hunters makes Bruce the last stand for certain endangered Great Lakes wildlife, but it also is friendly to the more common species. Woodchucks and rabbits abound. In winter, when the summer visitors are gone, deer stroll among weathering cottages and browse on the tastier shrubbery.

While it is hoped the Bruce can endure in its present naturalness, it may not. Incessantly, the hamburger drive-in culture presses in.

A trip on the highway running along the spine of Bruce Peninsula is a beautiful experience, but the full wildlife story is seen best along the hiking trail. Canada politely warns visitors to prepare well. Even experienced outdoorsmen do not make a mile an hour through some of the tangled vegetation or up the steep rock faces. Many hope that civilization of the Bruce will be equally slow.

A strong swimmer, the moose seeks a home near water for better forage and protection from enemies.

From the ski-plane over Isle Royale, Dave Mech, Purdue Wildlife Management graduate student, focused his field glasses with all alertness on the moose cow below. He had seen that she was in the path of a nose-to-tail column of sixteen wolves, which had picked up her scent. Mech had three very hard winters invested in the chance to study this upcoming encounter. He yelled to the pilot over the noise of the engine, "Keep her in sight."

Three winters of tracking by snowshoe and aircraft had yielded few eye-witness views of the heart of the study, the actual attack and defense, crucial to understanding future population probabilities.

White-bearded and rugged, wildlife professor Durwood Allen had started this project by pointing out to Purdue graduate students the research potential of this national park island in Lake Superior: "About 600 moose on it. But fourteen years ago a few gray wolves walked across fifteen miles of ice from Canada. They say there's twenty to twenty-two of them now. It's a battleground."

Allen posed interesting questions. Will the moose stamp out the wolves? Will the wolves control the moose population to a level the browse can support? Or will the wolf population explode and wipe out the moose? Will the moose endure and the wolves starve?

"Might take ten years," he said, "but we'd come out with important answers."

On the 210 square miles of this wilderness island, Dr. Allen and two Purdue graduate students have been tracking some of the continent's few remaining wolves. Harried by bounty-hunter poisons, traps, and guns, gray wolves are down to perhaps 150 around the upper Great Lakes.

Tracking the largest of the three wolf packs, Allen and company found they had killed a moose approximately every fourth day, but not easily. They learned that wolves have deep respect for moose hooves. They avoid the bull in favor of the cow, and if a moose stands and fights several times, wolves will skulk off. The researchers found that the wolves had tested twelve moose for every one killed.

The team noticed that before ice forms, the moose can usually win if it can get to water. Standing knee deep it turns to face attacking wolves. If they do lunge into the water, it flounders them by kicking.

While the rest of the Canidae family range the whole region, the bounty-hunted gray wolf is largely found north of the Great Lakes, except for upper Minnesota and Wisconsin, and the Upper Peninsula of Michigan. Can they make a comeback if protected?

Dr. Allen's men were getting more questions than answers. Why were the wolves not multiplying? Did something tell them that one wolf per ten acres was the right number? Were pups being born but not surviving? The wolves must be aging. Were as many dying as were being replaced by pups?

And the moose—indications were that they were producing 225 calves per year, yet the herd population remained static. Were they losing exactly 225 per year?

Autopsies on the kills showed that the wolves were killing the oldest, youngest, and sickest moose. Moose between one and six years of age are healthiest, and they fight off wolves successfully two ways in winter. They stand and fight, or they take off into deep snow, where the chase exhausts the wolves.

When the wolves are more successful, the pack may leave one wolf to finish off a failing moose while the main party goes after another quarry. The guardsman wolf waits until the tiring moose tries to lie down, then he charges. The moose rises. Repeated, this process exhausts the moose.

Dave Mech watched from the ski-plane, thinking that the failing light might favor the moose's defense. He spotted the pack of sixteen wolves pushing through the snow in column with ears rigid, tails straight out. A hundred yards away the cow saw them coming. She began moving away, instantly triggering the predators' charge. They flew up the slope in ten-foot leaps, surrounding the cow. Backed up against some spruce trees she counter-charged. Ears flattened, head low, the cow was eight hundred pounds of alertness. When she had the wolves at bay, she tried to run. The wolves charged, several attaching themselves to her flank. She brushed them off against the trees.

However, she was running toward the edge of a fifty-foot embankment. The observers felt she would turn and face the wolves there. Instead, she plunged down the bank, and immediately the sixteen wolves swarmed over her and killed her.

This gray wolf, filmed from the air on Isle Royale, is a rare survivor of a century of bounty hunting.

Another winter, when the three Purdue men returned to Isle Royale by air, they sighted their large wolf pack and began counting.

"Seventeen!"—that was the first pup to their knowledge in four years.

NATURALISTS ALL OVER the world worry about Point Pelee. In science journals they read that this nine-mile needle of Canada in Lake Erie is endangered by wave action cutting away the east side two feet a year and by winds repiling the dunes on the west and ripping up vegetation.

This fantastic sand spit, only ten feet above the water and thinly clad at the tip by a scrabble of tough plants, is a haven for nearly every animal species in the Great Lakes region. It contains a two-thousand-acre marsh protected by Canada from man but not from nature. Water plants fight the open ponds; waves and winds rearrange the point, clipping three miles off it in three hundred years. Yet the spit survives and supports a rich variety of creatures in its disparate environments. Moles burrow the sand, mink cavort in the ponds, cottontail rabbits scoot through the brush, whitetail deer browse the woods.

The point is especially famous among bird lovers, as a terminus or way stop on major flyways. In spring the air vibrates under the arrival of great squadrons of tired birds from the south. Six hundred and fifty whistling swans will flap in one day, followed the next by twenty thousand white-throated sparrows, and the next by an armada of waterfowl. When they all arrive, Point Pelee has the most cosmopolitan bird population in the Great Lakes. By late spring, over a hundred species will have checked in.

Thus Point Pelee, Bruce Peninsula, and Isle Royale are living laboratories of many aspects of present, past, and future Great Lakes wildlife.

Bear territory generally lies north of Saginaw Bay and excludes the two lower-lake regions. Black bears, which may actually be dark brown or black, are five to seven feet long, weighing between 225 and 475 pounds, and standing about three feet high. Woods and swamps are their native environments.

Strangely enough, the bear is still partially a mystery. Lynn Rogers, a bearded two-hundred-pound bear of a graduate student at University of Minnesota, has been trying to remedy that for years. Rogers puts together enough small grants to devote his life to four-hundred-odd bears with which he is in radio contact. The radio collars he puts on his bears allow him to aim his jeep through the woods and recapture them periodically to record changes in their growth, biography, health, and habits. He has located and recaptured some of the bears more than two hundred times for study.

Most bear investigators shoot tranquilizing darts, but not Rogers. A dart-tranquilized bear may fall out of a tree or otherwise injure itself. Rogers climbs the tree, administers the shot by hand, and carries the monster down.

Citizens in several counties have resented Rogers' taking such good care of the bears. Some fear the bears; others like to go bear hunting at will, legal or otherwise. Several illegal hunters have looked up from their kill to find an enraged Rogers bearing down on them in his jeep. After many months of watching Rogers, the people now respect his work, phoning him day or night when they sight hunters or a wounded, trapped, or sick bear.

Heavy hunting endangers bears because they repopulate so slowly, the mother giving birth to one or two cubs only in alternate years. Rogers is optimistic, however, that bears are well equipped to survive. They are secretive and stay out of the way of loggers, hunters, and canoeists who invade the five square miles each needs for forage (within wilderness units at least fifty square miles in size).

The chain pickerel, like other members of the pike family, is a favorite among Great Lakes sport fishermen.

THE GREAT LAKES fish population changes dramatically from overfishing, new predators, government stocking, and man-made changes in spawning streams.

In the century of French domination, Atlantic salmon weighing up to forty pounds were taken easily in major tributaries of Lake Ontario. Numerous enough in autumn to be seined, they were a cash crop for homesteaders paying off mortgages.

Giant sturgeon, which could live a century and a half and grew to eight feet, swam up the Great Lakes tributaries to spawn. Commercially overfished in the late 1800s, they are gone now except in a few waters.

Other species have had special importance to Great Lakes natives. Whitefish were a delicacy, highly prized by commercial fishermen. The smaller Lake Erie whitefish was especially famous as a best-hotel gourmet fish. It has been starkly diminished by commercial overfishing, and especially by the advent of high-efficiency gill netting,

which almost depopulates a fishing area. There is little chance to evade a small-mesh gill net, which extends very deep in the water and captures young and mature alike by the gills. When the net is retrieved, the young fish are seldom released and many are dead.

A great game fish that sportsmen loved was the smallmouth bass, which was overfished commercially. Today it is generally protected by law as a game fish by both nations and may be making a comeback.

A twelve-pound walleye on light tackle may not give a man the challenging half-hour workout of a bass of comparable size, but it is exciting enough to lure fishermen back to western Lake Erie every Sunday. Natives call the olive-brown, prickly-skinned fish the walleye; visitors often call it a pickerel or pike perch. The walleye, similar to the blue pike and sauger, delivered a record commercial catch of nearly 8 million pounds in 1955. Then it began waning, until today the commercial catch is less than a third of a million pounds.

Most experts seem to think the walleye diminished, not

from overfishing or lake pollution, but rather from changes in its spawning tributaries. It is believed that fish may find their home spawning ground by scent. Chemicals, pulp, and suddenly overenriched plant life may change the homing fragrance and unfavorably change the spawning streams. At any rate, the walleye female, which once produced one hundred thousand eggs per spawn, now seems to wander like a fish without a country in spring.

ENFORCEMENT OF COMMERCIAL FISHING regulations has varied. On the Canadian side it was relaxed during World War I, and on the American side it fluctuates. Regulations are nearly unenforceable in their finer points, such as not taking fish during spawning runs, not catching them at all depths, and not harvesting below a certain size. The modernizing of commercial fishing gear (unbreakable nylons nets, bigger vessels, sounding gear) gave species less chance to survive, and thus to propagate. Belatedly, commercial fishermen have supported regulation.

When a species is wiped out or depressed, others fill the void. Smelt eggs from Maine were planted in Crystal Lake, Michigan, in 1912. By 1930 smelt were all over Green Bay. By 1935 they were all over Lake Michigan. By 1940 they were in Superior waters in prodigious numbers, and a few were caught downstream in western Lake Erie. The commercially important fish in the lower lakes today are yellow perch and smelt, the latter being nearly 100 percent of the Lake Erie catch.

Once man's canals had opened a through route from the Gulf of St. Lawrence, two major predators swam upstream to violently change the Great Lakes. It is nearly impossible for ocean fish to get upstream against the seaward flush of Niagara, the rapids, and the canal-lock sluices. However, there is an ugly creature, the sea lamprey, which is equipped to lock his suction-cup mouth onto any large fish that might manage the upstream trip and ride along. To man's surprise, it could also lock onto the barnacles of a wooden ship. Once the sea lampreys had stowed away and made it upstream of the Welland Canal in 1920, they continued migrating one lake at a time, multiplying prodigiously and attacking large lake trout.

Sport fishermen living today on the upper lakes still get wet in the eye when they tell of pulling in a trout to find him carrying a pair of these writhing outrages. Horny teeth hold fast to the trout while a drill-tipped tongue punches a hole in the host and sucks him dead. The lamprey grows to twenty-four inches.

Lampreys had nearly wiped out the trout before the United States and Canada took action in 1958. The U.S. government installed electrically charged wires to block the tributary spawning streams. Still, in high water, the lamprey evaded the charge. Later a mild poison killed lamprey larvae, achieving a temporary 80-percent drop in Lake Superior. At this writing, however, the population is back up, holding to within 10 to 20 percent of its peak.

In 1936, 5 million trout were caught in Huron alone. Today a single trout catch is reason for a round of drinks.

On May 5, 1949, a sportsman in a small boat off Manitou Island, Georgian Bay, caught a small fish he didn't recognize. He took it to a friend and said, "What in hell is this?" Together they took it to a commercial fisherman, who thought they were pulling a joke on him. He knew it was impossible for them to have caught this little fish; it was from the sea. A third specimen caught off Milwaukee came to the attention of a now-forgotten official in the Michigan Department of Conservation. Through the newspaper he warned—"Watch out."

It was too late.

The alewife is a mild-mannered little fish that appears to be no threat to any aquarium. However, it multiplies in hordes. Somehow the alewife got upstream of the Welland in the 1930s. It does not attack large competitors, but by sheer multitudes, it monopolizes all the forage, starving out its enemies. Unfortunately, the natural control opponents of the alewife—large trout and burbot—had been annihilated by the sea lamprey. So alewives have taken over, comprising nearly half the total Great Lakes fish population today, and are little valued by commercial or sport fishermen.

MAN—IN NUMBERS of any political significance—is only recently beginning to realize how precise are the environmental needs of wildlife and how little tolerance the wild things have for man-made changes. In addition to such refuges as Bruce Peninsula, Isle Royale, and Point Pelee, the Great Lakes states and provinces are gradually establishing really substantial legal sanctuaries and protected wilderness areas. Michigan, Wisconsin, Minnesota, and Ontario presently seem to be the most zealous in preserving the wild side of Great Lakes America.

Part Two
THE COMING OF MAN

Beginning some ten thousand years ago, the Great Lakes region was sparsely populated by eleven successive races of prehistoric peoples, who probably crossed over from Siberia via the Aleutian Islands in pursuit of game. The more sophisticated American Woods Indian who occupied these lakeshore forests when Europeans first came into them, whether he descended from the earlier inhabitants or migrated from somewhere else, can be traced to about 1000 B.C.

"The Moose Chase," by George deForest Brush.

CHAPTER 6

HIAWATHA'S PEOPLE

First came the prehistoric mound builders, to be followed
by the Algonquin, the Iroquois, and the Sioux

AT I:30 A.M. in an area called Africa, on a dirt road off U.S. 23 near Delaware, Ohio, the distinguished archaeologist Raymond S. Baby was on an urgent manhunt. When it began to rain, he left his tent with a roll of plastic drop cloth, which he spread over a particular part of the excavation, "Thought I could cover it a little better so we could start here in the morning. Not much time left, you know."

Dr. Baby and his associate, Martha A. Potter, are in charge of a crew excavating in search of missing persons. One would not expect them to be in such a hurry, since the trail is eleven thousand years cold. But the bulldozers are about to move in to build a dam. In fact, in this race to learn more about the prehistoric peoples who inhabited the Great Lakes area, Dr. Baby and his crews are only a jump ahead of the bulldozers all over Ohio, as a wave of highway construction, shopping centers, and condominiums unknowingly destroys his clues.

Over in Illinois outspoken Northwestern University archaeologist Stuart Struever had a crew also working a jump ahead of the bulldozers in Koster's cornfield on the Illinois River. They have screened one hundred thousand cubic feet of dirt and have delved through fifteen prehistoric towns stacked on top of one another. "We're down eight thousand years now, and if we can finish before rising land values take it away from us, we think we'll get down eleven thousand years."

Similar searches are going on all over the Great Lakes area as scholars race construction crews for clues to mysterious populations who roamed the territory hun-dreds of years before the arrival of the American Indian.

A carpet of cedar bogs followed the Wisconsin glacier's retreat north, supporting a large number of animals. The cold, moist path of the glacier favored cedar, spruce, fir, and pine, and their roots could make the most of the stony, newly ice-free soil. These plants in turn favored the giant beaver, musk-ox, tapir, and mastodon. Tracking the smaller game—and trying to avoid the large—were short, black-haired, bent-kneed men who fought a daily battle against dangerous animals and climate.

Despite shelves of volumes about them, our knowledge of these prehistoric peoples is still faint, but certain distinct populations have been established.

Paleo people (from Paleolithic Age)	
First group: Fluted-Point Complex (from pattern on their chipped spearheads)	9000 to 6000 B.C.
Second group: Plano Complex	7500 to 6000 B.C.
Archaic	6000 to 1500 B.C.
Old Copper people	4000 to 1000 B.C.
Glacial Kame (from burial ground in glacial kames)	2500 to 1000 B.C.
Adena (name of farm where first found)	1000 B.C. to A.D. 700
Hopewell (name of owner of farm where artifacts were found)	300 B.C. to A.D. 600
Cole	800 B.C. to A.D. 300
Erie and Fort ancient peoples	A.D. 1000 to 1654

The Koster site dig in Illinois is yielding a rich store of information about prehistoric Indians; the pioneers
who built their farmhouse here in the 1830s were the thirteenth culture on this site.

The Old Copper people around the Keweenaw Peninsula made crude cutting tools millennia before Christ.

IT IS BELIEVED that when the glaciers built up for the last advance on the Great Lakes region, they consumed so much of the earth's water that oceans fell three hundred feet, unveiling enough of the tops of formerly submerged mountains to create intermittent land bridges across the present Bering Strait and the Aleutian archipelago so animals and then men could cross from Siberia to Alaska and over many generations work their way south on the west side of the Rockies. When they were south of the glaciers, they began filtering east and north, following game and the improving climate created by the recession of glaciers.

Relics of the first four groups of primitive men—the Paleo, the Archaic, the Old Copper, and the Glacial Kame peoples—show a painfully slow inching forward in

sophistication. The eight thousand years from 9000 B.C. to 1000 B.C. reveal a gradual progression from plain flint spearheads to fluted spearheads to the use of the atlatl, a grooved stick that was a spear launcher, giving the hunter leverage for more distance and accuracy.

Nomadism decreased slightly; some very primitive agriculture began; a few crude tools were devised; and a spiritual life built around the burial ceremony was developed. Some use of copper occurred. Spread over eight thousand years, however, the pace of cultural change was snaillike.

MOVING DOWN THE CENTURIES to 1000 B.C., we come to a turning-point population in the Great Lakes country, the Adena people (so named because they were first identified from diggings on Adena, the homeplace of Ohio's sixth governor, Thomas Worthington). The first to span the B.C.–A.D. point in time, they also were the region's first mound builders; and they began to farm pumpkin, squash, and march elder in substantial quantity, judging by seeds found in their excavated campfire pits. They girdled trees, apparently to open their gardens to the sun, indicating a longer stay.

With this group, the nomadic characteristic waned sharply. Settlements consisted of two to four huts by a stream. Sometimes a four- or five-foot circular wall of earth surrounded such a village. Adena houses were the most sophisticated yet. Short posts were set in the ground a yard apart in a circle, slanting outward; then vines were woven among them to form outer walls. Four tall posts rose in a square in the middle of the circle, supporting roof timbers radiating to the short walls. These were covered with bark. The outward slant of the outer walls shed rain away from the base of the house. The firepit was in the center of the four support posts.

Adena spiritualism apparently was highly ritualized. Relics of shaman costumes appear to have been made in a standardized way of wolf heads and skins, along with leather bags of objects believed to be the witch doctor's magic kit.

The Adena people demonstrated more craftsmanship than their forebears. They made pottery by rolling long coils of clay, forming them into circles, piling circle upon circle, then firing. They also smoked clay pipes. Animal-skin clothing came into fashion with awled holes for lacing;

Much can be learned about prehistoric Great Lakes peoples from their burial places. As spiritual life developed, funerals became important and elaborate, as shown in this University of Michigan diorama.

ornaments included bracelets, beads, and finger rings, many inscribed with serpents.

The mounds for which the Adenas are known were used for burial, around which event their most elaborate ceremonial and spiritual life developed.

The later Hopewell people (whose artifacts were first found on the lands of Capt. M. C. Hopewell, Ross County, Ohio) built mounds of a more spectacular type; however, the Hopewell Indians spanned a region far beyond the Great Lakes country.

The Adena mounds were huge and conical; the most spectacular, however, was an exception—the Great Serpent Mound. This thousand-foot serpent in Miamisburg, Ohio, is neither a burial site nor a fortification. Apparently

it is merely the Adenas' monument to the serpent. Today thousands of tourists annually stare at it and ask, "Why?"

From excavated graves, we know that the Adenas practiced head deformation. Infants were strapped to timber boards to flatten the back of their heads. Some skulls show depressions in the forehead, too, presumably from the bindings.

Within the Great Lakes region evidence of Adena occupation has so far appeared only as far north and west as Indiana, Illinois, Ohio, and Pennsylvania. They endured, most researchers believe, into the sixth century A.D.

The Hopewell people, who arrived on the scene a little later, were more advanced and more ceremonial, and they were prodigious builders of nearly one hundred thousand

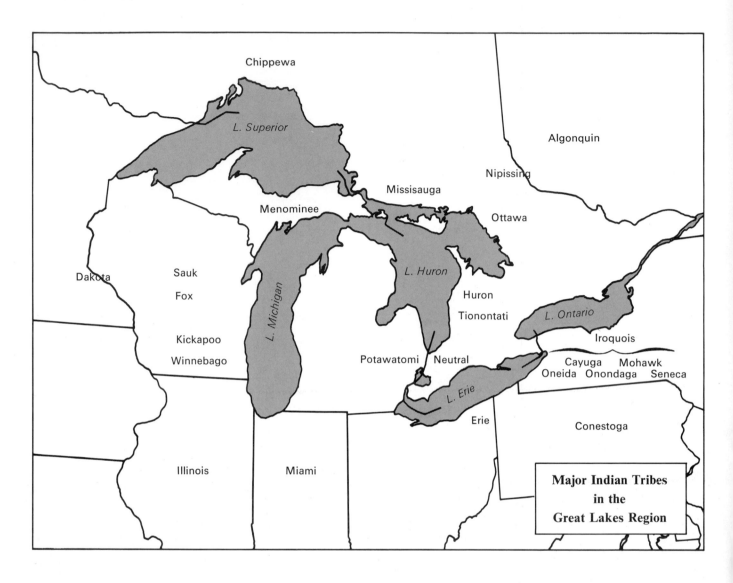

Chippewa

L. Superior

Algonquin

Nipissing

Missisauga

Menominee

Ottawa

Dakota

Sauk

L. Huron

Fox

Huron

Tionontati

L. Ontario

Kickapoo

Iroquois

Winnebago

Potawatomi   Neutral

Cayuga   Mohawk

Oneida Onondaga   Seneca

L. Michigan

L. Erie

Erie

Conestoga

Illinois

Miami

**Major Indian Tribes
in the
Great Lakes Region**

mounds in twenty eastern states. They were followed by a people scholars call the Intrusive Mound people, who did not build their own mounds but excavated existing ones, making new graves in them. At their highest state of civilization, evidence of these latter people abruptly disappears, suggesting famine, epidemic, or war.

While we have fragmentary knowledge of some additional minor cultures scattered around the Great Lakes—including the ill-fated Erie people, who lived in moated and picketed fortifications until their slaughter and extinction—there is generally a great thousand-year dark age from approximately A.D. 600 to A.D. 1650—a gap between the prehistoric peoples and the American Indian.

Some believe that the American Indians are descended

from these prehistoric peoples; others believe them to be a whole new wave of immigrants. The answers still lie buried under the earth of Great Lakes country.

IN A.D. 1600 the crudely estimated 117,000 American Indians of several dozen tribes in the Great Lakes region divided themselves loosely into three large groups: Iroquois, Algonquin, and Sioux. These groupings were not geographical, religious, or nationalistic but were based on language similarity.

Indians speaking Siouan-type languages, numbering only about 5,000, were established in Wisconsin, Minnesota, and western Ontario. Iroquoian language tribes, a population of about 43,500, were around Lakes Erie, Ontario, and eastern Huron, and astride the St. Lawrence River. The sprawling Algonquian-speaking population of about 69,000 was generally in the center: Michigan, Illinois, Ohio, eastern Wisconsin, and Ontario.

The boundaries, however, were not clear-cut. The fifty or a hundred villages of one tribe would sprawl across 800 to 1,000 miles, necessarily crossing and intermingling with the villages of the other two language groups.

A lifetime would be needed to trace the odysseys of the migrating and warring tribes over the years. One man who recently did much to extract from all sources the Indian picture of the whole region is William J. Kubiak, an artist and lifelong student of the Indian. His task in tracking individual migrating tribes was complicated by the tremendous variation in the naming of tribes. Chippewas, for example, have twenty-six different names. Seven of these names look and sound something like *Chippewa;* nineteen

are totally different, including their own name for themselves, *Anishinabe* ("first man").

None of the three language groups had a strong central leadership. Each contained certain confederations of tribes having a common geography or common enemy to ally them. In general, tribes within a language group made war less often upon each other and had some similarities in travel, warfare, torture, and religion.

During the two centuries from 1600 to 1800, as the Dutch, English, French, and Spanish fought a bitter contest for control of the continent, these Indians survived white men's wars in which they were treated as only a nuisance or a force to be used for leverage. The Indian was unable to organize, except on a too-local basis, to wield his balance of power effectively.

What he did accomplish is remarkable when we consider the wonder of a primitive man's first encounter with gunfire, hearing its stupefying thunder in a forest that had

Mysticism pervaded the everyday life of Indians in the lake region. This rendering of the Winnebago medicine dance appears in a volume by that foremost authority on Great Lakes Indians, Henry Schoolcraft.

BY SETH EASTMAN, STANFORD UNIVERSITY LIBRARY

long been silent. His perception of distinctions among nationalities and even in the politics and objectives of white men who looked and spoke alike—the British and the American colonists—seems amazing. That he learned to communicate in both French and English is startling.

When Europeans assaulted the continent in 1520, the Indian tribes lived in isolated, independent villages. The Algonquian and Siouan language groups were nomadic; the central Iroquoian tribes were doing some farming—fourteen kinds of maize, fifty kinds of beans, several species of squash. These were not confined to small patches; fields stretched for miles in strips along the river bottoms. All three language groups had very effective canoe designs and traveled the rivers and the Great Lakes knowledgeably without maps.

The three groups differed in living habits. The Sioux favored the wigwam, a conical frame of saplings lashed together at the top around a smoke hole and covered with skins and bark. Contrary to the souvenir-store offerings, these were not neat and symmetrical.

The Iroquois, more settled, favored the longhouse, where six to twelve families lived. To build it, two parallel rows of saplings forty to eighty feet long were stuck into the ground. The tops of the saplings were bent to the middle and lashed together, forming a tunnel. Transverse saplings were woven in, and the long arch was covered with bark and skins. Despite smoke holes, many Indians were ultimately smoke-blinded. Jesuit missionary guests or prisoners complained of smoke, noise, dogs, and dirt.

The Algonquins favored a dome-shaped hut, of similar construction to the long house.

The spiritual world of the Indians was complex and highly developed, peopled with gods of good and evil with retinues of specialist archangels and devils for hunting, fishing, fighting, and living long. Dreams and visions played a large part, and shamans of various sorts worked with horrible accoutrements and magic objects.

WHILE IT IS NOT FEASIBLE either to describe life in every tribe nor to let one tribe represent all, a look at three influential tribes is revealing: the Chippewas, the Ottawas, and the Five Nations.

When the famous Chippewas were allied with the Potawatomis and Ottawas in the Three Fires Confederacy, they were the greatest power in the western lakes.

They centered first around Sault Ste. Marie, moved to La Pointe, south of Superior, and later to the region north of Superior. *Ojibwa* is what neighboring Indians called them; Englishmen pronounced it "Chippewa."

Algonquian-Language Tribes
Ottawa
Miami
Illinois
Chippewa
Potawatomi
Algonquin
Abnaki
Fox
Kickapoo
Mascouten
Menominee
Missisauga
Nipissing
Sauk (Fox or Sak)

Iroquoian-Language Tribes
Erie
Huron (Wyandot)
Iroquois
Neutral
Tionontati (Tobacco Huron)
Wenrohronon
Conestoga (Susquehanna)
Seneca
Cayuga
Onondaga
Oneida
Mohawk
Tuscarora

Siouan-Language Tribes
Winnebago
Dakota
Tutelo

The Chippewa was tall—the compassionate U.S. government Indian agent Henry Schoolcraft estimated that half the Chippewa men were six feet tall. While Chippewa women paid unusual attention to their appearance, combing and braiding their hair elaborately, Chippewa men

Sault Ste. Marie was always a strategic Indian site, commanding as it did the entrance to three lakes, and it changed hands several times. Paul Kane painted these Ojibways there in 1845.

tended to be sloppy; their deerskin jackets still had patches of hair on them and drooped to mid-thigh, belted low. Around his head the Chippewa wrapped strips of deerskin, turban fashion.

The Chippewa was an excellent beaver trapper, using a rather complex trap baited with beech sapling to trigger the drop of a heavy log on the prey. Indian dogs, according to Jesuit missionary Paul Le Jeune, were trained to pursue and catch beaver, too. But possibly their greatest contribution was the design of the Chippewa canoe, widely emulated because of its steadiness in rapids, shallow draft, and high cargo capacity.

In 1764 the Chippewa were estimated at 25,000; in 1794—15,000; in 1843—30,000.

The Ottawas—from *adawa*, "to trade"—were so named by other tribes because they traveled and traded furs, skins, tobacco, roots, and herbs. They inhabited the south shore of Lake Erie, nearly the entire eastern and southwestern shores of Lake Michigan, as well as the Bruce Peninsula, Manitoulin Island, and the north shore of Georgian Bay.

Ottawas were especially appearance conscious, wearing tattoos, nose rings, and ornaments, and in winter fur robes to the ankles. Champlain met three hundred Ottawas between Lake Nipissing and Georgian Bay, and named them *Cheveux Relevez*, writing, "Not one of our courtiers takes so much pains in dressing his locks."

The most distinguished Ottawa was Pontiac, who built an alliance with the Chippewas and Potowatomis to harass the British. When Pontiac was murdered in 1769,

Awbonwaishkum, chief of the Ottawas, a people widely known for their painstaking personal grooming.

Red Jacket, chief of the Senecas, the largest tribe of the powerful Five Nations confederation.

the Ottawas contracted their population onto Walpole Island in Lake St. Clair and onto Manitoulin and Lockburn islands and the Canadian shore of Lake Huron. Today there are Ottawas living on Michigan's Lower Peninsula.

I F ONE HAD TO SELECT the best-known and most influential Great Lakes tribe, he would probably be compelled to choose the Iroquois.

"Tribe" is a flexible concept, and tribes confederated and deconfederated from time to time over various disputes. The most enduring confederation was the Five Nations, a hundred-year union that often dominated the region and its destiny.

This union was probably formed around 1600 by five small tribes in a lateral line across the Finger Lakes of New York, where they had moved from the St. Lawrence near

Montreal when the French came. In the New York location the league stretched from Lake Champlain to the Genesee River and from the Adirondack Mountains south to the Susquehana River in Pennsylvania. From east to west, it included the Mohawks, Oneidas, Onondagas, Cayugas, and Senecas. This group was called by many names, most commonly Iroquois, Confederate Indians, Five Nations, Mingos, and Six Nations (after the Tuscaroras joined them).

The Mohawks were the fiercest. The Onondagas ("People of the Hills") had their villages on a hill in the center and ruled the league. Most numerous were the Seneca.

Fierceness was the confederation's salient characteristic, and a sense of outrage its principal mood after the arrival of whites. These Indians are closest to the model of the warlike woodland Indians appearing in art, literature, and history. Most Iroquois men wore the shaved head with center tuft; the Mohawks wore the famous crescent-

Great Lakes Indians understood and respected their unique environment. These are Menominees, as artist Paul Kane observed them, spearing fish at night by the light of pine-knot fires.

shaped cockscomb. They painted their faces and upper bodies elaborately for war, and some used a primitive chest armor made of plaited branches and small shields made of bark.

Between major wars, the Five Nations conducted what might be called training wars, constant small attacks on other Indians and whites. Young braves gained experience and trophies, and veterans stayed keen. Thus, they were always in a state of taut readiness. The warrior was revered in this culture as other tribes revered the hunter or trapper. To make up for heavy losses in war, the Iroquois adopted Indians from defeated tribes so extensively that adopted members sometimes outnumbered native Iroquois.

While all Indians tortured captured prisoners, the Five Nations' tortures were probably the most excruciating and vicious. While their warlike cruelty could turn the stomachs of strong men, it was nevertheless the only thing that elicited from the white man respect and honest dealing.

White men who defaulted on a bargain with them were caught and turned over to the women. They ultimately begged to be killed.

The fierceness of the Five Nations is not typical of Great Lakes Indians, even though nearly all tribes did torture and practice cannibalism. When the inevitable European tide gained momentum against them, however, the impression one gets from Jesuit notes and the journals of Indian agents, surveyors, and troops is a milder one. The picture comes through of a bewildered people of the forest —who had learned the laws for making peace with that forest—trying desperately to appease the strange world of gunpowder, commerce, and European ideas of territorial possession.

Even in the midst of bloodshed, without benefit of hindsight and nostalgia, frontiersmen like Henry Schoolcraft, William Johnston, and William Henry Harrison wrote of the Great Lakes Indian with affection and admiration.

CHAPTER 7

THE EARLY EXPLORERS

Frenchmen who claimed and built a fragile empire while seeking an elusive waterway to the wealth and spices of China

THE FIRST GREAT LAKES EXPLORERS had no better designed itinerary than most other advance men of history. However, because for two centuries their goal was a route to China, Europeans' search was totally waterborne; therefore it was canalized by major waterways into a crisp and strategic shape—a vast arc from the Gulf of St. Lawrence through the Great Lakes to the headwaters of the Mississippi and thence down to the Gulf of Mexico.

Europe's navigators first entered the continent through the northern waters, hence a huge arc of discovery preceded exploration of the seaboard shelf east of the Appalachians. While English beachheads like Boston and Jamestown were still learning to survive winterkill, experienced French voyageurs were already climbing the water stairway into *Lac Supérieur*, two thousand canoe miles from salt water. By 1682, La Salle planted the last of a long series of flags at the Mississippi delta on the Gulf of Mexico and these flags were French. A huge arc surrounded the eastern-seaboard civilizations.

Seeking not fame but only fair weather, French and Portuguese fishermen commonly worked the cod waters off Newfoundland in the early 1500s. Certainly some discovered the mouth of the unnamed St. Lawrence, sailed up it, and landed on its shores. But these were nameless men in nameless ships. The schoolbook discoverer of the St. Lawrence, and deservedly enough, is a French seaman who grew up on the seacoast of St. Malo, Brittany—Jacques Cartier. When King Francis I became earnest about finding a shortcut to the wealth of China, he selected

from those who applied this weathered young Breton master pilot. Slight in stature, Cartier approached the shore world with a deferential courtesy, but when he walked a deck, his demeanor turned quietly commanding.

Cartier was in his early thirties in 1534 when he headed out from St. Malo with two small ships. He had made it to Newfoundland before; this time the navigational challenge would be finding that rumored waterway to China. He braved the grim cliff of Newfoundland and combed the waters of the gulf, looking for an opening. But the Gulf of St. Lawrence is a vast sea in itself, and its shores are scalloped with identical bays, often shrouded in cold fog.

Trying to make his way around Gaspé Peninsula he was hit by a driving storm. The jutting rock off Gaspé Bay interrupted the wind, so he took shelter behind it and dropped anchor.

Going ashore in a long boat, he planted a thirty-foot timber cross with a pageantry that impressed the Indians favorably until the crew hung on it a flag with a fleur-de-lis and the words "Vivre le Roi France." The chief knew no French, but he recognized it as some tribal totem of ownership, and he challenged Cartier angrily. Cartier, in the quickly learned art of deceiving natives, pantomimed to the chief that it was only to guide ships. He proffered a hatchet, which soothed the chief, and two red hats, which intrigued the chief's two young sons. Cartier then made the chief understand that he would like to take these boys back to France for a visit. Strangely, the chief consented, sending beaver pelts as a kind of dowry.

Cartier had to put out before winter. He had not found

Jacques Cartier's explorations opened the North American continent to France. On his second trip he sailed up the St. Lawrence as far as the Indian village of Hochelaga (Montreal).

A professional navigator, Jacques Cartier was commissioned by Francis I to sail to China.

France's claim to Canada was based on Cartier's first voyage, in 1534, when he discovered the mouth of the St. Lawrence, landed on the Gaspé Peninsula, erected a cross, and took two Indian boys home to France.

the great river, but when he tied up at St. Malo, the two Indian boys and the beaver fur became the conversation of high-level Europe.

It seems odd at first that nothing much was made of the fact that Cartier had claimed a continent for France. However, the enormity of the land mass was not yet realized, and the real need of kings at the time was not land but that rumored northwest water passage to the gold and spices of China.

Francis I commissioned Cartier for a second attempt, this time with three vessels—the *Grande Hermine*, *Petite Hermine*, and *Emerillon*. Cartier retraced his route quickly to Gaspé. His return with the two boys gained him the trust of the Indians, who now helped him locate the river mouth. He named it St. Lawrence, because it was on that saint's feast day that he entered it.

As they sailed up the St. Lawrence, hopefully to China, the French seamen were awed. The water was too broad

to be a river. White whales and seals frolicked in it, and cliffs loomed above them—silent, primeval, and foreboding. This crew became the first Frenchmen to tilt their heads back and look up at that forbidding rock promontory—Quebec.

Around the ships crowded the canoes of the Huron-Iroquois of Stadacona village. They yelled in approval when Cartier displayed his two Indian boys. Through these lads Cartier asked, "What place is this?" The probable reply was "*kanata*," Iroquois for "the village." Whatever—Cartier pronounced it "Canada."

They told of a larger *kanata* upstream—Hochelaga. Cartier built a small log fort on the bank of a tributary opposite Stadacona, then moved upstream in his smallest vessel, the *Emerillon*, to Hochelaga, a highly developed village with long bark houses.

Cartier and his men, in gleaming chest armor and helmets, were greeted as gods. The Indian leaders took him to the top of the mountain by their village, and he dubbed it *Mont Réal* (Mount Royal). As he looked toward China, the view was breathtaking but marred by a violent white-water cascade boiling down a series of rock stairs, which he knew his ships could not climb. He named them Lachine rapids for China, turned the *Emerillon* down-stream, and spread sail to return. But he found himself locked in the St. Lawrence by ice.

On the first spring day when oarsmen were able to push one of the small deck dories through the floating slush, Cartier gave orders to prepare sail, and he invited Chief Donnacona aboard for a farewell feast. While the dining and oratory were in progress, Cartier hand-signaled the first officer. Seamen raised anchor quietly and spread sail. With kidnapped Donnacona aboard, the *Emerillon* was under way, as were three and a half centuries of white trickery against red men.

Francis I, though impressed with Donnacona, was dis-appointed in the exploration results. Preoccupation with a Spanish war further disinterested him in Canada. By 1541, however, he felt the only way to maintain his claim to Canada until he was ready to exploit it was to establish at least one formal settlement there. A large expedition was fitted out under two leaders: the Sieur de Roberval, viceroy in charge of the settlement, and Cartier, who was in charge of navigation, exploration, search for treasure, and finding the route to China. From the outset the two leaders were at odds, finally splitting the expedition, each half going its own way. Both failed, and eventually Cartier was sent one more time to take de Roberval's dying settlers off Canada.

For fifty years the Indians would be left alone, except for Breton fishermen going ashore occasionally to trade knives for pelts of mink, otter, and especially beaver.

HENRY OF NAVARRE ascended the throne of France with a different plan. After destructive religious and Spanish wars, he was determined to expand French power. He wanted Canada; and he wanted the fur trade to be under official French auspices, not siphoned off in-formally by fishermen. For this he employed an effective formula that would become the pattern for French colo-nizing. He gave large land grants and exclusive fur trade charters to noblemen and businessmen who would agree to emplace settlers and towns, using their own capital in

Samuel de Champlain, though he arrived late (1603), colonized and so is known as the Father of Canada.

exchange for exclusive fur rights. To assign these rights intelligently, the king needed to know the shape and size of the land. For this exploration he selected the man usu-ally considered the father of the Great Lakes country and New France—Samuel de Champlain, a young army of-ficer with a boyhood and family heritage of seafaring who had demonstrated his own seamanship, daring, and execu-tive ability in campaigns to the West Indies and Mexico.

In 1603, Champlain set out for Canada accompanied by Sieur de Pontgravé, who was to engage in fur trade at Tadoussac. While Pontgravé dealt with the Indians, Champlain sailed up the Saguenay, discovering its great breadth, depth, and waterfalls.

The next year Champlain made a second trip, bringing this time the Sieur de Monts, who held monopoly fur rights and the responsibility to colonize. Pontgravé came along also. On this voyage they built the colony of Habi-tation at Port Royal (now Annapolis Royal, Nova Scotia).

CULVER PICTURES

*Champlain cast France's fate with the Algonquins at Lake Champlain, forcing England to ally with the opposing Iroquois—
a pivotal decision that influenced affairs on this continent for one hundred years.*

Meanwhile Champlain carried on his life's mission of exploring and building the Canada empire for France. Sailing up the magnificent, silent St. Lawrence, using Cartier's landmarks, he chose a small shelf at the foot of a great cliff to locate a second French colony. *Kèbec*, the Indians called it—"*place where the waters narrow.*" The French spelled it *Quebecq*.

The fur-trading monopolists defaulted badly in their commitment to colonize. The king took away charters and commissioned new men who did no better. What early French development did take place in Canada was accomplished by Champlain, who nurtured Port Royal, Quebec, and Montreal. For a quarter century, whenever Champlain could escape the administrative duties of building Quebec, he paddled up the myriad waterways with Indian guides, exploring and mapping and looking for the water route to China.

As much as he traveled, it is amazing that Champlain did not personally locate the Great Lakes. However, he was indirectly responsible for their discovery.

On his sixth voyage (1608), Champlain's design was to put strong young Frenchmen of adventurous bent among the Indians for extended periods to learn the various Indian languages and explore the thousands of rivers. This scheme should put future French colonization on a sound basis of real knowledge of the land and its routes, resources, and native peoples.

One of these young men was the brilliantly daring seventeen-year-old, Étienne Brûlé. Tough, energetic, burdened by little conscience, religion, or patriotism, Brûlé was a shrewd selection. He would become the instrument for the first full revelation to white man of the location, size, shape, and complexity of the Great Lakes' waters and land masses.

At the end of his first year among the Indians near Ottawa, Brûlé reported back to Champlain at Quebec

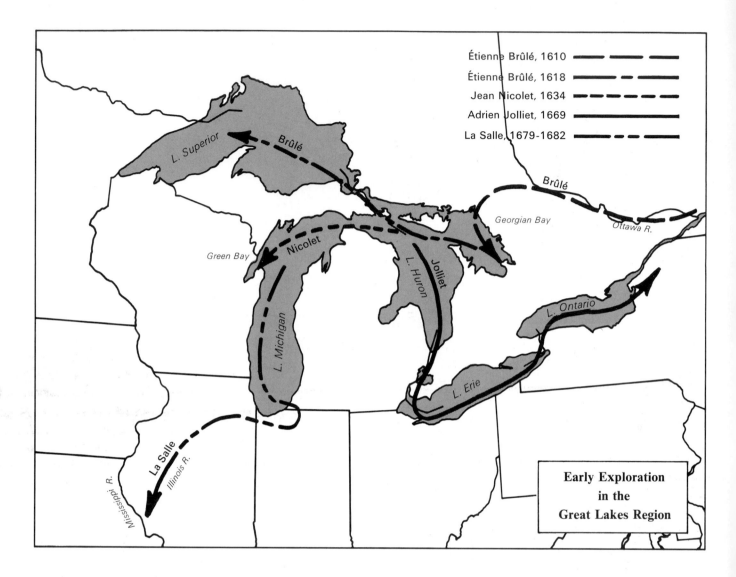

Étienne Brûlé, 1610
Étienne Brûlé, 1618
Jean Nicolet, 1634
Adrien Jolliet, 1669
La Salle, 1679-1682

**Early Exploration
in the
Great Lakes Region**

dressed as an Algonquin, speaking Algonquian and insultingly eager to hurry back to the Indians. From then on Brûlé's experience and exploration among the Indians became the most concentrated of all explorers'; at the same time his reports and his loyalty to France became thinner.

Indian men found him bold, strong, and a good fighter, and their women accepted him into welcoming brown arms at night. While the Jesuits criticized him for this, it was normal Indian conduct—and he had become Indian.

Ultimately, the Indians took Brûlé up the Ottawa into Georgian Bay, making him the first white to see the short route from the St. Lawrence to the upper lakes and the first to see Lake Huron. Later they showed him the extension—up the white waters of St. Mary's River to Sault

Ste. Marie and out onto the broad surface of Gitche Gumee, the "shining Big-Sea-Water"—Lake Superior. Thus the upper lakes were, strangely enough, discovered before the lower lakes, Erie and Ontario.

For two decades Brûlé conducted these dangerous explorations. Even his detractors conceded that he had discovered more of the region than all the other explorers together. Champlain's fatherly feeling for the young man fought with his disgust over Brûlé's thin patriotism. He forgave Brûlé repeatedly until 1629, when his protégé betrayed him to the British, resulting in his capture.

In 1633 Champlain, released from captivity, became governor of New France. He cut off Brûlé's French pay and sent word among the Hurons that he wanted Brûlé delivered up for court-martial. Instead the Hurons took over the punishment. Brûlé was brutally quartered, broiled, and eaten.

IN THE DECADES THAT FOLLOWED, scores of explorers filled in the growing map of New France and pushed its boundaries west and south. Jean Nicolet, on orders of Governor Champlain to pursue a newly rumored route to China, became the first white man to push west through the Straits of Mackinac. China was not there, but he did discover Green Bay, which he claimed for France.

Adrien Jolliet, returning from Lake Superior in 1669, took a fateful detour. He normally paddled north to the Ottawa and down it to Montreal, avoiding dangerous Iroquois to the south, but reports of a peace treaty had emboldened him to paddle downstream on Lake Huron. He continued through its outlet and found himself on a new lake—Erie. He crossed Erie, portaged around Niagara, and paddled on across Ontario, thus opening a broad new route and eliminating scores of portages.

The most capable governor since Champlain arrived in 1672—Louis de Buade, Comte de Palluaue de Frontenac. In addition to administrative flair, he had Louis XIV's favor for a strong-handed extension of New France from Newfoundland to Texas. An empire builder, Louis sought to do with French mercantilism what England had done with navigation. New France was vital to his plan.

Frontenac moved forcefully on several fronts to expand exploration. First, he built Fort Frontenac at the present site of Kingston and used it to force a peace agreement from England's powerful but frightened Five Nations Indians, who controlled Lake Ontario. This gave him freer movement on Ontario. Second, Frontenac took firm control of the fur trade, which had drifted into fragmented ownership. Third, he activated exploration with the specific triple mission of seeking the most strategic fur stations, strongest fort sites, and as always, the route to China. The route to China mission, however, was subtly modified: China—yes, if possible—but in any case push

This map of Louis Jolliet's 1673 expedition from the Great Lakes to explore the Mississippi reflects France's dawning ambition: to link the two great watersheds into a vast crescent empire of French power and commerce.

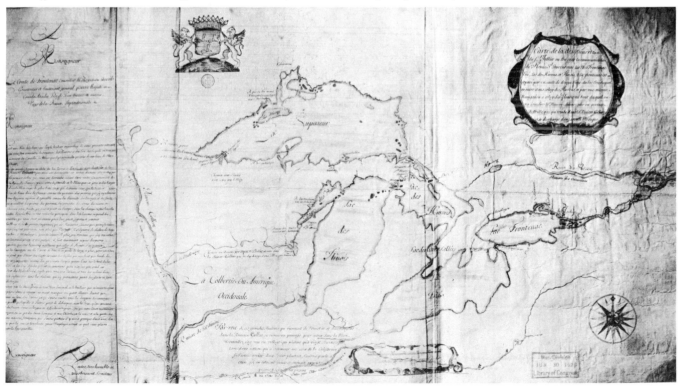

René Robert Cavelier, Sieur de la Salle, pushed French territorial claims all the way to the Gulf of Mexico.

New France all the way south to a full half-circle by water behind the English colonies. *Frontenac knew that if it came to a confrontation, Frenchmen could traverse their watery empire quickly from strategic strongholds; the English, locked to the land, could only crawl their armies and supplies through roadless forests.*

This strategy, along with a desire for a warm-water entrance to the continental interior, pressed Louis Jolliet and Father Jacques Marquette into the search for the rumored, mysterious "Mees-ee-see-pee" or "Messip"—the old, big, deep, strong, and muddy river.

Frontenac commissioned Louis Jolliet to organize this mission in exchange for customary fur rights. Jolliet chose five capable voyageurs. The head of the Jesuits selected Father Jacques Marquette to accompany the expedition.

On May 17, 1673, the party pushed off in two canoes from St. Ignace, moving into Green Bay, down its length, and into the Fox River. As they paddled upstream in the Fox they were intercepted frequently by Indians who, as Marquette reports in *Jesuit Relations* vol. 59, ". . . did their

best to dissuade me. They represented to me that I should meet nations which never show mercy to strangers but break their heads without cause . . . finally that the heat was so excessive it would inevitably cause our death."

At Maskoutens they pulled the canoes out of the river and made a laborious portage of 2,700 paces to the Wisconsin River. "Thus we left the waters flowing to Quebecq, four or five hundred leagues from here, to float on those that would take us through strange lands."

In a tremendous voyage, they discovered the Mississippi, traveled down to the Arkansas, saw the Great Plains, and returned. Another would complete that exploration. Frontenac invested his biggest hopes for discovery and trade in an aloof, brooding man who had firmly grasped the continental vision and the entwined roles of empire building and fur trading—René Robert Cavelier, Sieur de la Salle.

A FORMER JESUIT STUDENT who found the life too limiting and coercive, twenty-three-year-old La Salle was a driven man. He acquired a grant on the St. Lawrence between Lachine and Montreal, and in feudal style entered the fur trade, with plans far beyond the existing trade. Meanwhile he brought a Jesuit's dedication to learning the Indian languages firsthand. He did not put on greasy leather or affect man-to-man equality with the Indians and other traders; instead he went into the forests in full continental garb with crossed sashes. He rubbed most whites the wrong way, but Indians generally sensed the character that supported his arrogance.

After mastering eight Indian languages, he heard in Seneca of a great river, the *O-hy-o*. It *must* flow southwest to California and China, so La Salle began the first white exploration of the Ohio River Valley. He located the confluence of the Monongahela and Allegheny (Fort Duquesne, Fort Pitt) in 1669 and explored down the Ohio River to the falls (Louisville). His men abandoned him there, as men would do several times in the future. Returning to his seat in Canada, he found he had been displaced and his property usurped.

La Salle's next great exploration was a trip with Iroquois hunters up Lakes Erie and Huron to Michilimackinac at the straits, then south across Lake Michigan, and from there, a prairie portage to the Illinois River and a glimpse of the Mississippi.

With his own eyes, then, he had seen from two directions the shape of the riches of the future Northwest Territory (the land circumscribed by the Ohio and Mississippi rivers). The view crystallized his great plan. He would consolidate the French hold on the continent with a chain of French stations from the Great Lakes to the mouth of the Mississippi. They would begin as fur-trading posts, doubling as strategic forts. He would begin by widening the fur trade's scope: ships, not canoes; settlements at the trading centers, not mere outposts.

His concept coincided with the arrival of Frontenac as governor, an equally bold planner. He embraced La Salle's strategic and commercial vision of canoe flotillas converging over the vast riverine net on large French posts (forts) with tons of furs to be transshipped by an armada of galleons over broad lakes to Montreal, and thence to Europe. By the time the English woke up, the center of the continent would be peopled with French commercial and military armies. Together, they began a great arc of forts, posts, and settlements, with fur as the way and the means.

La Salle—through many chapters of adversity—traveled south on Lake Michigan to the mouth of the St. Joseph River (then the Miami), where he built Fort Miami. He paddled up the St. Joseph to the present site of South Bend, where he portaged over an Indian trail to Kankakee and beyond to the Illinois River. New Year's Day, 1680, brought him to the capital of the Illinois tribe, where the huge promontory of Starved Rock towered above timber. He noted it for a fort site while he sent his men up a dozen rivers to Indian villages to make fur alliances and establish small fur stations. Later in January his party paddled down the Illinois to Lake Peoria. He set his men to building Fort Crèvecoeur ("Heartbreak") and also a ship to sail down the Mississippi.

That ship would never sail, but La Salle embarked on another expedition down the Mississippi. This time he made it all the way to the marshy bayous. Pushing on to the very mouth, he stood at the Gulf of Mexico, and on April 9, 1682, in accord with rules of possession by which the nation that holds the mouth owns the valley, La Salle claimed the entire Mississippi watershed for France. In honor of his king, he named it Louisiana.

By 1700 the early discoverers had mapped the vast crescent from the Gulf of St. Lawrence through the Great Lakes, and down the Mississippi to the Gulf of Mexico.

This drawing from Father Louis Hennepin's account records La Salle's arrival at Niagara in 1679.

Outlining this huge semicircle was a chain of forts and fur stations built on high ground at key constrictions, commanding large regions about them. The gateway, Quebec, sat on a three-hundred-foot rock at the point where the St. Lawrence narrowed. Montreal commanded the junction of the St. Lawrence and the Ottawa, the great water road to Georgian Bay and the upper lakes. Fort Frontenac at Kingston and Fort Niagara bracketed Lake Ontario. Fort Pontchartrain, at the strait (*détroit*), was built to control all ascent to the upper lakes. The forts at Sault Ste. Marie, St. Ignace, and Michilimackinac guarded the complex entrances to the three upper lakes. Fort Miami at the south end of Lake Michigan was in line with Fort St. Louis and fur posts yet to be built down the Mississippi to the Gulf of Mexico. These posts flew the white flag with the golden lilies, and their residents spoke the several dialects of New France.

Today the arc is easily retraced by the French-named cities on a road map.

CHAPTER 8

THE BLACK ROBES

*Jesuit missionaries who mapped a new land—its peoples,
customs, and topography—at a sometimes terrible price*

THE VOLUMES HAD THE POPULARITY of illicit literature and were so hard to acquire that they were
passed hand to hand among French youth until
shredded and then were repaired, carefully wrapped, and
often carried fifty leagues on horseback. They were *The
Jesuit Relations*, ultimately seventy-three volumes of them.
North America was being won for France, not so much by
regiments of troops as by a small corps of the world's most
astonishing men—the Pope's commandos—and *Jesuit Relations* was their story, published annually in France.
French noblemen worried to find their sons reading each
new volume—these compilations of the reports, notes,
maps, diaries, and thoughts sent back by the Jesuits to
their superior in France. The volumes enticed second sons
away from home and from promising careers.

The men sending these reports were highly educated,
often formerly wealthy, physically toughened members of
an elite band that then numbered less than one thousand
in all Europe. They were a Catholic marine corps. It was
France's North American policy to send with each expedition and large fur party one or two Jesuits. Their aim was
to convert the Indians to Christianity. The governor
general's aim was to convert the Indians to France. Actually, neither the government nor the fur men at first
wanted the priests distracting the Indians from the job of
fur trapping.

Young Jacques Marquette of Laon longed to enlist. He
had read of the order's founding by Ignatius Loyola and
its approval in 1540 by Pope Paul III—the Society of
Jesus, mobile, versatile, ready to take on the most im-

possible missionary assignments. Their enemies, who outnumbered their friends, dubbed them "Jesuits," a name
the men arrogantly adopted.

If neither the government nor the fur traders welcomed
them in Canada, how did the Jesuits become such a basic
force in its development?

When Champlain returned to France from North
America with tales of thousands of heathen Indians, Father Pierre Colon, then confessor to Henry IV, told the
king to send Jesuit missionaries to Acadia (Canada).
Henry IV liked the idea, but for the wrong reason. He
knew the Jesuits held suspect his sudden conversion from
Protestantism to Catholicism on assumption of the throne.
His Huguenot friends told him his best move was to get the
Jesuits shipped to Canada. Therefore, in 1607, when a
merchant explorer, the Sieur de Poutrincourt, sought a
charter to establish trading settlements in Canada, it was
granted with the condition that he take along a priest to
begin converting the Indians.

The Jesuits elected Father Pierre Baird for this first
mission. He closed up his theology class in Lyons and hurried to the port of Bordeaux to catch Poutrincourt's ship
when it stopped there en route from Dieppe. The Sieur
and his Huguenot partners did not want to defy the king,
but neither did they want a Jesuit. Therefore Poutrincourt
took aboard a non-Jesuit priest at Dieppe, Father Jesse La
Flèche, and sailed directly from Dieppe, leaving Baird at
the dock in Bordeaux. The plan was that if Father La
Flèche could convert thousands of savages to Christianity,
then the king would not insist upon Jesuits.

*Strong of body, quick of mind, undaunted by hardship, torture, even martyrdom
—Jean de Brébeuf was typical of the Jesuit missionaries to New France.*

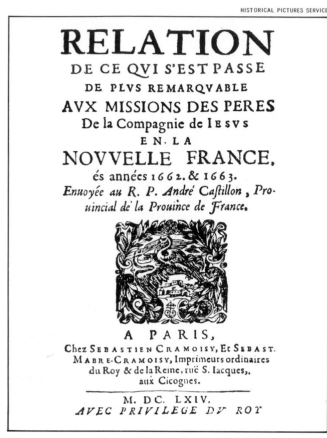

RELATION
DE CE QVI S'EST PASSE
DE PLVS REMARQVABLE
AVX MISSIONS DES PERES
De la Compagnie de IESVS
EN·LA
NOVVELLE FRANCE,
és années 1662. & 1663.

Enuoyée au R. P. André Caſtillon, Pro-
uincial de la Prouince de France.

A PARIS,
Chez SEBASTIEN CRAMOISY, Et SEBAST.
MABRE-CRAMOISY, Imprimeurs ordinaires
du Roy & de la Reine, rüe S. Iacques,.
aux Cicognes.

M. DC. LXIV.
AVEC PRIVILEGE DV ROY

The seventy-two volumes of Jesuit Relations *give a full and colorful account of early Great Lakes history.*

In Acadia, La Flèche did in fact convert as many Indians as he had presents. When the presents ran out, the conversions fell off, and some that were made came undone. Francis Parkman, the region's first comprehensive historian, explained that "an Indian would be baptized ten times a day for a pint of brandy."

Henry IV was assassinated in 1610, and many blamed the Jesuits.

POUTRINCOURT'S SON, BIENCOURT, returned to France for supplies. When the vessel was loaded at Dieppe and ready to return in 1611, two robed figures stepped out of the shadow of the warehouse, slung their duffle neatly up over the ship's rail, and climbed aboard—Father Baird and a giant named Father Ennemond Massé.

The Huguenot shipowners and partners in the expeditions put guards on the mooring lines and ordered the priests off. They would not invest in any enterprise involving Jesuits, whom they regarded as Spanish agents. From the slash in Father Baird's robe came a purse. He turned to young Biencourt, offering to invest 3,800 livres in the Poutrincourt venture in Acadia. He added that at a reasonable interest he was authorized to loan an additional amount at his discretion. This immediately wiped out the prejudice against Jesuits. The vessel cast off.

In Acadia, before he began converting Indians, Father Baird established the simplest yet most profound priority for taking over a continent—learn the language. Working patiently with the Indians, his quill scratched page after page of Indian language. He would be followed by increasing numbers of Jesuits moving deeper inland, recording the language of scores of tribes.

These pages, along with the Jesuits' minute descriptions of the customs, tortures, lands, rivers, lakes, conversions, and hardships, would be assembled annually in the volume of *Jesuit Relations* and sent back to Europe to be copied. It meant that the oncoming stream of black robes could arrive in North America having already studied Indian languages. Further, explorers and traders could learn the customs and differences of the various tribes, and the best routes inland.

While England and Spain were merely transplanting Europe to North America, the French were adapting to the new continent, learning the land, languages, shape, and waterways. The Jesuits were pivotal in accomplishing this amid unbelievable hardships of hunger, cold, Indian torture, and loneliness, which would have destroyed most men. Reading of the Jesuit exploits, Jacques Marquette applied for admission and was accepted at age seventeen. Along with all other Jesuits he continued reading *Jesuit Relations* and pressed for service in Canada. But there were too many applicants ahead of him.

This first mission ended abruptly when the priests, seeking a place apart from commercialism to establish a wholly Jesuit colony, were captured by a British ship and deported to England. But in 1625, six Jesuits went back to Quebec, headed by Father Paul Le Jeune and guided by Father Massé. They moved into a mission of hospitable gray Recollect friars, established by Champlain but now languishing.

Establishing a mission at Quebec, Le Jeune and Massé evolved a master strategy: bypass at first the hostile Iroquois and the nomadic northern Algonquins, who had no attachment to place; work first with the more settled, village-building Algonquins—the Hurons—farther west on the Great Lakes. When these Hurons were substantially converted, there would be a better chance to convert the nomadic Algonquins and the Iroquois. They began their work of convincing the Hurons of the superiority of their God through acts of service, faith, ceremony, and courage—and by speaking the Indian language.

ONE OF THE GREATEST MISSIONARIES was the huge Father Jean de Brébeuf. In battle with the British in 1629, he was captured and returned to England. He swiftly found his way back to Canada and moved deep west

among the Hurons with Fathers Daniel, Davost, Martin, and Baron. In the *Jesuit Relations* he reported that trip, showing others how to follow, "I have kept count of the number of portages and found that we carried our canoes thirty-five times and dragged them at least fifty. I took a hand in helping the savages; but the bottom of the river is full of stones so sharp I could not walk them barefooted, though the Indians do."

He explained that the way to get transport inland was to wait until a clan of Indians from the upper lakes, having brought their fur to Quebec, were ready to canoe back to their western lands. He prepared his colleagues for hardship: "In regard to provisions, frequently one has to fast, if he misses the caches that were made [when the Indians

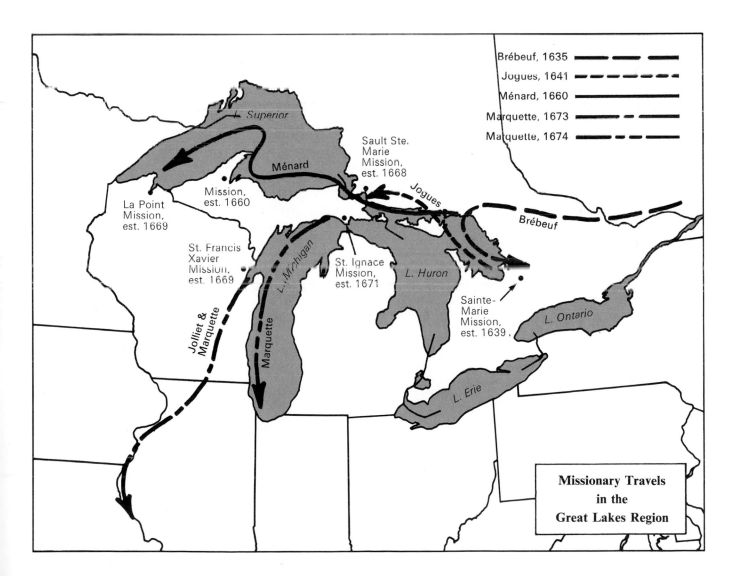

Brébeuf, 1635
Jogues, 1641
Ménard, 1660
Marquette, 1673
Marquette, 1674

L. Superior

Sault Ste. Marie Mission, est. 1668

Ménard

Mission, est. 1660

La Point Mission, est. 1669

St. Francis Xavier Mission, est. 1669

Jogues

Brébeuf

L. Michigan

St. Ignace Mission, est. 1671

L. Huron

Jolliet & Marquette

Marquette

Sainte-Marie Mission, est. 1639

L. Ontario

L. Erie

Missionary Travels in the Great Lakes Region

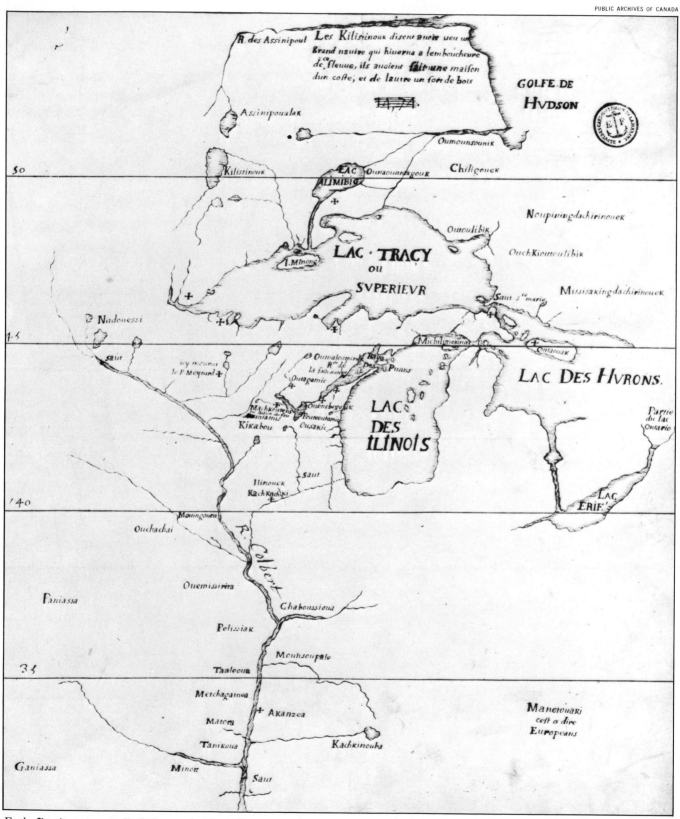

Early Jesuit maps expedited the travels of ensuing waves of missionaries, explorers, and fur traders.
The configuration of Lake Superior here is indicative of the remarkable accuracy of these maps.

Father Brébeuf, esteemed by the Hurons, was brutally tortured and killed by their enemies the Iroquois.

treated," he explained. "The Indians stole from him much of his little outfit. They compelled him to throw away his small steel [grain] mill and almost all our books and paper, of which we have great need. They deserted him at an island."

When Davost finally reached the Huron country, he was worn out and sick. Father Daniel, Brébeuf wrote, "was abandoned and compelled to seek another canoe, as also was little Martin, who was very roughly treated and at last was left behind with the Bissiriniens, where he remained so long that he was about two months on the trail. Baron was robbed by his savages on the very day he arrived in these regions; and he would have lost more if he had not compelled them, through fear of his arms, to give him back part of what they had taken."

For the guidance of a long, thin line of black robes who would be following him, Brébeuf set down instructions for traveling with Indians: "You must be prompt in embarking and disembarking. Tuck up your gowns so they will not get wet, and so you will not carry either water or sand into the canoe . . . you must have your feet and legs bare; while crossing the rapids you can wear your shoes and in the long portages, even your leggings. Be careful not to annoy anyone in the canoe with your hat."

On Lake Simcoe, between Lake Ontario and Georgian Bay, these Jesuits built missions and began the work of converting the Hurons. The Indians were alternately intrigued, then bored, and then angered by the process. Therefore the Jesuits often needed to resort to magic. One magic item was a clock. "[The Indians] all think it is some living thing. They cannot imagine how it speaks by itself; and when it is going to strike they look to see if we all are there and if someone has not hidden in order to shake it. They think it hears, especially if for a joke some one of our Frenchmen calls out at the last stroke of the hammer, 'That's enough,' and then it immediately becomes silent. They call it the captain of the day. When it strikes they ask what it says. They ask about its food, and they stay a whole hour to hear it speak again."

Brébeuf found that the greatest wonder to the Indians was written language. "For they cannot conceive how what one of us, being in the village, had said to them and put down at the same time in writing, another, who meanwhile was in a house far away, could say readily on seeing the writing. I believe they have made a hundred trials of it."

descended from Huron lands to Quebec]." Even if caches are recovered successfully, he warned that Frenchmen would go hungry, "for the ordinary food is only a little Indian corn coarsely broken between stones and taken whole in pure water."

Although Brébeuf was a strong man, he was not accustomed to the dawn-to-dusk paddling forced upon him by the Indians. The relationship was strange and constantly changing. While at certain times the Indians were in awe of a Jesuit, at other times the Jesuit was their slave and subject to their utter contempt and physical abuse. At the portages, Brébeuf wrote, the Indians would hurry off at a run with their own baggage leaving him to carry his own or be left behind.

Portages were generally several miles long. Brébeuf managed to keep up, but then sank exhausted on his paddle. "Father Davost, among others, was very badly

WHILE THE USE of such magic helped gain respect for the Christian message and warded off violence, it also had one dangerous effect. When the Indian crops turned out well, Indians came and thanked the Jesuits; but when the drought came, the Indians upbraided and threatened and abused the Jesuits. Worse, the French unknowingly brought the Indians smallpox, to which they were themselves somewhat immune. Indians thought the priests had called fiends down on them. As the disease began to devastate Huron clans, they saw that only Indians were dying, not French, so the surviving Indians blamed the Jesuits.

Indian persecution of Jesuits accelerated in 1645, increasing as the epidemic increased. Jesuits considered the persecution as launched by the devil to prevent their work. They therefore stepped up their conversion attempts—which increased the Indians' anger and assaults.

The powerful bodies of the Jesuits began to weaken under cold, hunger, diseases of filth, physical attacks, and wounds. Still, the black-robed line continued filtering west, weighted down under backpacks laden with paper, books, colored pictures of saints, sometimes a heavy metal altar cross, medicine, and a handgun.

The black robes, with the cross swinging from their rope belts, worked their way in twos and threes and singly throughout the Huron clans, teaching and converting. However, the ranks of the rugged young men from France were thinned by the hard life among the Indians. One apologized to his superior for his poor handwriting—the Indians had left him only one finger.

Sometimes the missions they built were crude bark huts; sometimes they were extensive clearings surrounded by pointed palisades doubling as small forts. But always the Jesuits were way out in front. Hardly a new strait on the lakes was discovered, or a new river, or a new Indian tribe without a priest in the vanguard. Most impressive to the Indians was the amazing Jesuit ability and courage. However, that did not remove their suspicions.

When a Jesuit would hear a dying child crying in a hut, he felt driven to go in and baptize the child before it died. He would talk his way in through the protective adults. Then, as if for the first time aware of the sick child, he would touch the young forehead with a wet handkerchief, and without moving his lips, mutter a baptism. If the child later died, the Indians would remember the wet handkerchief and the touch as a Jesuit death curse.

Isaac Jogues, later canonized, was the first of many French Jesuits to be martyred by the Indians.

Huron persecution took the form of stoning, destroying Jesuit property, and turning the priests out of Indian villages. This—by their own Hurons.

IT WAS NOT THE PERSECUTION, the Jesuits decided, that was handicapping their work in converting Hurons. It was the Iroquois. When the Hurons were already understrength from smallpox, the Iroquoian Five Nations from New York were sending powerful war parties into Huron country north of the Great Lakes to cut off the Ottawa River fur route. The first few attacks found the Iroquois warriors weakened from the long trek; they were beaten off. But they returned repeatedly, stronger each time. If the priests were to be effective, they must go among the brutal Iroquois.

Father Isaac Jogues and Father Charles Raymbault, who went to the hostile Mohawks, had as hard a time as any. It took all their ingenuity to calm down the Mohawk rages. Father Jogues occasionally resorted to the diversion of a piece of cut glass with eleven facets. Placed over an object, it would produce eleven identical images. He also had a prism that would turn sunlight into many colors. These and other objects saved the priests several times. But in one of the battles against the Hurons, the Mohawks turned on Jogues and tortured him. He escaped after thirteen months and was rescued by the Dutch in New

York country, who sent him back to France on their ship.

Young Jesuits in France heard that a wounded Jesuit had come home, but they did not get to see him because within the same year Jogues was back in North America working among the Iroquois. That trip to France was his last, for he was again set upon, and this time became the first of many Jesuits martyred by the Five Nations.

The ultimate Iroquois campaign struck with full force in midsummer 1648. It was a highly organized whirlwind

Barbarous tortures at the hands of the Indians were the fate of the Jesuit martyrs. This composite painting commemorates ten of them: Father Jogues kneels at left; Fathers Lalemant and Brébeuf are tied to stakes.

attack on three Huron villages by Senecas and Mohawks. The Huron warriors were away at the time, and the village residents were killed and scattered. The following winter the Iroquois struck fifteen Huron villages, including three missions. Father Daniel was killed as he was finishing mass, his body thrown into the flames of his church hut.

The older men and women and children were hastened out of the villages while the Huron warriors stayed to fight. Brébeuf and Father Gabriel Lalemant stayed with them, urging them to defend their villages and helping them do so.

Ultimately they were overwhelmed, their villages left in flames. Some Indians escaped; others were captured. The two Jesuits were seized and taken to St. Ignace, where they were bound to stakes. The Iroquois wrought their most revolting tortures upon Jesuits, and seven of twenty-nine missionaries were killed in the holocaust.

Physically powerful Father Brébeuf, who had worked among the Hurons for twenty years, endured the ordeal for only four hours before he expired; Father Lalemant, of delicate physique, survived for seventeen horrible hours. Witnesses reported, however, that Brébeuf suffered the successive administrations with unbelievable calm. The fact that he would not cry out incited the angered Indians to even worse punishments; but it also won their admiration, for after his death they ate his heart, hoping thereby to acquire his courage.

Back in France, young Jesuits read that the decades of good work by scores of priests had largely been undone by the scattering of the defeated Hurons among whom they had worked. Had a century's effort been wiped out?

THE CROWD AT TROIS RIVIÈRES, halfway between Quebec and Montreal, stared unbelieving as the venerable Father René Ménard waved aside assistance and made his way down to the flotilla of sixty large merchant canoes belonging to fur traders Radisson and Groseilliers, ready to run northwest up the Ottawa to Nipissing Lake, south into Georgian Bay and on to the Straits of Mackinac, eight hundred twisting miles.

It was 1660, and Ménard was making one more trip to the west. How could they let the old man risk himself again at this age? He had come here young, established a dozen missions, and survived. Why could not a younger priest make this mission to the hard country? There was a

reason. This was the most important trip of all so far; Ménard was the logical Jesuit in the East to make it.

The mission was to try to salvage the decades of work performed by black-robed Jesuits, to seek out the remnants of the Hurons who had learned Christianity but had scattered and vanished under the Iroquois' fury. Old Ménard would know where to look for these Indians, and he would be able to recognize them even though they were assimilated into various other tribes. Older Indians would recognize him, as well. He must seek them out in scores of obscure villages, bolster their faith, get them to spread it among all Algonquins, and pass it down the generations. Otherwise decades of Jesuit deaths would be wasted. The Jesuit record was in his hands.

This time the trip up would be easier. Instead of traveling with petulant, dangerous Indians, this journey would be made under the protection of prosperous fur trappers, aware of a debt to the black robes. They would see to the old man's every need and comfort on the way northwest. It was with real regret that they cast him loose in his small canoe when they arrived at the Sault.

Ménard proceeded along the southern shore of Superior, paddled by Indians who remembered. On October 15 he reached the head of Keweenaw Bay, naming it for St. Theresa. Knowing the old man's mission and fearing it, his Indian guides abandoned him there, but he found solace: "I had the consolation of saying mass which repaid me with usury for all my past hardships."

Here he began a mission, "composed of a flying church of Christian Indians from the neighborhoods." He put out the word among them—stragglers from the Iroquois war who remembered the Jesuits should come to him here. Few came. Therefore in the spring he left Theresa Bay and, accompanied by a single Indian and a voyageur, Chaquainegan, furnished by the fur company, he pushed westward toward the head of Lake Superior. They took the route through Portage Lake, and while the voyageur was carrying the canoe across a portage, Ménard wandered off the trail into cold hemlock forest and vanished.

Father Claude Allouez, also a veteran of Canada, took up the mission. From Quebec he traveled part way with a flotilla of four hundred Indians. He pushed north across Superior beyond Keweenaw Peninsula to Chequamegon Bay. At La Pointe he built a mission in 1669. He circled the rocky Superior shore looking for lost Huron Christians, at the same time mapping the Superior shorelines.

*Jacques Marquette, one of the last and greatest
of the Jesuit missionaries in New France.*

BACK IN FRANCE JACQUES MARQUETTE had applied for
Canada many times, but his name had been far down
the list. He knew the names and stories of all the great
priests, but it looked as if he would miss all the adventure.

Finally, in 1666, his call came. He was by this time
twenty-nine and proud to be following in the footsteps of
his heroes—Jogues, Ménard, Allouez, Brébeuf.

Little did he know that his mission would be perhaps
the greatest of all: salvaging the work of his heroes, pushing
it to completion, and establishing missions in the upper
lakes region.

Among the senior and veteran priests, Ménard was
gone, Allouez was aging, Dablon was elevated to the head
of the Jesuits and out of the field into administration.

In the wake of the martyrs, Jacques Marquette was
finally sent up through the Sault to the mission at La
Pointe to relieve the great Claude Allouez, who moved on
in 1669 to establish the mission St. Francis Xavier among

the Sacs and Foxes, Potawatomis and Winnebagos at
Green Bay. Periodically Marquette worked with Allouez,
and as he watched Indians venerate the great priest, he
felt it was all true—that the courage and integrity and
loyalty of the Jesuits had reached the Indian.

Marquette had around him at La Pointe remnants of
Hurons, Ottawas, and Sioux. The Hurons and Sioux were
battling, with the Hurons losing out and withdrawing to
the Sault. Marquette went to the Sault to serve them and
was joined by Father Dollier.

In 1671, Marquette went among the Hurons north of
the Straits of Mackinac, where he worked at the mission at
St. Ignace. He helped a new man, Louis Andre, start a
mission for the Ottawas in their withdrawal to Manitoulin
Island, and he reestablished missions to replace those destroyed in the Iroquois invasion.

Marquette's return from the famous trip to discover the
Mississippi River (see chapter 7) had shown him the need
for new missions in the Illinois country. The next year he
traveled down the west shore of Lake Michigan and into
the Chicago River to establish them. With two colleagues
he built a hut to shelter them through the worst of the
winter. His strenuous labor in this country, however, had
swiftly aged his powerful body. In January he was weak
with fever and chills, and by spring he felt he was coming
to the end. He made it to the Indian town of Kaskaskia, but
his illness worsened, and his party decided to get him back
to the St. Ignace mission.

On the way north, in Lake Michigan, the end came.
Marquette's party put ashore and buried him near the
mouth of the river now named for him. He was thirty-
eight years old.

Two years later, according to Father Dablon's account
in volume 59 of *Jesuit Relations*, thirty canoes of Iroquois
and Algonquins came ashore, dug up the body, boiled the
bones clean, wrapped them in deerskin, took them north
to St. Ignace and "buried them with ceremony."

The French Parliament forced Louis XV to undercut
the Jesuits. Pope Clement XIV suppressed them throughout the world. By 1773 only eleven Jesuits remained on
duty in Canada. But by that time they, along with priests
of other orders, had mapped the entire region, taught the
French people the Indian languages, built missions from
Gaspé to Duluth, and helped discover the Mississippi,
which completed the crescent empire of New France;
their missions became cities from St. Laurent to St. Louis.

CHAPTER 9

THE FUR MEN

Competitive ploys of four nations to establish trade, build outposts, and entrench empires—all on the back of the beaver

EUROPEAN FASHION first shaped the destiny of Great Lakes America.

Fur was the continent's cash crop and beaver its gold standard. It directed the exploration, colonization, and conduct of warfare in the region.

As a device for colonizing and financing, European kings granted monopoly fur rights on North American lands. They gave the recipients of these rights little help or support, so they generally exerted minimal supervision as long as the taxable shares reached the governments. This freedom in turn created powerful French and English fur companies with quasi-governmental authority. Since the companies generally had to enforce their own territorial monopoly rights against all independent operators, the fur trade became a fur war, declared and undeclared.

The chief French fur companies were two, the Northwest Company, operating the big stockaded fur post, Grand Portage, on the northwest cliff of Lake Superior, and the Mackinaw Company, whose key trading post was strategic Mackinac in the straits at the juncture of the three large lakes.

Several English and Dutch companies operated south of the lakes in New York, but the French controlled the waters and the best Indian traders (the Hurons). The English responded by trying to flank the French from the north, through Hudson Bay, forming the powerful Hudson's Bay Company, which endures today.

English colonies, and later the American states, did not use the governmental monopoly formula. Hundreds of independent fur traders entered the business, fragmenting it. Out of the swarm of operators emerged one fur baron, John Jacob Astor, whose powerful American Fur Company bought and ultimately destroyed competition.

These four giants, emerging through many transitory stages, swept thousands of men into the forests armed with traps and paddles, and other thousands with muskets.

When the first French fishermen ventured ashore at the Gulf of St. Lawrence and found that for a few knife blades and a tierce of brandy they could buy from the Indians a year's fishing wages in beaver pelts, the destiny of upper North America was cast.

In England, under heavy trapping, beaver had disappeared by 1520. In France and Germany they were scarce; even Poland had few left. In a high-fashion era, the garment trades in Europe were famished for fur. When North American pelts came ashore in France, rumor of the low price and high quantity and quality exploded. Every merchant who put the silky pelt to his face could smell unbridled fortune, while dukes and kings could envision revenue vast enough to float navies.

Why beaver? There were mink, rabbit, bear, and marten in abundance, but the soft underfur of beaver had a special fashion property: after being processed, it could be brushed to a flat, feltlike material for rakish brimmed hats that held shape and style through rain, snow, and hard wear. Each beaver hair is shielded by microscopic interlocking scales that seal out water, an ideal property for hats. These were not utilitarian hats to keep the head warm; they were coveted, high-style hats for which Europeans would pay long profits and longer wars.

The powerful "voyageurs," who paddled the great trading canoes, typified the adaptation to native ways and wilderness living that made French fur men successful in the New World.

The independent fur trader traveled a circuit of Indian villages that saved their pelts for him; his trading goods were cloth, knives, ax blades—smaller items than the bulky goods traded at the fur posts.

If vain fashion was a profane use of millions of creatures and the beginning of two centuries of destruction, it was also the prime mover of history. French rulers soon noticed that if they let freebooting vessel captains run the fur trade, this tremendous flow of potential revenue largely evaded government coffers and resulted in no permanent French settlements to hold the territory. Henry IV of France therefore in 1600 granted a ten-year monopoly of all St. Lawrence River fur trading to Pierre Chauvin in exchange for which, besides paying taxes, Chauvin must establish a colony of five hundred people. This was the magic formula under variants of which French kings, without investing a franc, planned to make the fur business colonize New France and enrich old France.

Chauvin quickly dispatched one large shipload of pelts which was a startling success. Then he died in 1602. His partner returned in 1603. But the important event was that in that party was a superbly capable executive, Samuel de Champlain. The potential he witnessed changed his life and the lives of many others.

Returning to France he organized a group of merchants and investors in St. Malo and Rouen as the Company of Associates. With a monopoly charter from the king, they arrived in Canada in 1608 and virtually controlled the fur trade for fourteen years. Far more than a fur trader, however, Champlain took seriously the responsibility in his charter to colonize for France and to explore. Delegating much of the trading to capable lieutenants, he invested heavily in exploration, relations with Indians, assisting settlers, and building forts. Even above La Salle and Frontenac, he is considered the Father of Canada.

Successive French kings were inconsistent in their support of New France, and even within a single reign, the degree of royal interest changed. In 1622 the king yielded to the pressure of two Huguenots, William and Emery de Caën, to cancel the monopoly fur charter of Champlain's group and give it to them. They held it until Cardinal Richelieu ascended.

A brilliant ruler in general, the gaunt, sophisticated cardinal mishandled Canada. He cancelled the De Caëns' charter and in 1627 authorized the "One Hundred Associates" of the Company of New France. These powerful men took over the business aggressively; but heedless of the experience of their predecessors, they lost money. A series of reorganizations and reformations rocked the French attempt to control the fur trade, resulting by 1664 in a new policy under which all French fur trade was to be carried on by just twenty-five licensed traders.

Probably the greatest of the official licensees was Robert Cavelier, Sieur de la Salle. Like Champlain, in addition to commercial daring, he was driven by a fierce

The beaver—the prize that sparked wars and opened up a continent (European artist's conception, 1715).

sense of Frenchness—a desire to spread France's empire. Commercially, he operated a fleet of large canoes ranging north far up the Ottawa River and its tributaries, and south into the Michigan Lower Peninsula, Mackinac, and Green Bay. He spent heavily, too, to explore for France. However, after several ups and downs, he had three superb fur seasons that recouped his exploration outlays.

With the arrival of Frontenac as governor of New France, La Salle became the government favorite. Frontenac was driving to tighten government control of the fur trade to entrench the empire. Therefore he leaned heavily on La Salle, whose bold thinking he admired. La Salle proposed to expand the scope of French trade by meeting the fur-bearing Indian canoes at the fur outposts, not with the usual larger canoes to bring the baled pelts into Quebec, but with ships. While other fur traders wished him a hearty failure because of his favored position, Frontenac gave his blessing to this major pioneering step.

On August 7, 1679, outside the entrance to the Niagara River, the *Griffon* loosed sail for Green Bay. The mission was complex. She was the first full-sized ship specifically designed and built for the fur trade and the first to sail the lakes. On deck was La Salle, who needed to make an overwhelming commercial success of her, for he had borrowed heavily at 40 percent interest.

The *Griffon* sailed the length of Lake Erie in three days and beat her way up the Detroit and St. Clair rivers into Lake Huron, to the astonishment of shoreline Wyandots. Though the ship's plans are unavailable, marine author James P. Barry has deduced that she must have been a high-sterned, square-rigged, three-masted galleon, probably seventy feet long and weighing forty-five tons.

North across Huron, she handled very well through a challenging storm and made it to Mackinac, where some of La Salle's advance party should have had cargo ready. That cargo was disappointing, but he proceeded into the mouth of Green Bay, loading substantial bales of fur assembled by his other advance group.

On September 18 La Salle dispatched the *Griffon* back to Niagara with the fur, not boarding himself. With a small crew he was preparing to explore Illinois and the south by canoe, planning ultimately to go down the Mississippi, planting flags all the way to Texas. However, the *Griffon* was barely under sail when she sliced into the western edge of a four-day storm. She never came out, creating the greatest ongoing mystery of the Great Lakes.

Divers still look for her—the most coveted prize in waters that have yielded a thousand wrecks.

Meanwhile, the limit of twenty-five licensees could not be enforced along the long, forested waterways leading to fur posts at the Sault, Mackinac, Detroit, Green Bay, Fond du Lac, Grand Portage, and dozens of others.

While only twenty-five official licenses were issued, a large unofficial corps of independents operated. Some traded with the Indians to acquire furs; a few did their own trapping. Both types sold their fur to the large traders from Montreal. They were bold, independent entrepreneurs. From a total French population of ten thousand, eight hundred Frenchmen slipped away from settlements into the forest either as traders or as *voyageurs*, paddling the canoes.

THE FUR MEN operated over tremendous distances by virtue of a remarkable canoe, patterned after the Chippewa masterpiece, which was the communications and intelligence system of the continent.

These giant bark canoes were thirty-five to forty feet long and about six feet wide amidship. A very high bow and stern crescent deflected icy spray in the rapids. The birchbark shell was so easily punctured that nothing but water was allowed to touch it inside or out (the crew did not run it up on landings, but debarked offshore), yet these vessels withstood the rapids because of their flexibility and buoyancy. Inside was a fairly rugged frame. Four four-inch timbers called *grandes perches* ran the length of the canoe, supporting the *voyageurs*' feet and the ninety-pound baled freight, lashed down.

With occasional patching, this canoe could endure the twisting action of ten *voyageurs* paddling fourteen hours a day almost without interruption to the steady beat of rowing *chansons* bellowed into the wind.

One canoe could carry ten to fourteen men from Montreal all the way up to Grand Portage on the north shore of Lake Superior, along with five tons of trade goods and support equipment. Its mission was to swap the trade goods (kettles, ax heads, knives, chisels) to the Indians or to French *coureurs de bois*, who came downstream to the post

La Salle's dream was to expand fur shipments vastly beyond canoe capabilities, so he built a full-sized ship, the Griffon, *above the falls at Niagara and launched it in 1679. On its first trip it sank.*

Large-scale traders Radisson (standing) and de Groseilliers, angered by the French licensing policy, struck out on their own and proposed to the British a Hudson's Bay Company to compete with Montreal.

over the vast net of rivers. After the swap, *voyageurs* paddled the heavy load of furs back to Montreal.

The vessels not only made the fur trade, they also made the *voyageurs* what they were—nearly unbelievable men. Generally short in stature, they developed tremendous shoulders and arms from paddling and extremely muscular legs from portaging on the run. Between the heavy shoulders and legs was an hourglass trunk made muscular by twisting all day. They developed lusty singing voices from the constant songs that kept the stroke.

When they came to a rapids too violent to navigate, they pulled the canoe out of the water, and two men carried it while the others each packed two ninety-pound packages of trade goods on their backs. A portage, made

at the trot, might be anywhere from five to twenty miles. Why would they run? Because the first canoes to the rendezvous post drew the best choice of pelts from the Indians or the *coureurs de bois;* and more important, the canoes carried only twenty-two to twenty-five days' rations aboard for the approximately two thousand-mile trips. In times of disaster they ate their candles, moccasins, or dead companions. Fatalities from drowning were high and marked by twenty to thirty crosses at some rapids where passing *voyageurs* took off their hats and crossed themselves.

These communicating canoes covered thousands of miles of waterways and reported to each other the geography and events occurring on hundreds of watersheds. One of these events was especially crucial. The farthest-ranging *coureurs de bois* were talking about a shorter route by which to get beaver to Europe—from Hudson Bay. They were talking about British explorer ships sighted there. The rumor coincided in the late 1660s with a newly stringent enforcement of the exclusive licensing law, which threatened many independent *coureurs*, who had been bringing their pelts openly into the Montreal fur mart.

Suddenly these men were told they were illegal. They could not do business. French rulers temporarily ignored the fact that these *coureurs* had constituted an unpaid French naval force, patrolling streams that laced the

Great Lakes forests. To such an ungrateful government, many *coureurs* suddenly put thumb to nose and paddled their furs south to English and Dutch traders—and many became men without a country.

The most damaging disaffection occurred because two of these *coureurs de bois* were very remarkable men: Médard Chouart, Sieur de Groseilliers, and his brother-in-law, Pierre Esprit Radisson. These two daring Frenchmen operated on a very large scale, sometimes sixty canoes. On one occasion they brought a flotilla of fur into Montreal only to be told they were unlicensed and illegal. They were fined heavily, even though they protested that the new

The voyageurs' day moved to the steady rhythm of paddles and a lusty "chanson." Speed was vital on these two-thousand-mile trips; rations lasted only twenty-two days, and first arrivals took the choice pelts.

BY FRANCES HOPKINS, PUBLIC ARCHIVES OF CANADA

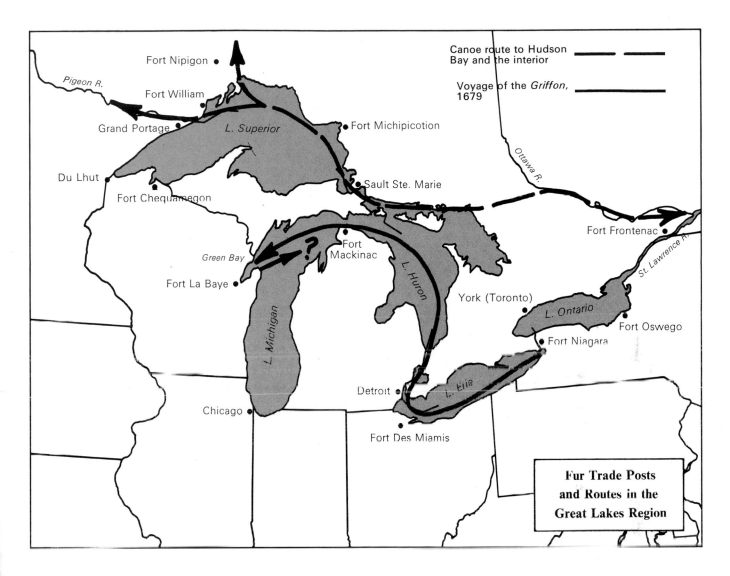

Canoe route to Hudson Bay and the interior

Voyage of the *Griffon*, 1679

Fort Nipigon
Pigeon R.
Fort William
Grand Portage
Du Lhut
L. Superior
Fort Chequamegon
Fort Michipicotion
Sault Ste. Marie
Ottawa R.
Fort Frontenac
St. Lawrence R.
Green Bay
Fort Mackinac
L. Huron
York (Toronto)
L. Ontario
Fort Oswego
Fort La Baye
L. Michigan
Fort Niagara
L. Erie
Detroit
Chicago
Fort Des Miamis

Fur Trade Posts and Routes in the Great Lakes Region

system was inaugurated while they were in the woods. France collected the fine, but it was to cost her dearly.

IT IS EASY TO SEE how the vision of French management sitting at Quebec was blinded. Their maps showed the tremendous penetration of Frenchmen deep into Lake Superior country, with the names of posts and forts like Deux Rivières and Lac la Croix. Headstones, already turning mossy by the rapids, were chiseled: *Jean, Baptiste, François, Pierre.* What the maps did not highlight was the proximity of Hudson Bay, and how a direct course could be steered there from England with no rapids.

The snubbed brothers-in-law went to the English with a plan, and on May 2, 1670, England produced a charter for "the Governor and Company of Adventurers of England Trading Into Hudson's Bay." The "adventurers" were London men of means who signed on Groseilliers and Radisson to lead them. On the very first adventure Radisson and Groseilliers delivered to the English ships a load of furs so profitable as to command full attention in England. The Hudson's Bay Company, as it came to be called, established three new fur-trading and processing posts on St. James Bay—Fort Albany, Moose Factory, York Factory—with a supply of Indian trade goods somewhat superior to that of the French. Indians from as far away as Lake Superior began taking their best pelts to the British at Moose Factory. The English could afford to give better trade goods, as they had none of the rehandling costs confronting the French around the St. Lawrence rapids. English profits were good. In 1676 the Hudson's Bay Company paid out trade goods worth 650 pounds sterling in exchange for 19,000 pounds sterling in furs.

The French trimmed prices to match the English, squeezing France's profit. At first competition led to skirmishes in the forests between competing *coureurs*—later to massed armies and the Indian wars. Although the French outnumbered the English around the Great Lakes, the English had the French sandwiched between their Hudson Bay operations and their thirteen colonies to the south. The English also incited their Iroquois allies to harass and kill French fur traders on the Ottawa and St. Lawrence rivers.

In a century of forest warfare over the fur trade, prices rose and fell, creating terrible waste. In one year of low prices most of the furs stored at Montreal were burned to bring up the price.

Fur traders' methods changed very little over the years. Even after the 1759 Battle of Quebec, when New France fell, the English adopted all the French methods, routes, maps, *coureurs* and *voyageurs*, and built the fur trade to unprecedented heights with increased profits. The English, however, did remove state control and allow freebooters. This unleashed ruthless, wasteful competition, which resulted in the killing of immature beaver and year-round trapping. By 1783, English Canada had formed, in addition to Hudson's Bay Company, the Northwest Company, operating to Grand Portage with two thousand employees —factors, clerks, interpreters, traders, trappers, and *voyageurs*. The Mackinaw Company was the third major competitor.

An idea of the scope of the trade is seen in the Colonial Office Papers of 1786, recording in the trade: 163 canoes; 163 flat-bottomed boats; 2,139 men; 56,324 gallons rum; 66,207 pounds gunpowder; 899 cut ball and shot.

After the Revolutionary War, American fur trade south of the lakes was fragmented among hundreds of operators competing for ever fewer pelts. A young German immigrant from Waldorf, Germany, John Jacob Astor, went to work in a furrier's New York warehouse beating dirt out of the pelts, and soon began buying a few to sell profitably. Later he went into the woods himself seeking better pelts among the Iroquois. Shipping his furs to England, Astor imported musical instruments for resale in New York.

German immigrant John Jacob Astor worked his way up from warehouse boy to czar of the fur business.

By 1790 he was buying "futures" in Montreal. He watched closely the 1796 treaty in which Britain theoretically gave up Detroit and Mackinac, and concluded: "Now, I will make my fortune."

By 1808 his fur-trading operations were so extensive that he changed his company name to the grander American Fur Company. He drove many competitors out of the trade by underselling. His toughest competitor was the Hudson's Bay Company, neither side respecting the national boundary.

To reduce Canadian competition, Astor bought the Mackinaw Company, acquiring their strategic fur post on Mackinac Island for his western headquarters, to be operated by his aggressive agent Ramsay Crooks.

Astor's major technique, however, was bending the fledgling United States government to his uses. Fur traders

Fond du Lac spans the full story of the fur trade: established by the French, the post fell to the British after the Battle of Quebec; despite the Revolution, they held it until after the War of 1812, when the U.S. took over.

were exploiting the Indians with liquor and a credit system that first enslaved them and then enraged them. To correct this, the government established official fur posts, an action that put the government in the fur business. Astor abhorred this but used it, persuading the government to go a step further—to build forts to protect the American fur trade against Canadian intruders. These forts largely protected Astor, especially Fort Howard at Green Bay.

After the government had assisted him against his Hudson's Bay competitor, Astor persuaded it to step out of the fur business in 1822. His own highly organized company stepped in to fill the void.

From 1817 to 1832 Astor was in full control of the fur country south of the lakes and even up on the northwest coast of Superior. He was willing to divide North America

with the Hudson's Bay Company, and not have to worry about competition from Canada's Northwest Company. When the international boundary was finally drawn, it ran down the center of Pigeon River into Lake Superior, just a few miles north of the great Northwest Company's fur post, Grand Portage. The Canadians had to move out, and the Northwest Company merged with the Hudson's Bay Company.

In his small, cluttered New York office, Astor watched the millions accumulate. He also watched the beaver diminish. Almost at the perfect moment, in 1835, he sold out.

The fur business did not end abruptly in a crash of cymbals; it slowly gave way to lumbering. Along the whitewater streams where *coureurs* and *voyageurs* had paddled for a century were endless stands of hemlock, balsam, and white pine; and America was ready to build cities.

Part Three
THE STRUGGLE FOR A CONTINENT

Even before the coming of the white man, Algonquins were fighting Iroquois around the Great Lakes. They continued the ancient enmity as allies of the French and British respectively when those two powers vied for the fur trade and domination of North America. Britain defeated France in 1759, only to face fresh hostilities with her erstwhile American colonies, in the Revolution and later in the War of 1812. At last, in September 1813, the Battle of Put-in-Bay wrote the final chapter in the struggle for the continent.

The Battle of Lake Erie, 1813.

CHAPTER 10

FRENCH VS. ENGLISH

The Battle of Quebec: a mad bid for personal glory and national power that sealed the fate of a continent

"THEY SAY HE IS QUITE MAD, General," Maj. Chevalier Johnstone commented.

As generals go, the handsome M. le Marquis Louis Joseph de Montcalm was known as a courteous officer, yet he did not answer. Instead, he stared down from the rock of Quebec at a chip of wood in the river, which he knew was the thirty-gun English sloop HMS *Terror of France*. The glass did not bring it much closer. From the Quebec heights one looks *down* on clouds. When these moving clouds parted, the marquis could see the backs of flying birds which appeared larger than the ship below them.

"I said, General—"

"Yes. Mad. And he is. And *that* is the worry."

Montcalm, being a successful general, recognized this requirement in another. He knew what the recent daring French victories at Oswego and Ticonderoga had cost him, and the touch of madness required to win both. Down below, looking up at him he knew, was a brilliant madman. Less experienced than he, perhaps more mad. There was a story that England's Duke of Newcastle, hoping to block James Wolfe's promotion over senior officers, had told King George that Wolfe was mad. The king was said to have replied, "Mad is he? Then I hope he bites my other generals."

Montcalm knew the outrageous losses Wolfe had already accepted in trying to storm the rock of Quebec. He knew the terrible pressure Wolfe had accepted. Wolfe must take Quebec in the short warm season. If he failed to get either inside Quebec City or out of the St. Lawrence before the freeze, his ships would be ice locked and Montcalm would harvest the British army like a crop of clover. There were only days left before the freeze. Wolfe would have to make his next move quickly if he was going to act. And Montcalm knew that Wolfe would take the most reckless chance rather than report failure back to England's William Pitt. Wolfe had been given every strength England could supply to take Quebec, because Quebec was now the key to North America.

Montcalm had watched Wolfe scout the shoreline for eighty miles looking for the slightest possible new weakness to attack. He had watched Wolfe repeatedly assault the Quebec shore and fall back with tremendous losses, as high as 430 deaths per attempt, without killing a single Frenchman. Quebec was nature's fort, a solid ninety-degree granite escarpment rising out of St. Lawrence water, topped by man-made ramparts and flanked by two unfordable rivers.

Montcalm had watched Wolfe attack at dawn, at high noon, in the evening, in the middle of the night, accepting murderous direct fire. He had watched Wolfe feint to the upstream side of Quebec and attack the downstream side, then feint downstream and attack upstream. He had watched Wolfe's boats disappear far upstream looking for a weakness week after week, in daylight and darkness.

But he knew Wolfe would come. He was a man hungering less for life than for a chapter in history; and this battle would climax a century and a half of it, and would be a full chapter in every account of the North American struggle.

Until approximately mid-eighteenth century, both

The Marquis de Montcalm, able commander of French forces in the New World, managed to hold back the British for two years—until the Battle of Quebec. Here he congratulates his men at Ticonderoga.

*French Lt. Gen. Louis Joseph, Marquis de Montcalm—
gallant, courageous, and an experienced veteran.*

*British Maj. Gen. James Wolfe—youthful, brilliant,
and driven by a reckless, ruthless ambition.*

French and English had surprisingly eschewed the solid
acquisition of the continent, the French in favor of the
pursuit of fur and the building of a sprawling system of fur
posts and forts, the English in favor of fur and the intense
colonization of the eastern seaboard.

The contest between French and English, though violent, had been diffused over a wide territory; and its battles
were waged independently by widely separated, autono-
mous commanders, hardly able to coordinate their attacks
in the vast forest and waterways. These campaigns were
waged not so much for control of the lands but for control
of the fur-trade waterways and the fur-trading Indians.

An exception to this was the more organized and enduring Iroquois campaign supported by the British against
the Huron Indian region east of Lake Huron and north of
Lake Erie. Beginning in 1740, the Iroquois mounted this
long campaign to disrupt the French trade route along the
Ottawa River and decimate their ancient enemies, the

Hurons. The campaign persisted for decades and spread
west to the French posts above the Straits of Mackinac, on
Lake Michigan, and in Illinois.

The fight was basically for the control of fur, and the
French had emplaced their fur posts and forts so strategically that they were able to exercise remarkable control.
The great chronicler of the region, Henry Schoolcraft,
notes, "It is surprising to reflect upon the . . . sound judgment of the French in seizing on the points commanding
all the natural avenues and passes of the lakes, particularly when . . . these selections must necessarily have been
the result of an intimate acquaintance with the geographical features. . . . A number of posts . . . were subsequently
fortified by the United States government while the Indians still held the Northwest."

For example, the French put up a crude fort at Mackinaw in 1671. Daniel Greysolon, Sieur Dulhut, was sent in
1678 to the land of the Sioux and Assiniboines; he planted

the French coat of arms at Mille Lacs (Minnesota) to warn off encroachment from north or west. The passage between Lakes Erie and Huron was crucial; Sieur Antoine de la Cadillac built and manned Fort Pontchartrain at Detroit in 1701. (The English wanted this key spot and in 1703 sent a force of Indians against it, partially destroying it. It was rebuilt in 1718 and became one of the strongest in New France.) The French emplaced a fort at Green Bay to dominate the key Fox–Wisconsin River portage and one at the mouth of Chicago River. They built numerous small forts along the northern shores of the lakes at river mouths, each manned by a small garrison headed by an officer called a governor, who was in fact more of an accountant, controlling the fur trade, not the terrain.

However, by 1750, both nations were settling into earnest battle for the heart of the continent and actual possession of its land. The English were awakening, finding the passes westward through the Appalachian barrier in larger numbers and doing more and more fur business with the Indians. When they cut through these gaps, however, they found themselves increasingly encountering Frenchmen, who were closer than they thought. The Marquis Duquesne de Menneville, governor of New France, had ordered construction of a chain of French forts to extend from Presque Isle (Erie, Pennsylvania) southward to occupy the upper Ohio River Valley, a territory claimed by both Virginia and Pennsylvania, and eyed by New York.

Virginia's Governor Robert Dinwiddie sent a young officer-surveyor, George Washington, north to the French at Fort LeBoeuf with the message that they were trespassing on English soil and must withdraw. Courtesy prevailed, but the French remained. Dinwiddie then sent William Trent to build an English fort at the forks of the Ohio River.

The French arrived in force, drove off Trent, completed the fort, named it Fort Duquesne, and remained. Twenty-one-year-old Major Washington was sent with a body of Virginia militia to dislodge them. En route he captured a detachment of French but was himself attacked by a larger body of French and forced to surrender on July 3, 1754. The French were in control of not only the Great Lakes but even the Ohio Valley right behind the English colonies. Those Ohio Valley Indians formerly friendly to the English would no longer risk the association in view of the formidable demonstration of French power.

As every schoolboy knows, Gen. Edward Braddock now marched north with a large English army to drive the French out of the Ohio Valley. His noisy and baggage-heavy army struggled slowly north through dense forest, the French and their Indians aware of his march much of the way. A few miles from Fort Duquesne, at a place of their own choosing, the Indians and the French ambushed Braddock's army and destroyed it so badly in 1755 that even the fierce Iroquois who had been on the British side came over to the French. At one point only the Mohawks remained loyal to the British.

Later that year an army of 3,000 New England and New York militia with 500 Mohawks under William Johnson marched up the Hudson River trail to drive the French off Lake Champlain and threaten the great fur capital of Montreal. They established a fortified base at the south end of Lake George, then attacked north. Although they were driven back by French, they were able to hold Fort William Henry and even to drive the French off with heavy casualties. The French withdrew to Fort Carillon (Ticonderoga) on Lake Champlain.

Two years later, Montcalm, recently appointed French commander-in-chief, swept south from Ticonderoga and destroyed Fort William Henry the French had again strengthened their hold on the continent. Beyond that they pushed far down the Hudson Valley toward the back door of New York.

By now the war had ceased to be only a Great Lakes war. France and England had declared war formally, and this war was fought on the seas, in the West Indies, India, Africa, and Europe.

In the first years England was losing on most fronts. Then, in the midst of broad defeat, William Pitt announced, "I know that I can save the country and that I alone can." Assuming office as prime minister, Pitt laid out a grand worldwide design to use part of the British fleet to lock the French navy ashore in France so the balance of the British warships could sweep the French vessels from the oceans and carry troops to seize French colonies on land.

By now one of the very choice colonies to be seized was New France. One of the strongest British land positions was Oswego on Lake Ontario from which they hoped to subdue Fort Frontenac, opposite, and control Lake Ontario, breaking French communications with the line of

George Washington, a colonel on Braddock's staff, helped troops escape, barely saving his own life.

French posts and forts strung from Frontenac to Detroit to Michilimackinac to Fort St. Joseph (on Lake Michigan) and down the Mississippi. Therefore at Oswego the British began building a fleet of seven warships. In the first engagement with the French fleet, in June 1756, the English were driven off the lake and back into Oswego. In August, General Montcalm, in a daring operation slipped out of Fort Frontenac with a fleet of small paddle boats. Hugging the east and south shores of Ontario, he fell on Oswego. Some of the English ships were alerted in time to cast off, but Montcalm attacked and seized Fort Oswego. He burned it and the shipyard to the ground, taking 1,600 prisoners, 120 cannon, 6 sloops of war, and 18,000 pounds in English money.

The French, with only eighty thousand people stretched thin over their vast crescent, were outfighting the English, who had about one and one-half million people in North America. However, three thousand miles away in London a civilian of formidable military understanding, William Pitt, sent out Lord Jeffrey Amherst with the mission: secure North America.

General Amherst reached Halifax, Nova Scotia, on May 28, 1758, and stormed Louisbourg, France's powerful guard-dog fort at the continental entrance. The next planned target was impregnable Quebec, atop the natural fortress rock at the place where the St. Lawrence constricts. In the fleet was a task force of eighty-five hundred men for that mission, headed by a homely redheaded prodigy, James Wolfe.

When Wolfe first looked up at the sheer rock face of Quebec, he was awed. It was even worse than the fortress of Louisbourg in the Gulf of St. Lawrence, which the British had already taken.

As Gibraltar controlled the Mediterranean, the rock fortress of Quebec bottlenecked mid–North America. Here the St. Lawrence inlet for the first time narrowed to a river. Towering above the stricture was a granite palisade capped by a heavily-gunned citadel. Wolfe, a student of generalship, knew that it was under the capable command of the young veteran Marquis Louis Joseph de Montcalm, one of the most respected officers on the continent under any flag.

Montcalm, a soldier at age twelve, a captain at seventeen, and a hero in the War of Austrian Succession, became commander of all French troops in North America at forty-four. Although he had held Wolfe at bay all summer, he constantly stared down from the battlement at the tiny English ships in the river.

F AR BELOW THE AWESOME fortified heights, Wolfe was ill—sick with fever and failure. He had a fishbelly-white complexion, with red hair tied on his nape in a short queue. His bulging blue eyes, undershot jaw, and scathing sarcasm repelled his top staff daily. His rapport with his regimental commanders was so bad that his orders were all transmitted in writing. He sat alone in his quarters reading poetry and writing puritanical rules of military deportment.

Wolfe's youthful arrogance was exceeded only by unforgivably profane ambition. His leadership ability rested on a single characteristic: awesome courage. He threw himself recklessly into his assaults, inviting glory or death.

Gnawing on him in September was a dispatch from his

General Braddock's attack on Fort Duquesne (Pittsburgh) in 1755 was his last battle and a historic disaster.

naval commander, Admiral Saunders, reminding him that the ships could wait only a few more days. To make the eight-hundred-league run to the open sea, the admiral would have to pull anchor before the ice locked in his majesty's vessels, leaving Wolfe's regiments to certain starvation and ultimate massacre at the hands of nine thousand well-fed French troops.

Wolfe had started with 8,500 men. By September 1759 his adjutant reported 4,423 effectives left. His field hospitals overflowed with sick and wounded. His cemetery had a full platoon working to camouflage it from the French Indian scouts.

Wolfe himself lay sweating with fever on his bed while the surgeon general ministered to that and bled him several more pints for his kidney trouble. Time was short and he had decided on his plan. It was a plan he would have dismissed scathingly as recently as a week ago, but he was a general down to his last chance for a place in history.

WOLFE HAD LONG KNOWN of a narrow cleft in the cliff face a mile and a half upstream of Quebec. It was distinguished from other such clefts by a little heavier vegetation, grown tough from fighting for a roothold in the rock face. From a defected French priest Wolfe learned that this place at Anse au Foulon was defended by Canadian troops of low morale commanded by a Captain de Vergor, who had been tried for cowardice at the surrender at Beausejour. De Vergor's company had replaced a superb company which had been positioned there personally by Montcalm. The switch had been made by a high ranking civilian.

This vertical cleft was blocked here and there by fallen trees, but the informer said there had once been a slippery footpath under the foliage zigzagging up the cliff. The only chance for ascent would be on a dark night, and early detection was possible because French boats patrolled the Canadian shore in close all night. Twelve French army tents were visible atop the cliff.

A French officer sent a messenger to Montcalm's headquarters to say that he was now seeing through the glass a large group of English officers embarking in landing boats probably for reconnaissance of the shoreline. They were disguised as Grenadiers but had not bothered to button their coats over braided tunics. And one wore a blue surtout with much gold lace.

Wolfe took his regimental brigade and regimental commanders on a daylight scouting survey of the possible landing site. To avoid having his three reconnaissance boats standing off the particular spot, Wolfe had caused them to be rowed many miles upstream and to float back down, then upstream and down. This went on for days, exhausting both the British oarsmen and the French troops atop the escarpment, who marched and counter-marched in parallel, keeping the boats under observation. This continued until September 10, on which date Wolfe received notice from Admiral Saunders that the fleet must now pull out. Ice skim was already reported downstream (the St. Lawrence flows sharply north) off Saguenay.

Wolfe ordered himself rowed out to the flagship. He told Saunders he could not believe the navy would jeopardize the whole campaign for North America for the sake of a few more days—which is how he, Wolfe, would have to report it. Saunders explained he could not risk the largest squadron of the king's navy for the sake of a few more failures—which is how *he* would have to report it.

Wolfe explained that he was ready to strike the winning blow. He would make a show of sending landing boats far upstream in daylight. In the dark they would come about and float down to Anse au Foulon. He would send 150 picked men up the cleft first; if they could make it and hold once they gained the top, then the entire command would follow. Saunders was to create a great noisy diversion downstream of Quebec. If the first 150 men could not make it to the top of the escarpment, Wolfe would pull out, load the whole force on the ships and withdraw in defeat. Saunders agreed.

Wolfe's final written orders to his brigadiers on how the operation would be conducted on the following day were so brief and vague that they had to write special requests for clarification of detail; he replied with petulant, reproachful notes.

The man was very ill. He tried to rest for the desperate attempt he would launch tomorrow.

Up on the heights, Montcalm watched and waited. He knew there was activity in Wolfe's camp.

The ice was coming.

The Marquis de Vaudreuil, governor of Canada, interpreted the English reconnaissance activity in the river as prelude to withdrawal, "Their grand designs have failed." Vaudreuil constantly interfered with the military and used such poor judgment that the professional officers were terrified lest one time Montcalm could not dissuade him from his suicidal orders.

Montcalm knew that his mad English enemy's hunger for acclaim required the strictest French alert. In addition to all his normal intelligence activities, Montcalm daily received reports from an officer in charge of ten canoes of Indians silently patrolling the enemy shore every night.

The French general never relaxed his alert, as a letter of September 2, found by author Christopher Hibbert, shows: "The night is dark, raining. Have ordered all of the tented troops to sleep fully dressed. I am in my boots; my horses are saddled. This is my usual way. I have not taken off my clothes since 23 June."

Bougainville, one of Montcalm's generals commanding three thousand troops, had instructions to watch every English move. "M. Wolfe is just the man to double back in the night."

ON SEPTEMBER 13, the English let the French see them sail upriver a convoy of landing boats and two transport ships of reserves. At two o'clock in the morning, they were silently drifting back downstream. The wind was behind them and ebb tide running at three knots. They dipped an oar only occasionally to square up in the current. A second wave of boats followed at a short interval. A half hour behind, armed sloops pulled anchor and drifted down.

The pivotal battle for the continent occurred on the Plains of Abraham at Quebec on September 13, 1759; the campaign took three years, the battle only about ten minutes.

Repulsed with heavy losses all summer, Wolfe finally discovered a crack in Quebec's defenses: he landed by night and scrambled up the cliff behind the fortress.

There was no moon. The men in the lead boat squinted for shore sentries. Suddenly a voice bounced off the water, "*Qui vive?*" The Englishmen froze on their muskets.

Then a young officer, Simon Fraser of the Seventy-eighth Highlanders, stood up and yelled, "*France! Et vive le roi!*"

"*A quel régiment?*"

"*De le Reine!*"

"*Pourquoi est-ce que vous ne parlez plus haut?*" ("Why don't you speak louder?")

"*Tais-toi! Nous serons entendus!*" ("Be quiet! We will be heard!")

Minutes later the lead boat could see the spit of land that marked Anse au Foulon, the way the base of a tree flares out a little. But there was a slather of noise as a shore sentry slid down the slope and demanded the password.

This time Capt. Donald MacDonald, also of the Seventy-eighth, called back in French, "Provision boats! Don't make such a racket. The damned English will hear!"

The sentry passed them on.

At the Anse the jutting land swirled current out to midstream. On orders the oarsmen now pulled against this offshore thrust, but they overshot slightly as they beached.

Captain Delaune, Fraser, and MacDonald leaped ashore and led the rush to the base of the cliff.

Very early in the rush were senior officers Wolfe, Barre, and Harvey Smith. They looked up the cliff face, shocked. Wolfe was heard to mutter, "I don't think we can by any possible means get up here, but we must use—"

They signaled each other silent. There were no shots. It was just after four o'clock. Then they heard the rumble of gunfire from Admiral Saunders' downstream diversion at Pointe aux Peres. The assault group started scrambling up the cliff grabbing at bushes. Loose rocks and soil rolled down making what seemed a horrible racket.

MacDonald and Delaune made it to the top. This let the twenty-two men just below them know at least that it was humanly possible. MacDonald moved quietly toward the cluster of thirteen tents on the top. Suddenly he and Delaune froze. MacDonald was challenged in French.

In the same imperious whisper he said he was sent to relieve the post. He ordered the sentry to go back and tell the duty officer to call off the other men on the cliff top. The sentry stopped to consider this, and the dialog gave the other twenty-two men time to reach the top.

No one has apparently recorded who fired first, but Captain de Vergor's camp was suddenly alive with musketry. De Vergor himself fell, hit in the ankle. The rest of the guard company, not knowing the enemy so far numbered only twenty-four, fled in confusion.

Wolfe and others waiting at the bottom heard the shots and expected the worst. Then came a yell in English, "Come on!" Wolfe ordered the second wave out of the boats and up the cliff. A courageous French corporal from De Vergor's company had assembled a few French and was directing a telling fire down the face of the cliff. But in the dark they hit only three English.

Wolfe threw his sick body against the cliff and began a frenzied climbing. Weak from days of medical bloodletting, he pulled himself from bush to bush in the greatest physical effort of his life. Around him, the cliff was alive with scrambling men and clattering gear. Men slipped, slid down, caught hold, and scrambled up again, their boots pushing rocks into the faces of the men below, who cursed "that redheaded jackass, probably asleep in his bloody bunk back on the ship."

SILENCE WAS LONG SINCE BROKEN. Get to the top before the handful up there get overpowered—before the whole French army wakes up! They must be awake already. Frenchmen must be rushing to preassigned posts.

Perhaps they would be drawn to the decoy firing downstream at Pointe aux Peres. Admiral Saunders' naval guns were firing at the French Beauport coast. He was also staging a vast play-acting scene. The cast was hospital cases embarking in attack landing boats, over-illuminated by fires on the shore. Cooks on shore were firing into the air. Ships fired at the coast. Would Montcalm detect that it was fiction? Would he look elsewhere for the real attack?

French shore batteries retaliated downstream. The sky there was illuminated by exploding powder. The noise was stupefying. Were Montcalm's batteries instructed to pretend they believed Saunders' staging?

At the base of Anse au Foulon empty attack landing boats returned to transport ships for more men. Others crossed the river to pick up Colonel Burton's shore-based troops. Confusion on the face of the cliff was staggering. There were 4,800 English in motion. By five o'clock the cliff was stripped bare of bushes. Soil was scraped off. Men were clinging to handholds in the layered rock, which crumbled and dropped them. Arriving at the top in the dark, some English were taken for enemy and fired upon in the terrifying confusion.

Night was fading as the last squadrons of English were scrambling over the top of the escarpment looking for their sergeants. In the gray half-light Wolfe strained his eyes toward the great fortification. On the downstream side of him stretched the broad Plains of Abraham, undefended except for a French mortar battery, which had discovered them and found their range. Wolfe saw that Colonel Howe's light infantry was already forming up in battle ranks; he sent a platoon to kill the mortar battery.

On orders, Wolfe's units were forming out of the confusion into parade ground ranks. They moved inland to Sillery Road as ordered, crossed it, and continued straight across the width of the plains until they came to Ste. Foy

Road, which they correctly identified although they had never seen it. Here they faced east—the walls of Quebec.

They were now stretched across the Plains of Abraham between the river and Ste. Foy Road in a line parallel to and facing the Quebec wall three-quarters mile to their front. The half-mile front stretched units very thin, only two ranks deep. The units now moved forward one hundred yards, perfecting alignment and straining to see in what formation French units would pour out of the two huge gates of Quebec—or would they elect to wait inside the fort and fight from a protected position?

Rain began. At about six o'clock the front rank made out white uniformed French forming on a ridge six hundred yards to their front.

At six-thirty a Frenchman who had been gazing out the hospital window on the St. Charles River broke in on Governor General Vaudreuil, "English have landed!" Minutes later, a straggler from De Vergor's guard company panted in with confirmation.

The governor general, as if not understanding how close the action was or mistaking it for a training maneuver, sat and wrote a long letter to General Bougainville at Cap Rouge, telling him to come and concluding, "It seems quite certain the enemy has landed at the Anse au Foulon."

Montcalm, fatigued from inspecting posts all night, was returning to Quebec from the decoy action downstream with two other officers. They were intercepted with the news of the Foulon landing. Montcalm assumed that Foulon was a counterfeint and the main attack would still come downstream. But as he reached the shore of the St. Charles River near Vaudreuil's house, he changed his mind. He could vaguely but definitely see the thin red line of British tunics stretched across the plain.

THE ENGLISH STOOD MOTIONLESS in the rain. The Highland pipers played a challenge.

"C'est sérieux," Montcalm murmured to Chevalier Johnstone. He sent Johnstone to order troops from Beauport to the St. Charles River and to summon twenty-five field pieces into position. Other officers assembled quickly around Montcalm.

The English had gained a tremendous opening advantage. It would take all Montcalm's generalship to dislodge them. He sat his horse calmly, made his plan, and sent mounted officers off to execute. Soon the heavy guns

The death of Wolfe: Though aloof and arrogant, Wolfe showed flaming courage at Quebec, refusing to concede his first three wounds. When a chest wound finally forced him down, he died smiling—he had won.

of Quebec were dropping shot among the British.

Montcalm assembled his top staff. The alternatives were: attack now before all the field pieces, Bougainville's troops, and other support arrive, or wait, allowing the British two hours in which to drag heavy guns up the cliff and dig in defensively.

Montcalm's officers were devoted. They unanimously said it would normally be shrewder to wait, but if they did, it would give the governor general time to intervene with some fantastic plan that could get them all killed. Montcalm agreed.

He had quickly available only five regiments of regulars for France's most pivotal North American battle. The rest of those available were Canadians and Indians, courage-ous and tough but untrained in the formal type battle this would be. If only the Canadians could have kept up the alert watch a few more days, Wolfe would have had to withdraw to beat the ice. But . . .

Montcalm rode out in front of his line on a black mount. He raised a sword so high his wide sleeves fell to the elbow revealing a white linen arm, a beacon in the gray light to help the regiments line up.

All that was best in Montcalm showed that morning as he rode along the front of his line encouraging and preparing his men. He knew they were tired from standing on alert in trenches along the cliff all night. He called out, "*Êtes-vous préparés, mes enfants?*"

Cheers roared back at him and he grinned. Many

*The death of Montcalm: Though aristocratic, Montcalm had an easy, paternal rapport with his troops. Also hit
in the chest, he clung to life for nearly a day, continuing to advise his officers from his deathbed.*

veterans of this battle told how great a general Montcalm
was that morning, how the cross of St. Louis shone above
his sword belt. Even though preliminary action was starting on the flanks and some in the middle of the plain, he
continued his ride along the front.

Quebec's guns were lobbing shot among the British,
who now largely dropped to their bellies to gain cover in
the brush and tall grass covering the prairie. On the left
flank Colonel Townsend took several squads and drove
French troops out of a house to prevent enfilade fire. He
put his own men inside. The French, observing this,
burned some other houses to prevent the English from oc-
cupying them as strongholds. Wolfe's men had got two
brass guns up the cliff. These were answering Quebec's

fire. On both flanks forward scouts of both sides were
closing in skirmish.

The level of gunfire crackling was rising. But Wolfe
was steady—waiting. He was pale but "surveying the
enemy with a countenance radiant beyond description,"
as one veteran said later. A French fragment dropped a
captain standing beside him. With unprecedented tender-
ness Wolfe knelt over the captain, holding up his head and
promising promotion when he recovered. To be sure it
would happen in case he himself died, he sent his aide,
Mouckton, to the rear to write the order up for signature
immediately. A later fragment shredded tendons in
Wolfe's wrist. Calmly he ordered Mouckton to bind it up.
The story grapevined, starting a new Wolfe legend.

133

Wolfe also walked his front line. A shell exploded in front of him, ricocheting a small fragment into Wolfe's belly below the belt. He stumbled, recovered, ignored the blood, and took up his combat position on the right wing between the Twenty-eighth Regiment and the Grenadiers, bleeding from the wrist and abdomen, waiting for the French to attack.

AT NEARLY TEN O'CLOCK a detail of English light infantry feinted at the French center along Sillery Road, which bisected both opposing lines. The French fired on them, and they retreated, apparently in bad disorder, yelling as if panicked. The act was so realistic Wolfe had to assure the rank behind him it was a trick to make the French attack prematurely.

No sooner said than the entire French line advanced, slowly at first—gray, white, and blue uniforms with bayonets fixed. They were six deep, deeper in the center. The center advanced with deliberate professionalism across the six-hundred-yard no-man's land. They were in close rank, no more than four feet between files, a wall of advancing French. Except for the distant large guns and a hollow French drumbeat counting out the steps, the advance was ominously silent.

The sun came out. The English rose from their bellies and stood braced.

The Indians and Canadians on the French flanks were the first to break cadence. They fired as soon as they came in range, dropped in the grass, reloaded, and came on firing. At a hundred fifty yards, the French regulars fired. Balls screamed through the British line. A few red coats dropped.

Wolfe yelled, "Hold your fi-ah!" As British fell, the French let out yells, quickening the advance and the firing. More gaps appeared in the red line.

"Hold fire! Hold your fire!"

The French had advanced so close that the bristling Englishmen could count their ammunition pouches. They stood silent, fingers on triggers, praying for the order to retaliate.

"Hold fire!"

The French came on firing at will, closing the gap to eighty yards—fifty—forty-five, thinning the red line.

"Fire!" Wolfe personally issued the order. Officers echoed it across the front, "Fire!"

The volley was so simultaneous a French survivor reported it appeared as a line of light a half-mile wide flashing out from center. It laid smoke in front of the British. They could hear the agony of the French through the smoke. The British reloaded in cadence and in synchronization fired into the smoke. Again the simultaneous shots hit the French like a huge fist.

Right out of the drill manual, the British advanced twenty paces while reloading, halted, fired. From this position they fired at will until the smoke rose. When it lifted, the British were as awestruck as their opponents as they gazed at the horrifying scene. French wounded writhed in every conceivable position of agony. Behind the decimated front French ranks, the reserves stood in stunned horror. A few were beginning to run for the Quebec wall.

The British stood firing for a matter of seconds, desultorily and without spirit. The pitiful scene on the field hollowed even the senior British veterans.

"Charge!" It was Wolfe. Unit commanders relayed the command, "Charge!"

The British advanced with bayonets. The Royal Rousillon French regiment made a gallant stand but were able to hold less than two minutes. The kilted British Highlanders had more heart for the butcherous pursuit. Charging through the wounded, they dogged the retreating French effectives, abandoning their muskets the better to wield broadswords.

Brave Canadian snipers trying to cover the retreat were able to drop some Highlanders and English.

Wolfe was wounded again slightly. But he was leading the Grenadiers and Twenty-eighth Regiment in the charge. The next few minutes of the charge are confused, but a bullet caught Wolfe through the chest, dropping him to his knees. Blood gushed out his mouth, but he was able to ask a lieutenant to stand him up so the troops would not know.

After the action many veterans claimed to have carried Wolfe off the field. Strongest evidence is that a Lieutenant Brown of the Grenadiers, an unidentified artillery officer, and two soldiers came to his side. Brown sent for the surgeon. Wolfe said, "No need. It's over with me." When the surgeon arrived, the general said, "Lay me down. I'm suffocating."

One of the men, a James Henderson later wrote home, "Then I opened his Breast. And found his Shirt full of

Within a year after Quebec fell, Montreal surrendered, under siege by three columns under Gen. Jeffrey Amherst, and New France became British.

Blood At Which he Smiled. And When he seen the Distress I was in, My Dear, he said, Don't Grive for me, I shall be Happy In A Few Minutes. Take care Your Self As I see your wounded. but Tell me O tell me How Goes the Battle. Just then came some Officers Who told him that . . . our troops was pursuin them to the Walls. . . . He Smiled."

As the retreat reached the St. Charles River, two hundred gallant Canadians held off nearly a thousand British, allowing French regulars to withdraw across a pontoon bridge. The British attack, so emphatically victorious, now lost all discipline as redcoats pursued French on an individual basis, stopping to loot French watches and rings.

Gen. James Murray, hearing Wolfe was in a bad way and Gen. George Townshend dead, assumed command and struggled for order. Townshend was not dead, however, and he came forward, also fighting for order with Murray's assistance. Together they got enough units realigned to scare off Bougainville's rescue cavalry, counterattacking from the inland flank.

Pushed back in the retreat, Montcalm took a shell fragment in the chest. He asked two soldiers to hold him up in the saddle. At four o'clock the next morning, he died. At dawn the British flag went up on the Citadel, Quebec.

Britain commanded the entrance to Canada. The rest would fall. A half continent had changed hands.

Wolfe did not live to hear history call it the most fateful victory of the eighteenth-century world.

CHAPTER 11

INDIAN VS. WHITE

Pontiac's Conspiracy, Little Turtle's League, and short term successes of these powerful red confederations

AFTER THE FALL OF QUEBEC, the British moved on Montreal. The French governor surrendered to save civilian bloodshed, and Canada became the fourteenth British North American colony. Maj. Robert Rogers, the leatherclad legend of Vermont's Green Mountain Boys, was to take over the French forts and outposts in 1760 even before the formal treaty of 1763. He was concerned about the mission. Who would believe that he and his rabble-in-arms were official representatives of the King of England, authorized to take over the French forts from French colonels? Why not send one of those braided regular army officers with the white breeches?

More on the mind of the woodsfighter was the naiveté of the high command in believing that French-speaking Indians would transfer their loyalty from the French to the English simply because of a treaty negotiated three thousand miles across the ocean. Rogers' concern was valid. The English takeover, and later the American, handled as they were, fostered the creation of powerful Indian confederations south of the Great Lakes, each led by a chief with little at his command but raw leadership and a flaming sense of outrage. Thus were kindled the sweeping wars of Pontiac's Conspiracy, Little Turtle's League, Tecumseh's Confederation, Black Hawk's War.

With his two hundred rangers in fifteen whaleboats, Rogers moved upstream out of Montreal on September 13, 1760, to take over Fort Pontchartrain at Detroit. By November 7, he had reached a river mouth on Lake Erie which he logged as the Chogage; most historians assume it was the Cuyahoga outletting at the future Cleveland.

Chief Pontiac, with a party of warriors, accosted him and asked what business he had in that area. Having dealt with many Indian chiefs, Rogers recognized in Pontiac the poise and nerve of an authentic leader.

After four days, Pontiac finally allowed Rogers to continue. As he moved west, Rogers entered the country of Indians still loyal to the French. They did not grasp the turnover of this land to the English. Four hundred such Indians waited for Rogers at the mouth of the Detroit River, but Pontiac's word of approval reached them while they were delaying Rogers. The fifteen whalers rowed upriver between a Wyandot camp on the left bank and Potawatomi huts on the right. In the distance Rogers could see the weather-silvered pickets of the fort flying a faded fleur-de-lis. He landed on the bank opposite the fort on November 29, pitched camp, and sent officers across to demand surrender of the fort.

The flag was lowered without resistance. Rogers left a cadre to take charge, and pushed west to Fort Michilimackinac. However, ice and storms on Lake Huron drove him back to Detroit.

In the spring (1761) the British took over Michilimackinac, Sault Ste. Marie, Green Bay, and St. Joseph. However, the Indians did not go with the property. At Michilimackinac, Chippewa Chief Minavavana declared, "Englishmen, although you have conquered France, you have not conquered the Indians. We are not your slaves. Those lakes, those woods and mountains were left *us* by our ancestors. We will part with them to none."

The curt, commanding ways of the British offended the

The British lacked the French knack for dealing with the Indians. Though Pontiac's plan to attack Detroit was aborted and his chiefs withdrew, red hostility would plague the white victors for decades.

BY FREDERIC REMINGTON, KENNEDY GALLERIES

Rogers and his rangers were sent west to take over the French forts. Stopped at the Cuyahoga by Pontiac, he learned that in the Indians' view defeating the French did not give the British rights to the land.

Indians, who even had trouble talking to them because few English had bothered to learn Indian languages. The English were not astute in distinguishing between tribes or between individual Indians. This was a costly error, particularly in the case of one superb specimen—Pontiac.

THE OTTAWAS were loosely leagued with Chippewas and Potawatomis; and Pontiac exercised easy authority in the league. In late 1762 he sent messengers beyond that league to the major tribes bearing war belts, red-stained tomahawks, and a complex message. It summarized the British transgressions, fort-strengthening activity, and contempt for Indian rights. The message described the key forts—Niagara, Detroit, Duquesne (re-named Fort Pitt), Sandusky, St. Joseph's Post, Michilimackinac, Green Bay. It further explained that separate attacks on these forts would fail. What was needed was an attack on all the English forts in the same season. Such an attack could not fail. The messengers finally asked for a commitment from each tribe to join this attack in its own area.

The signal for the time of attack would come later by a messenger carrying a red tomahawk. Until then, absolute secrecy was necessary (the Pontiac Conspiracy).

Except for the Iroquois, the tribes responded favorably. Although the communications required many months, the secrecy was well kept until Pontiac was nearly ready. The first leak came from an Indian trader who had overheard a half-breed bragging that next summer his shirt would be fringed with English hair. Maj. Henry Gladwyn, commandant of Fort Detroit (previously Fort Pontchartrain) laughed off the warning. Ensign Holmes, commanding at Fort Miami, did not laugh, however, when in March 1763 an Indian friend told him his tribe had received a war belt from Pontiac with a plan for destroying Fort Miami. When Holmes sent written word to Gladwyn at Detroit, Gladwyn replied that the three Indian villages near him were peaceful.

Pontiac assembled his chiefs in council April 27 at Ecorse near Detroit. Representatives of most of the notified tribes came with their squaws, children, and dogs. "It is important, my brothers, that we understand the English will not let us live as the French did. When I visit the English chief and inform him of the death of any of our brothers, they make game of us. If I ask him anything for our sick, he refuses. It is plain they want our death. We must first destroy them. There is nothing to prevent us; there are but a few of them."

Major Gladwyn received on May 5, 1763, a settler named St. Aubrie, who said his wife had gone to an Ottawa village to buy maple sugar. While there she had seen Indians cutting off the ends of their guns, making them short. Gladwyn dismissed the story. On May 6, a Potawatomi girl, Catherine, brought Gladwyn the elk-skin moccasins he had bought from her. As she handed them over, he saw tears. "What is the matter?"

Under pressure she explained, "Tomorrow Pontiac will come to the fort with sixty chiefs and demand a council. He will offer you a peace belt, holding it with the wrong

Pontiac's opening plan was to ambush a conference inside Fort Detroit with concealed sawed-off guns. However, an Indian girl revealed the plot to an English officer, who alerted the fort.

side up. This will be a signal. The chiefs will have short guns under their blankets, and . . ."

Gladwyn believed.

Pontiac was startled when he entered the fort the next day. In requesting the meeting he asked, "Why do I see your young men standing on the street with their guns?"

"We hold a parade this afternoon."

The Indians sat on mats and kept their blankets around them. In the meeting, Pontiac stepped forward and held out a wampum belt in his left hand. When he did that, a platoon of armed troops rushed in with raised bayonets. Pontiac continued calmly. He spoke the specious peace talk used by all men on the frontier. His men watched him carefully. If Pontiac turned the belt so the white side was uppermost, that was the signal.

The chief prolonged his speech while he studied the Englishmen. He did not turn the belt over. He and his chiefs walked out carefully.

Pontiac followed that aborted attack with an open attack on the fort by Ojibways, Ottawas, Potawatomis, and Wyandots. They only wounded five troops. However, Pontiac considered Fort Detroit pivotal. He ordered the attack sustained five days. That failing, he decided to blockade the fort and starve it. It was a sound plan, but Gladwyn managed to sneak a scout out to Niagara to bring help.

MEANWHILE, THE CAPABLE PONTIAC was in motion supervising attacks on twelve other British posts. On the morning of June 15, his Indians loosed fire arrows against Presque Isle near Erie, Pennsylvania, commanded by Ensign Christie. Christie surrendered the next day.

Fort St. Joseph fell, Le Boeuf, Venango, Miami, and Fort Sandusky. (Ensign Pawlly, commander of the last named fort, was captured and threatened with death at the stake. An elderly widowed squaw wanted him, so he was spared for her.)

Forts Detroit and Pitt held out against the blockade. The English pieced together the picture that all their forts were under attack and marveled that such coordination could have been achieved by an Indian. They were yet to see another marvel—ingenuity.

On June 4, the king's birthday, the gates of Fort Michilimackinac were thrown open so the troops could go outside and watch the Ojibways playing baggataway (lacrosse) against the Chippewas, observed by their squaws and a few converted French traders. What attracted the garrison that day was the intensity of this closely fought game. The British troops began to take sides and yell.

Suddenly a Chippewa rifled an amazingly long, high pass to his receiver near the open gates of the fort. The receiver raced ahead to get in position, but he missed it. The ball hit the ground, bounced high through the open gates into the fort.

Both teams charged after the play, stopping only briefly at the sidelines to pick up some concealed equipment from the seated squaws. Once inside the fort, the Indians slammed the gates shut and proceeded to attack the English garrison inside with tomahawks and short guns. Outside, new teams of Chippewas and Ojibways suddenly appeared, attacking the surprised British troops. It was over in minutes, complete with the capture of Capt. George Etherington.

In addition to striking the forts with startling adherence to schedule, Pontiac had more remote villages simultaneously fall upon small settlements on the Pennsylvania frontier, killing about two thousand whites and burning their cabins.

Forts Detroit and Pitt continued to survive, expecting reinforcements. Fort Green Bay survived because Lieutenant Correll there, who had received a warning from Fort Michilimackinac, was well regarded by the Menominees, Sacs, Foxes, and Winnebagoes. He told them his plight, turned the fort over to the Indians, and marched to the relief of Etherington at Michilimackinac—in vain. For Pontiac, this effectively deactivated Green Bay as an English post.

To Pontiac's conspiracy, the British had lost the upper Great Lakes.

Major Gladwyn was amazed at the persistence of the renewed Indian blockade of Detroit, which now featured intermittent attacks. To keep the warriors supplied, Pontiac purchased rations from Frenchmen in Detroit. He issued promissory notes on birch bark picturing the supplies and signed with an otter.

At great cost in lives the British succeeded in getting supply vessels into Detroit from Fort Niagara. The *Gladwyn* sailed out for Niagara, returning September 3 with more ammunition and rations, bolstering its staying power enormously.

Pontiac increased his Detroit force to one thousand Indians. He had directed a brilliantly successful campaign, but he had three tough islands of resistance—Forts Pitt, Detroit, and Niagara, which supported the other two. Pontiac also directed a Detroit-style siege against the Fort Pitt stronghold, commanded by Capt. Simon Ecuyer, a Swiss officer working for the British. Ecuyer had 330 men—troops, traders, and frontiersmen—at a strong position: moated on two sides by the confluence of the Monongahela and Allegheny rivers. He was expecting reinforcement from Col. Henry Bouquet, who was advancing west across the Alleghenies with 500 troops. When Bouquet reached Bushy Run, twenty-five miles from Fort Pitt, his advance guard was cut up by Indians. He soon discovered he was up against no mob, but a

Under land blockade by Pontiac's troops, Major Gladwyn brought in supplies by ship to save Fort Detroit.

directed force. He made a formal battle out of it, extricating his force with twenty losses and proceeding to the relief of Fort Pitt.

Indians attacking the various English forts did not know how well their distant cousins were doing in the vast triangle from Mackinac to Niagara to Fort Pitt. Many awestruck Englishmen, however, did know how close Pontiac was to victory. His campaign stunned them with its coordination and persistence. The English had lost the upper lakes, and if their allies, the Six Nations, were to throw in now with Pontiac, they would lose the lower lakes as well.

It was time to acknowledge they were up against a master. Colonel Bradstreet was equipped with three thousand troops in Albany for a major counterattack to regain the West. He arrived at Fort Niagara, reinforced it, and proceeded toward Detroit.

Pontiac desperately sent messengers to Frenchmen as far away as New Orleans for a resupply of arms. The French failed him. Pontiac's hungry Indians began leaving their posts to seek food.

Bradstreet pushed on toward Detroit. When Pontiac saw the immense army, he realized he could not muster enough armed warriors quickly and feared that possibly hundreds of his people would be killed.

Sir William Johnson issued an invitation in all languages for a big council at Detroit.

Pontiac, from his Ottawa headquarters on the Maumee (near Toledo), lifted the blockade and gave his chiefs leave to attend Johnson's meeting. Pontiac did not go, and the conspiracy crumbled.

AFTER THE AMERICAN REVOLUTION the Indians had a new enemy, the United States. There was little difference in appearance between the English and the Americans, but the new enemy was more aggressive in pushing into Indian lands, and established a government in the West, Northwest Territorial Headquarters, first located at Fort Washington (Cincinnati).

Maturing in the valleys of the Ohio country was a Miami Indian of such bearing, intellectual power, and sincerity that he was becoming the focus of every council where he was present. He was not legally a chief, because his mother was a Mohican. But whenever a proposal of importance was made, chiefs and sachems turned to see

Little Turtle of the Miamis built an effective alliance that routed two American armies.

what they could read on his placid square-jawed face. This man was Little Turtle.

The territorial governor, Gen. Arthur St. Clair, told his translator, when in any group of chiefs, to put the words into Miami language and aim them at Little Turtle.

Little Turtle had already instructed chiefs in the Ohio country about United States law. By congressional act of 1787 the territory north and west of the Ohio River and east of the Mississippi was ceded to the Indians forever—which turned out to mean several weeks.

English-Americans immediately pushed into the territory, buying and stealing Indian land. Territorial Governor St. Clair, following instructions, was purchasing Indian lands for the United States, but he did it by assembling councils of chiefs (from the Wyandots, Potawatomis, Miamis, Delawares, Ottawas, Ojibways, Sacs, and Chippewas), paying them, and having them sign away vast territories far beyond their authority. Even as

he collected these treaties, St. Clair suspected he was building trouble, because Little Turtle would not attend the councils. Without Little Turtle, a western treaty was probably just a souvenir. But the general forwarded the paper to Washington.

Little Turtle saw what was happening. Pleading unity, he called his own council of the senior chiefs, beginning with the powerful Blue Jacket of the Shawnees and Buckongahelos of the Delawares. The three then traveled among lesser tribes, carefully piecing together a league centered around the dominant Miamis, Shawnees, and Delawares, between the two Miami rivers.

As Americans arrived to settle their illegally purchased lands, Little Turtle's League devastated settlements, killing or capturing fifteen hundred settlers within four years.

George Washington ordered Gen. Josiah Harmar to attack from Fort Washington north through the Indian villages toward Lake Erie. This mission was also to show strong presence to the British, who, despite the outcome of the Revolution, were not evacuating their Great Lakes forts. Harmar marched with three hundred regulars and twelve hundred militia. The size of this force reported to Little Turtle was so staggering that he knew he needed some totally new strategy. The one he chose went down very hard with the Indian villages, angered to recklessness by the approaching troops. These Indians had laid out fields, built villages, and erected corn storehouses. "We cannot leave," argued an aging chief. "They will burn our houses and fields with dried corn still on stalks. We stay and fight."

Little Turtle held up his open hand. "My father, they can cut off our villages one finger at a time, unless—" and he made a fist—"we close the hand."

General Harmar was nervous. His 150-man advance guard under Capt. John Armstrong was reporting back that he had made it north of the first three Miami villages without resistance. "Not a Miami in sight. Burned villages and fields."

The troops trudged north, passing through charred villages. Boredom set in. Flanker scouts were pulled in closer. The advance guard unit shortened the lead of its advance scouts. Men ceased carrying muskets at port arms and slung them over their shoulders. The advance guard troops found easier footing if they stuck to the main trail. Deeper and deeper they penetrated into the silent Miami country.

None of the leading troops thought much of the piercing prolonged call of some wild thing, though in later years some recalled arguing whether it was beast or fowl.

Then the forest erupted.

Every tree became a yelling Miami firing into the troops. It was a rout.

"I'd never seen such a massacre," reported a surviving corporal at the court-martial of General Harmar. "I doubt any force on earth could have stopped those Indians. They fought like madmen. I saw one kill a soldier with a shot; then use his gun as a club on three others."

When the main body of the army dispatched a counter-attack group, it met the same fate.

Little Turtle and his league now harassed every cluster of cabins in the Miami and Maumee valleys with righteous fury. The Philadelphia Congress realized the Northwest Territory would never be opened if Little Turtle's League were not subdued. They voted for a powerful force to drive the Miamis west of the Mississippi. Carrying out their wishes, President Washington summoned back to Philadelphia the territorial governor, Gen. Arthur St. Clair, for new orders. In this meeting the president put a hand on St. Clair: "I . . . add only one word— *beware of surprise!* The Indians have a leader of great bravery and skill in Little Turtle."

Late in the fall of 1791 St. Clair moved north with a powerful army of two thousand, which included the veteran Indian campaign regiments plus militia, two batteries of light cannon, four companies of cavalry. The watchword was alert caution. There were a few skirmishes on the flanks of the ponderous American column, directed by young Tecumseh, the Shawnee. These quick strikes gave the Americans confidence. Little Turtle had apparently been overrated.

However, on November 3, 1791, St. Clair's army camped at St. Mary's on the upper Wabash. The cold bothered St. Clair's rheumatism and gout. Col. Winthrop Sargent, the territorial secretary, was in effect commanding the army. The militia, feuding with the regulars, camped across the river separately. Snow began falling after dark.

When the military blankets on the ground first began to stir a half hour before dawn, no one paid any particular attention to the prolonged whirring of an owl . . .

Gen. Anthony Wayne, America's toughest soldier, was recalled from retirement to subdue Little Turtle.

"They burst out of the ground," wrote one survivor, "and appeared everywhere at once on all sides." Many soldiers never rose alive from that night's sleep but were scalped in their blankets. The snow turned red in three hours of bone-splintering confusion.

The path of the plunging twenty-nine-mile retreat to Fort Jefferson became a bloody trail of fallen men and horses. It was the worst defeat thus far suffered by an American force, a loss of more men than in any single battle of the Revolutionary War. Little Turtle lost only thirty-six men.

American boats stopped coming down the Ohio River from Fort Pitt. Squatter wagons stopped rolling in from the East. Ground cleared by former settlers healed over with second-growth trees. Little Turtle's League had won a striking victory. The Turtle himself was so highly regarded among Indians that the great literate Mohawk statesman-chief, Joseph Brant, was brought to Philadelphia to meet with President Washington, who asked him to act as intermediary with this giant of the Ohio country. Brant later wrote, "I was offered a thousand guineas and to have the half-pay and pension doubled that I use my endeavors to bring about peace with Little Turtle. But this I rejected."

LITTLE TURTLE's VICTORY was so highly respected that other tribes now voluntarily joined, and the independent Six Nations even passively assisted. His league had become a worthy opponent of the republic of the United States. President Washington recalled from retirement his Revolutionary War firebrand general, Mad

Anthony Wayne, who had stormed and won Stony Point, New York, from the British at night without ammunition. Wayne accepted the assignment on the condition that he could have a full year to train his troops.

On October 7, 1793, with 3,630 men, Wayne's legion moved north out of Cincinnati against the Miami league. Little Turtle studied the movement. What he saw led him to go before the council with a hard message. "There are more long knives under the black snake (Wayne) than ever came against us. They are led by their best chief. He never sleeps. I believe we should ask for a treaty of peace."

But Little Turtle's past victories and long successful suppression of the whites had made the tribes bold. Buckongahelos joined Blue Jacket in demanding to fight.

After training intensely for a year and cautiously building forts behind their advance, Wayne's legions crushed Indian resistance in the Ohio country at the Battle of Fallen Timbers.

BETTMANN ARCHIVE

The Treaty of Greenville (Ohio), 1795, set a new U.S.–Indian boundary, the Greenville Line. More important than those who signed it was one young chief who did not—Tecumseh, the Shawnee.

Little Turtle stepped down; Blue Jacket became leader.

Wayne, even after leaving 200 men at the forts he built in his wake, had 3,000 troops as he approached Lake Erie. Blue Jacket had approximately 1,400. Wayne had an eager young officer corps, including a future president, Capt. William Henry Harrison, his aide.

Blue Jacket had cannily selected the spot where he would make Wayne fight. Near the confluence of the Auglaize and Maumee rivers, a tornado had blown down a forest, making a formidable jungle of trunks, limbs, and roots. This could cancel out Wayne's cavalry and his heavy guns. On August 20, 1794, Wayne advanced on Fallen Timbers.

The Indians' opening surprise volley was superb. They won the first skirmish. But wave upon wave of Wayne's men kept coming in a disciplined fashion never experienced by the Indians. The red men were relentlessly driven back through the fallen timbers and out into the open to defeat.

Indian power in the West was broken. At the 1795 treaty proceedings at Fort Greenville, where ninety chiefs appeared at Wayne's invitation, Little Turtle watched them make their mark on the parchment, signing away 25,000 square miles of Indian country that he had held for seven years.

One young chief did not sign. It was a signature that would later preoccupy every military headquarters from Fort Wayne to Washington—Tecumseh, the Shawnee.

CHAPTER 12

ENGLISH VS. AMERICAN

How a young American republic created the Northwest Territory and defended it against Tecumseh and the British

THE CONQUEST OF NEW FRANCE in 1759 united the northern part of the continent as fourteen British colonies. However, before a man-child born that year reached militia age, North America was to be divided once more.

The conquest of New France was a major cause of the American Revolution. The staggering cost of shipping British troops across the ocean and up the St. Lawrence to conquer Quebec, and the ensuing cost of regulating the Indians in the vast newly acquired western territory was not peaceably borne by the English citizen. The British government, financially depleted from its worldwide war with France, was determined that North American colonies should pay North American costs. The resulting Stamp Act and tea duties outraged Americans—"taxation without representation."

Additionally, the British Quebec Act of 1774 fanned revolution. This act decreed that the Ohio and Mississippi valleys would be closed to settlement. They would remain fur trading areas controlled from Quebec. The other thirteen colonies were thus prevented from expanding westward, though several of their original charters granted them lands "from sea to sea." Connecticut, for example, was theoretically a thin strip of land 69 miles deep and 3,000 miles wide.

The first Continental Congress, convened in Philadelphia in 1774, dispatched a double-edged invitation to Canada to join in a boycott of British goods: "A moment's reflection should convince you which will be most for your interest and happiness, to have all the rest of North America your unalterable friends, or your inveterate enemies." Canada declined.

The Americans decided they could not afford to leave Canada out of it and loyal to England. Therefore, in 1775 American armies attacked. They occupied Montreal but were unable to take the rock, Quebec.

The American Revolution went forward without Canada, and yet it created Canada, geographically and demographically. The post-Revolution treaty of 1783 created Canada's southern border. Additionally, over forty thousand Americans who had remained loyal to the king quickly migrated north to Canada. Following them came the "late loyalists" for the free land grants offered to loyalists by Canada. Other thousands came who simply did not pay any attention to boundaries.

As the bankrupt new United States organized itself hurriedly to become a nation, there developed a great pressure of settlers pushing into the newly won territory west of the Alleghenies. The separate states of the United States fell into dispute over who owned that vast domain. Certain individual states, now belatedly honoring their charters from their former king, claimed it belonged to them. Virginia, Pennsylvania, and Connecticut had large claims. The small states with no sea-to-sea charters claimed the West belonged to the federation.

Meanwhile, action was required to stop individual settlers, squatters, and claimants from going into the territory until the new republic decided who owned the new land. How would this land be dispensed? How would the rights of Indians and whites be maintained? Beyond prac-

The Battle of Tippecanoe, prematurely triggered by Tecumseh's brother, dealt Indian hopes a serious setback; one day it would give Governor Harrison a rallying cry in his climb to the presidency.

AFTER A. CHAPPEL, CULVER PICTURES

147

tical decisions like those were more profound concerns. What should human life be like in this vast region? How should it be governed? What guarantees to citizens there should be enforced by the federal government, and how? Should it be a colony? A territory? A state or states? How many? What should be the criteria for forming new political units out of this region, or for that matter, any others to be discovered or annexed in the future?

DESPITE TREMENDOUS SPECIAL INTERESTS pressing them from all quarters to open the West, the remarkable men sitting in Congress from 1784 to 1787 insisted on time to answer these questions well and in a form that would endure future stresses and create an ideal. Amid excruciating conflict and turmoil, they forged a landmark document, the Ordinance of 1787, "for the Government of the Territory Northwest of the River Ohio." It designated as a *territory* the land lying west of Pennsylvania and north of the Ohio and Mississippi rivers, and it created the form of initial government by a territorial governor and three territorial judges, with provisions for expanding that structure to include an elected representative legislature and, when five thousand qualified citizens were in the territory, representation in Congress. Other progressive steps toward full statehood were prescribed, based on settlement.

The ordinance was a kind of constitution governing what kinds of laws could be made in the territory. It provided that the territory ultimately become at least three, but no more than five, states. A district would be able to apply for statehood when sixty thousand qualified settlers were inside its boundaries.

(Ever since the close of the Revolution, colonial statesmen had been planning how the acquired territory should be arranged and treated. Thomas Jefferson had made a plan which divided the future Northwest Territory into fourteen new states, naming them elegantly. The northwest corner of the region was to be Sylvania; astride Lake Michigan were to be the states of Michigania and Chersonesus. South of these, where Illinois and Indiana now lie, were Asenisipia and Metropotamia. Below those lay Illinois, Saratoga, Polypotamia, Washington and others.)

The ordinance also provided a bill of rights guaranteeing certain freedoms basic to what human life should be like in the extension of the new nation.

It specified education as an essential to the ideal human

condition, stating that it "should be forever encouraged." Implementation of that clause enabled the general government to insist that in every township surveyed section 16 should be set aside for support of education.

The territorial government, basically seated first at Fort Washington (Cincinnati), moved westward as new states formed.

The first district to gain fifty thousand people (by that time the requirement of sixty thousand had been reduced), and thus the right to apply for statehood, was Ohio (1803). As the first new state to be admitted from the territory, Ohio had to break the old pattern of kingship. Gen. Arthur St. Clair, the first territorial governor, ran the buckskin territory in the authoritarian manner of the old satin-trousered British colonial governors-general, adjourning the legislature when it displeased him or not convening it at all. Operating in the manner of the king's man in the West, he delayed statehood for Ohio, quarreling with the local leaders over liberal provisions they wanted in their proposed state constitution.

Following Ohio, no new states would be formed from the Northwest Territory until after a long period of settlement and a short war.

WHILE THE GREAT LAKES REGION was not the major theater of the War of 1812, it was an important one. Many British-Canadian officials still had hopes of undoing the Revolution. From posts just north of the lakes they looked hungrily south. To another major population segment, the oncoming war appeared as an opportunity to throw the Americans out of the heartland they had usurped. Watching with keen intelligence was the greatest Indian federation builder yet to appear in the region described by Northwest Territory boundaries—Tecumseh, the Shawnee. He had not signed the Greenville Treaty of 1795 that followed the crushing Indian defeat at Fallen Timbers.

After that treaty, there was a vacuum in Indian leadership. The great confederation builders were discouraged or dead or too aged to rise against the new wave of intrusion represented by the existence of the new flag of the state of Ohio. But this morose young leader who walked with a colder hatred and a bolder idea knew that previous plans for Indian unification had been correct, merely too small. He constantly looked for a miraculous means to

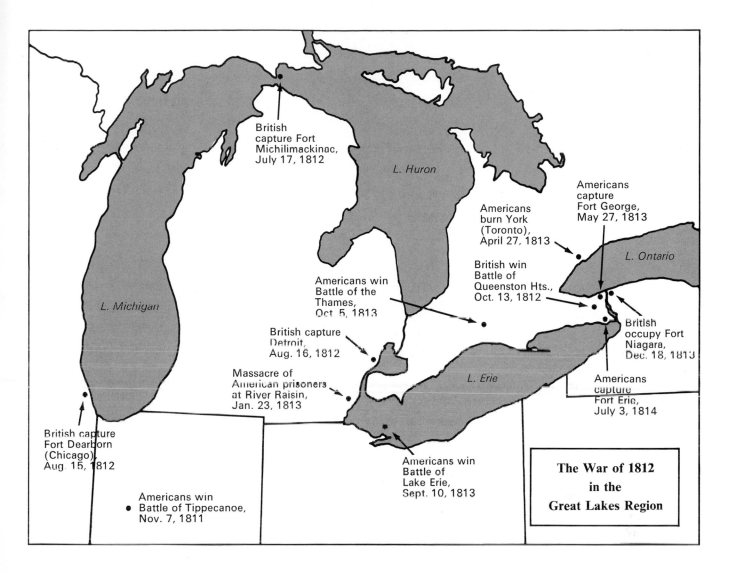

British capture Fort Michilimackinac, July 17, 1812

L. Huron

Americans capture Fort George, May 27, 1813

Americans burn York (Toronto), April 27, 1813

British win Battle of Queenston Hts., Oct. 13, 1812

L. Ontario

Americans win Battle of the Thames, Oct 5, 1813

British occupy Fort Niagara, Dec. 18, 1813

British capture Detroit, Aug. 16, 1812

L. Michigan

Massacre of American prisoners at River Raisin, Jan. 23, 1813

L. Erie

Americans capture Fort Erie, July 3, 1814

British capture Fort Dearborn (Chicago) Aug. 15, 1812

Americans win Battle of Lake Erie, Sept. 10, 1813

Americans win Battle of Tippecanoe, Nov. 7, 1811

The War of 1812 in the Great Lakes Region

build a solid Indian wall from the Great Lakes to the Gulf of Mexico. That miracle was presented to him in 1805 by his less profound but daring brother, Elkswatawa. While Tecumseh was quietly poised and commanding, Elkswatawa noisily clamored for respect that seldom came.

In 1805 Elkswatawa drew attention to himself by claiming a mystic seizure. With it, he said, came a vision. The path for Indians was to go back to the old customs and abandon the white man's strong waters and weak religion. He changed his name to Tenskwatawa and preached widely among the Delawares and Shawnees in Ohio and Indiana, stirring anger against whites.

Increasing reports of this unrest alarmed William Henry Harrison, then governor of the Indiana Territory, seated at Vincennes. To expose Tenskwatawa as a fraud and thus avert war, he sent a challenge to the Delawares in April 1806: "Ask him to cause the sun to stand still, the moon to alter its course, the rivers to . . ."

Tenskwatawa accepted. On June 18 he would hide the sun and turn the day to night. Upon this prediction anticipation grew among the tribes.

When the appointed day came, in the presence of hundreds of witnesses from many villages, Tenskwatawa in elaborate costume paced the center of the Indian village at Greenville, Ohio, site of the hated Greenville Treaty. He performed certain ceremonies, glancing repeatedly skyward. Suddenly he stood rooted, raised an arm at the sun and commanded it—out!

William Henry Harrison, governor of Indiana Territory, had an interesting relationship with Tecumseh, alternately reasonable and hostile.

As hundreds of Indians squinted sunward, day turned slowly to dusk. Indians fell to the ground and prayed. When the witnesses dispersed back to their villages, a powerful religion grew up around Tenskwatawa, the Prophet. Harrison dispatched couriers with the true explanation, that the Prophet had simply overheard white men speaking of the expected full eclipse of the sun in 1806. The Indians were not dissuaded.

While the Prophet used his new power to elicit adulation, Tecumseh put it to work. Knowing the story would travel hundreds of leagues, and that Indians from the lakes to the Gulf of Mexico would have seen the proof in the sun, Tecumseh had the mystical cement for his solid Indian line.

White settlers saw Tecumseh's confederation forming and begged Harrison to act. The governor met with Tecumseh, but with no result. Tecumseh and the Prophet moved from Greenville to the confluence of the Tippecanoe and the Wabash rivers in Indian Territory. This place would become a major Indian capital. In very few months the Wyandots, Mingos, Ottawas, Fox, Sacs, Delawares, Potawatomis and Kickapoos agreed to confederate to resist white westward motion.

Tecumseh did not send agents south; he went in person, enlisting tribes. While he was deep in the south, on September 15, 1809, Harrison assembled as many chiefs as he could at Fort Wayne and made offers to buy their lands. Only a few would sell. That night Harrison ordered whisky kegs opened and kept open several days. This induced land cessions rapidly—3 million acres for thirty-five cents an acre.

Tecumseh returned, learned of the larceny, and sent out a chilling message that doubled the guard at Fort Wayne and Vincennes. He gave the guilty chiefs one way to redeem themselves: see to it that no American surveyor lived to complete a survey line.

Harrison sought a meeting with Tecumseh. Meetings were held over many months and respect grew, but not agreement. In one meeting Tecumseh sat so close to Harrison as they talked on a log that the governor had to move away a little. During the talk Tecumseh continued crowding. The governor's aides were nervous. Finally the governor complained. The chief said, "That is the way the whites are treating my people. But you don't hear us."

HOSTILE INCIDENTS INCREASED. Large numbers of Indians were killed by whites. Harrison punished only a few. But when Potawatomis killed a party of white Indian-hunters, Harrison sent messages to the brothers demanding extradition of the guilty. Tecumseh refused.

At one meeting Tecumseh told Harrison he was leaving on another trip to the south. He would leave orders behind that Indians should not attack whites until he returned. He expected Harrison to control his whites.

With thirty warriors Tecumseh canoed south recruiting Chickasaws and Choctaws. During his absence, Harrison broke the pledge in a move to crush the Prophet's rising power. Marching 910 men on September 26, 1811, to the Wabash, he camped near Terra Haute and built Fort Harrison. Then he marched on the Prophet's town, Tippecanoe. Four hundred fifty warriors there from various tribes felt they could defeat this advancing column, but the leaders urged restraint.

The Prophet and chiefs debated most of one night. If they attacked Harrison, they threw away use of the great confederation Tecumseh was building. The Prophet feared his brother's anger, yet if he voted for peace, many young Indians would probably die here.

The governor was pulling on his boot at four in the morning when he heard a sentry fire and an Indian scream. The battle was on. It was all over in two and a half hours.

Harrison invaded Tippecanoe, burning it flat. A slogan

"The Prophet," Tecumseh's brother who was the inspiration of the Indian confederation—and its downfall.

growing from this action would one day elect Harrison president ("Tippecanoe and Tyler too!").

Tecumseh returned. Crushed by what he found, he repledged total vengeance against Americans and looked for another chance. It came to him soon. The United States was challenging Britain, largely over impressment of American seamen. Shortly after the United States opened the Great Lakes phase of the War of 1812, Tecumseh negotiated favorable terms for his Indians with the English based at Windsor across the river from Detroit.

Maj. Gen. Isaac Brock, lieutenant governor of Canada, came to Fort Malden with three hundred men, taking command. With his short manpower Brock saw Tecumseh as salvation. Tecumseh outlined to him the correct way to take Detroit and Brock acted on the strategy within twelve hours.

Watching from a firing port at Detroit, American Gen. William Hull was stunned. Approaching through a clearing between two stands of forest came an unending column of English and Indians. He summoned staff to watch. Hull

In the War of 1812, General Van Rensselaer attacked the Canadians at Queenston Heights. He was defeated while 5,000 militia who might have saved him watched from across the river, claiming it was out of their jurisdiction.

had 3,300 Americans well dug in and fortified. But this formidable *column!*

Hull ordered the white flag run up.

Brock and Tecumseh took Detroit without burning powder. The Americans, stunned by the small force of British and Indians who now confiscated their arms, heard Brock present Tecumseh, "—the greatest field general I have ever met." He explained Tecumseh's plan: As soon as the Indians at the head of the column crossed the open field and entered the second woods, they cut back on the run bent low behind a slight rise until they joined the tail of a British platoon and proceeded again across the open field in view of the fort. They repeated this several times.

The story of Tecumseh's maneuver traveled and rein-forced the confidence of many of the tribes: the Indians could win. To Tecumseh's dismay Brock was called east to defend Fort Niagara. The chief served under Col. Henry A. Procter who took command at Detroit, resenting Tecumseh's rank as brigadier general.

In the treaty ending the Revolution, England had agreed to evacuate her posts at Oswego, Niagara, Presque Isle, Detroit, and Mackinac, "with all convenient speed." However, it was not convenient for several years. The Americans had agreed to amnesty for returning Loyalists and restoration of their confiscated property but this was low on the priority list of the harried new nation. Britain retained the Great Lakes posts for security and continued fur operations.

Wounded American prisoners captured by General Procter at the River Raisin (near Detroit) were massacred by his Indian allies, triggering the American war cry, "Remember the Raisin!"

As the War of 1812 opened, there were only five thousand soldiers in Canada, sparsely strung along the St. Lawrence and the Great Lakes. Britain could not afford much reinforcement when the Americans struck, for she was engaged in a survival struggle with Napoleon at the time. If Americans had pushed boldly into Canada, the war probably would have ended quickly. Instead, after only a short foray across the Detroit River, General Hull pulled back into the security of the fort, which he later surrendered. This emboldened Canadian British to retake their previous gateway positions south of the boundary.

On Mackinac Island the fifty-seven-man garrison under American Lieutenant Sinclair awoke one morning to find themselves looking into muzzles aimed by a rabble of a thousand Canadian trappers, Indians, and soldiers. Fort Dearborn (Chicago) was ordered abandoned. The garrison of ninety-six people destroyed their guns and ammunition, and were escorted out by Indians who turned from protectors to captors, slaughtering sixty-three of the Americans on August 15, 1812. In the Niagara area, the British easily moved on Buffalo Village and burned it.

The administration wanted a decisive attack launched against Canada above Lake Erie. Brig. Gen. Henry Harrison began the march north from southern Ohio.

The emboldened British were reaching deeper into Ohio, attacking Fort Meigs below the rapids of the Maumee. Procter met resistance from Harrison there but veered boldly east to the Sandusky River and up that to attack Fort Stephenson (Fremont, Ohio). Fort Stephenson's garrison of 150 men was commanded by twenty-one-year-old Maj. George Croghan, who was a great-nephew of the flamboyant Indian fur trader largely responsible for starting resistance to the early French intrusion into the Fort Duquesne region. Young Croghan was ordered to abandon Fort Stephenson. Instead, by brilliant use of a single cannon (the storied Old Betsey), his small garrison held off 1,200 British.

Meanwhile Harrison continued assembling troops and supplies at Fort Meigs and Upper Sandusky for his drive into Canada.

AMERICANS HAD HAD NO TELLING VICTORY on the lakes. One reason was the control of Lake Erie exercised by the substantial British fleet there; it could shuttle supplies and troops to British shore operations and deny the lake to the Americans.

In a tour de force of shipbuilding, the Americans built a fleet at Erie, Pennsylvania. On March 27, 1813, the future commander of the fleet arrived—Oliver Hazard Perry. He was only twenty-eight years old but already a veteran who had worked his way up through the ranks and had seen service at Tripoli.

By two in the afternoon of September 10, 1813, this new nine-ship fleet was receiving a terrible pounding from six British warships on western Lake Erie. Commodore Perry's flagship *Lawrence* was a crippled wreck of smashed rigging cluttering a bloody deck with only 16 of 130 men left in action and all guns silent. The British Navy was at the moment only minutes away from total control of Lake Erie.

Suddenly Perry ordered a boat lowered to transfer him to the *Niagara* with eight oarsmen. As the small boat leaped away from the ship, it came under raking canister, but Perry successfully boarded the *Niagara* and took command. His quick eye found the rigging undamaged, guns undamaged, and crew intact except for three casualties.

At 2:45 Perry ran up his pennant on the *Niagara* and cut out of line, heading due north under full press, aiming to cut right through the British line between the *Detroit* and the *Hunter*, broadsiding both at half pistol range.

British Capt. Robert Barclay's *Detroit*, attempting to swing to broadside the *Niagara* as she cut through, fouled with the *Lady Prevost*. Perry dashed between the *Detroit* and

the *Hunter*, firing out of both sides double-shotted canister and grape at point-blank range, his longer-range guns even raking the *Queen Charlotte* and the *Lady Prevost*. In this single blazing pass, Perry seriously damaged four British vessels, wounding Captain Barclay.

He came about, preparing to make another pass, but he could see the gallant English crews were pitifully lacerated. The *Detroit*, *Lady Prevost*, and *Hunter* struck colors. The *Little Belt* and *Chippewa*, seeing the disaster, pressed sail and ran.

When the smoke lifted from the intermingled wrecked fleets, Perry put ashore a message to Brigadier General Harrison waiting at Fort Meigs to invade Canada, "We have met the enemy and they are ours; two ships, two brigs, one schooner, and one sloop." To the surprise of the

Commodore Perry was only twenty-eight years old when he broke British power in the Battle of Lake Erie.

BY J. L. G. FERRIS, SMITHSONIAN INSTITUTION

Tecumseh—whom Harrison called the greatest general in history—died covering the British troops' retreat. Three American colonels claimed to have killed him.

British seamen and their terrified Indians, Perry went aboard the captive British vessels to ensure attention to their wounded.

With British control of Lake Erie broken, Harrison could now move troops and supplies over water to invade Canada. Tecumseh was supporting newly promoted British General Procter, who, when he heard Harrison's six thousand troops were being ferried across to Canada, elected to evacuate Fort Malden.

Tecumseh was not informed, but when he saw the preparations, he confronted Procter. "You always told us you would not draw your foot off British ground! Now we watch you getting ready to run without seeing the enemy… like a fat dog with its tail down." Procter mumbled about the unevenness of the forces.

"Father, you have got the arms and ammunition which your Great Father sent for his red soldiers. If you have an idea of running away, give them to us. We will defend our land, and if it be His will, leave our bones here." The speech so affected the other Indians that they jumped up and threatened Procter. He promised to run only as far as the Thames River, where he would make a stand.

At the Thames, Tecumseh was the backbone of the crumbling British defense. He was wounded three times and then killed, his body hidden by the Indians. For a half century a hundred Americans bragged that they had killed Tecumseh. For a full century, search expeditions combed the battlefield to find his bones.

Several veteran officers of both armies in later years called Tecumseh the greatest field commander they had ever seen. His enemy, Harrison, wrote that Tecumseh was the superior of any American general in the history of the country.

With the close of the War of 1812, the Great Lakes boundary between the United States and Canada became firm, and the flag of the United States was established in the Northwest Territory, which contained one state and room for five more.

CHAPTER 13

THE BIRTH OF SELF-GOVERNMENT
The attainment of statehood by settlements in U.S. territories; the formation of the Dominion of Canada

WITH OHIO ADMITTED AS A STATE, the balance of the Northwest Territory became known as Indiana Territory. By 1804 the settlers in that territory voted to advance to the second stage, which, while not statehood, gave them the right to have a nine-man legislature.

Although Harrison was considered an outstanding territorial governor, many settlers were restive under the powerful veto privilege of his office and sought the repeal of those parts of the Ordinance of 1787 that conferred those powers. They did not succeed on this attempt, but already the western frontier was seeking more freedom and more voice in government.

In 1811 the unicameral legislature of Indiana Territory passed a resolution to Congress asking statehood. Congress did not approve it but passed a resolution that when population in Indiana Territory reached thirty-five thousand east of a line drawn due south from the tip of Lake Michigan, Indiana should be admitted. So the required population minimum fell substantially from that required of Ohio.

The legislature of Indiana Territory did not meet in 1812 because of the war. In 1813 they thrashed out the matter of a capital site, which had five contending locations, and the next year they authorized a census, hoping to count thirty-five thousand people.

In 1816 Congress approved Indiana's petition for statehood with a few changes. Forty-three delegates to a state constitutional convention met at Corydon in a square stone courthouse with walls two feet thick, built for a territorial headquarters at a cost of $3,000. The delegates were mostly farmer-settlers. However, among them were twelve ministers, ten lawyers, one stone mason, and one physician.

They were not intimidated by the task of drafting a state constitution. Largely, the delegates lifted articles from the constitutions of Ohio, Pennsylvania, Kentucky, and Virginia. Article I, for example, which included a long bill of rights, was practically copied from the Ohio constitution. Thus consistency existed among the constitutions of new states. Indiana ensured flexibility with its article VIII, providing that every twelfth year a vote of the people should be taken as to whether or not a convention should be called for possible amendment of the state constitution.

Indiana's constitution, as passed, added a handful of advanced concepts. Article IX, regarding education, specifically charged the general assembly with responsibility for handling funds from those lands set aside for support of education; as soon as possible, furthermore, laws were to be written to create a general system of education all the way up through a state university, "wherein tuition should be gratis and open to all." This enlightened article also provided for a penal system with the objective of reform "and not of vindictive justice." Ten percent of the revenue from sales of town lots in county seats was reserved for public libraries. Provision was made for state assistance to the aged and the indigent.

At that time, ratification of the constitution by the people was not required. It went into effect the day the convention adjourned.

With Indiana a full-fledged state in 1816, the balance

One by one six Great Lakes states were carved out of the Northwest Territory. Here a newborn Illinois swears in its first governor.

of the Northwest Territory comprised Michigan Territory (closely paralleling the boundaries of present-day Michigan) and Illinois Territory. A census of Illinois Territory authorized in 1818 showed eastern Illinois Territory lacking 5,000 of the then required 40,000 population necessary for statehood. A supplemental census, however, looking deeper into the woods and counting transients as well as the population of Prairie du Chien, a town outside the eastern Illinois proposed state boundary, tallied 40,258.

A constitutional convention met in Kaskaskia and proceeded with more dispatch than either previous state, achieving statehood for Illinois on December 3, 1818.

By that time Michigan Territory, too, had the population to be eligible for advancement to the second territorial status, representative government and a delegate to Congress. However, the citizens voted against it on the basis of increased costs. Additionally, the large French population in Michigan, descended from fur traders, were indifferent to the advantages of self-government. They had always had the freedom of the forests. However, since Michigan had enough population, Congress proceeded anyway to grant the territory the right to elect a delegate to the national legislature.

In 1822, the people again declined to claim their rights. They had lived under a governor and judges successfully, and liked it. Nevertheless, in 1823, Congress gave Michigan a legislative council of nine men appointed from eighteen chosen by the voters. The legislature was given power to submit to voters at any time the question of establishing a full general assembly.

Michigan was content and might have continued in territorial status for a long time. However, Michigan Territory was in a boundary dispute with Ohio that dragged on for years, both polities temporarily exercising jurisdiction over a thin strip of land along Ohio's northwest boundary. When the Miami Canal extension became imminent, the narrow strip became more important. Michigan leaders began pushing for overt action. Twenty-two-year-old acting Territorial Governor Stevens T. Mason recommended that they first gain admission to the Union so they could contend on equal footing with Ohio in the dispute. Therefore, in 1835, Michigan drew up her constitution and applied for admission.

Congress passed a law giving Michigan provisional admission if she would make major concessions in the land strip controversy. Michigan declined. However, if she was not admitted in 1836, she would lose her state's share of the $400,000 federal treasury surplus. A compromise gave her compensatory land in the Upper Peninsula and retroactive rights to her share of the $400,000, while granting Ohio the disputed strip, which included Toledo.

Wisconsin had been part of Indiana Territory from 1800 to 1809, part of Illinois Territory from 1809 to 1818, and part of Michigan Territory from 1818 until 1836, when it became Wisconsin Territory, headquartered at Belmont. Henry Dodge was the first territorial governor. Twelve years later, in 1848, Wisconsin was admitted to the Union, the thirtieth state.

In 1854, Wisconsin citizens worried about passage of the Kansas–Nebraska Act, which made slavery possible in the North. They held a protest meeting in Ripon in February and created a new political party. A prominent Whig, Alan Bovay, named it "Republican," and it was made official a year later at Jackson, Michigan.

When Wisconsin became a state, beautiful Minnesota (Sioux for "sky tinted water") was still in the wilds. Only four thousand hard-to-find white men lived there. Still effectually owned by Sioux and Chippewas, it did not become a territory until 1849. President Zachary Taylor appointed Alexander Ramsey governor.

In 1851, the Indians gave up 28 million acres west of the Mississippi by the treaties of Mendota and Traverse des Sioux. Congress opened the region to a tremendous pressure of settlers who were only awaiting Indian removal. In 1858, Minnesota entered the Union as the thirty-second state with a population approaching 150,000.

Governments south of the lakes had stabilized just prior to the Civil War.

NORTH OF THE LAKES a giant was thrashing around. If there was anything the ten provinces of Canada cherished in 1866 it was their utter unconfederability. Two of them, Upper Canada and Lower Canada, chafed in a frayed harness. The others could as well have been on planets of their own.

Canada was a 3,700-mile strip of cussedly independent peoples scattered in subarctic forests. Nova Scotia's proud-sailing grandfathers had fled the American Revolution in order to remain English, and their descendants wanted no alliance with French Canada. Prince Edward Island, New

Confederation of Canada's aloof, disparate provinces was difficult but essential for their defense; in 1867, through the efforts of John MacDonald (standing center), unity was achieved.

Brunswick, and Newfoundland residents lived from the sea, and they wanted no traffic with the river people of the St. Lawrence. English Upper Canada felt no kinship to French Lower Canada. Inhabitants of Hudson's Bay Company lands—called Ruperts Land—answered only to the Crown. Louis Riel's empire of Metis Indians on the Red River in Manitoba was hostile to the East. British Columbia's few settlers considered themselves United States Americans. A dozen scattered enclaves of Indians, Eskimos, and Icelanders had allegiance to no one. Confederation? Unthinkable.

But John A. Macdonald and George Brown, two brilliant political opponents in Ottawa, knew confederation was essential for survival, and quickly. The urgency was the United States. In 1864, just south of a nebulous boundary was a large battle-trained and soon-to-be victorious United States Army talking about "Manifest Destiny" and annexation of Canada. Western and Pacific Canada particularly could fall overnight to the United States, for the westerners were already more American than Canadian.

Canadian leaders remembered Oregon. Americans had merely moved into that broad, vacant British territory and built houses, farms, and local governments. Suddenly their mail came from Washington—a bloodless annexation. Again, heedless of boundaries, Americans had trekked from exhausted California gold fields into British Columbia, where gold was discovered in 1856. By the 1860s, settlement had passed west beyond Minnesota country and U.S. farmers stared greedily at rich, empty Canadian plains to the north. Charles Sumner, chairman of the powerful Senate Foreign Relations Committee, had openly proposed annexation.

To resist these pressures would require at the very least a confederated Canada. Opponents of Prime Minister John A. Macdonald had a joke: "Big John can't run the two Canadas, so he wants to run *all* the provinces."

The opening move came at 10:00 A.M. September 2, 1864, in Charlottestown, capital of the tiniest colony, St. Edwards Island, in the lee of Nova Scotia.

The selection of this particular site gives a clue to interprovincial politics. Macdonald and Brown buried the hatchet. They knew they could not lure Maritimers to Ontario or Quebec to talk confederation, but they also knew that the Maritime governors had casually planned to talk about confederating *only the Maritimes*: Nova Scotia, St. Johns Island, Newfoundland, St. Edwards Island, and New Brunswick. The governors really were not seriously interested, however, and had not even scheduled a meeting to explore the idea.

So Brown and Macdonald now asked if Upper and Lower Canada—being interested in a total confederation —could send delegates *as guests*. This nudged the Maritimes to scurry around and choose a time and place. The only meeting place the large Maritimes could accept without insult was the tiniest province—St. Edwards. It posed no threat. The only governor they could elect chairman was St. Edwards' premier, John Hamilton Gray.

Organized hastily, they wrote the Canadas that their delegates could come, strictly as guests. However, when they arrived, the delegates from the Canadas were so impressive in physical presence and accomplishment, and even in their royal yacht, *Queen Victoria*, that although they were at first seated in a gallery *as guests*, the awed Maritime delegates kept forgetting to *treat* them as guests.

Further, while the Maritimers reluctantly arrived, expecting to ad lib their thinking at the conference table, the sophisticated Canadians arrived with their thinking all done and in writing. They were impressive and authoritative in their planning and in their delivery. After presenting their confederation plan in splendid style, they were astute enough to retire from the limelight and restore the Maritimers to their role as hosts.

The delegates met for five days in September in Charlottetown. Most of them had not met before, so they were not friends; several were political opponents. Though they wore sober, long-tailed black suits and boots, they were young men, most in their early forties. Not one of them had seen all the provinces or colonies in the region north of the Great Lakes, and they had a great suspicion of being locked to any other province.

At one point in the five days the Canadians entertained the Maritimers on the *Queen Victoria*, opening special champagne. Among the rival colonials on the deck in the glow of evening sun and champagne, a relaxed camaraderie set in briefly. There were hundreds of complex, contentious financial and constitutional problems ahead that would spawn bitter debates, but at this moment one young delegate rashly raised his glass, "If anyone can show just cause or impediment why the colonies should not be united in matrimonial alliance, let him now express it or forever hold his peace!" Many fell silent, soberly considering the premature remark. George Brown and John Macdonald, however, quickly looked at each other and seized the moment. They saluted with their glasses and broke the silence, "Hear! Hear!"

THIS MEETING ON ST. EDWARDS was the most important single gathering. Without it, the ensuing meetings in Quebec and Ontario could not have occurred. Macdonald and Brown had seized on a tiny, strictly local and exploratory Maritime meeting, and they had blown it into a nearly nationwide confederation agreement.

The British Parliament had to approve the confederation. There was so little awareness that they were creating overnight the second largest nation in the world that on the day the British House of Commons was to debate this British North America Act, three-quarters of the members did not show up. They were waiting for the important dog tax bill that was to hit the floor for debate an hour later. Those who did debate the North America Act concentrated less on substance than on what name to authorize. "Confederated Canada" could arouse the United States. "United States of Canada" could also alarm them. Too big. "British North America" could someday bring war. How about "Dominion?" It had a diminutive tone— subordinate, nothing big. That would be it.

The second largest nation in the world was authorized. The Dominion of Canada would include Upper Canada, Lower Canada, four Maritime Provinces with provision for admission later of the colony of Red River, the Northwest Territory, and British Columbia.

The *Toronto Globe* of July 1, 1867, said, "Prince Edward Island has chosen to remain out in the cold, and Newfoundland is not quite ready to throw in her lot with the sister provinces. But . . . the Dominion of Canada is a *fait accompli*."

Sir John A. Macdonald knew that it was not. Chief designer of confederation, pragmatic politician, and to many the greatest of all Canadian prime ministers, he knew that the 1867 confederation was only a piece of paper that could be shredded by the first powerful regional leader to come along. He knew of several already practicing for the role—for example, Louis Riel, the fanatically admired Metis Indian leader of the Red River area.

To block them, Macdonald must make confederation work. For that purpose, his cabinet, including Brown, had a three-pronged national policy: (1) to build a transcontinental railway; (2) to raise tariff against imports; and (3) to promote western settlement vigorously. These moves, Macdonald truly believed, would build a strong enough East-West current of commerce and loyalty to overpower the southward suction of the United States. The tariff would let Canadian industries get started. Promoting western settlement would put Canadians on the land, making it clear it was not up for Yankee grabs; and it would create a farm surplus for export as well as a market for eastern manufacturers—all joined together by the railroad.

World leaders smiled at the naiveté of trying to bind 3,700 miles of separate peoples together with two long strips of railroad iron, and it is true that enormous schisms faulted this union. Nevertheless, in November 1885, in the mountains of British Columbia at Craigellachie, the last spike was hammered into the last steel rail, and Canada was in fact confederated.

*Sixteenth-century map by Vollard of the East Coast and St. Lawrence estuary,
showing the landing of Jacques Cartier in Canada in 1534.*

By the mid-eighteenth century, France and England had settled into earnest battle for this land of the inland seas—which ultimately became a struggle for the entire continent.

It was a period, initially, of competition for furs, of building forts, and ultimately of military confrontations on the lakes and in the cities.

There were later wars, Indian wars and the Revolutionary War and the War of 1812, that were necessary preludes to the development and peaceful settlement of Great Lakes country. With the passing of a century, great commercial fleets were sailing the lakes, the Erie Canal was a reality, and railroads were making their daily runs from the eastern seaboard to the western frontier.

*Overleaf: An authentic representation of an Indian encampment on an island
of Lake Huron, circa 1845, painted by Paul Kane from sketches made
on one of his journeys through the Great Lakes country.*

161

Father Hennepin, taking credit for the discovery of Niagara in 1678,
may have been the first white man to see and describe it. Thomas Benton mural.

Edwin Willard Deming's
"Jean Nicolet's Landfall on the
Shore of Lake Michigan"
shows Nicolet in a damask robe,
expecting to land in China.

Jacques Cartier's landing (1534) as portrayed in a segment
of a twentieth-century mural by Thomas Hart Benton.

165

Today, Indian drawings can still be seen on these Minnesota picture rocks.
This Francis Lee Jaques painting shows voyageurs *passing them at an earlier time.*

"Shooting the Rapids," by Frances Ann Hopkins, was painted circa 1879. The artist (in straw hat) is seated amidships, next to her husband. The North canoe, made of birch bark and measuring as long as thirty feet, was a favorite mode of transportation for Hudson's Bay voyageurs.

Overleaf: "The Death of Wolfe," by Benjamin West, was painted in 1770. British Maj. Gen. James Wolfe died in the Battle of Quebec in 1769.

Commander Oliver Perry transfers from his destroyed ship Niagara *to the* Lawrence *during the Battle of Lake Erie, 1813. Painting by William H. Powell.*

The Erie Canal connected Buffalo with Troy. Shown here is the junction with the Champlain Canal, running north from Troy. From a W. J. Bennett painting.

By 1836, a decade after the opening of the Erie Canal, Detroit had become transformed from a sleepy frontier fortress to a flourishing city. From a painting by W. J. Bennett.

*Once a strategic bastion, Fort Mackinac controlled
the strait between Lakes Huron and Michigan.*

*Fort Niagara, at the junction of the Niagara River and Lake Ontario, is now a state park.
Old Fort Niagara, built by the French in 1725–27, still stands.*

THOMAS D. LOWES

A tier of the original locks on the Erie Canal, completed in 1825, still remains at Lockport, New York. New locks replaced these in 1918.

Part Four
DEVELOPING A RICH NEW LAND

In the middle decades of the nineteenth century waves of European immigrants, fleeing famine, oppression, or war in their homelands, poured hopefully into the fertile Great Lakes country. They harvested its forests, plowed its soil, mined its underground riches. Simultaneously, a busy network of transportation—steamboats, canals, railroads, turnpikes—developed to link these advance platoons of American civilization with the industrial and commercial command posts back east.

Suspension bridge near Niagara Falls, 1856.

CHAPTER 14

THE WAVES OF EUROPEANS

Immigrants who traded crop failure and revolution in the Old Country for dreams of a better life in the New

I
N A NATION OF IMMIGRANTS, who is the immigrant?

A Duluth school principal, A. C. O'Neil, studied the ethnic background of his 332 students and found 49 Slovene, 47 Italian, 46 longtime American, 39 Serbian, 30 Polish, 22 Austrian, 22 Swedish, 20 Croatian, 9 German, 7 Finnish, 6 Scottish, 6 Slavic; 4 each were French, Bohemian, and Jewish; 3 each, Scandinavian, Lithuanian, Irish, Ukrainian, and Greek; 1 Russian and 1 English.

On a worldwide scale the most massive human migration in history has been from Europe to the western Great Lakes states and Canada. These waves of Europeans generally were not random. While a steady trickle of individuals and families did sustain over the years, the more important pattern was huge movements leaving Europe in certain years for specific reasons. Once arrived, these waves did not splash haphazardly about but flowed pointedly toward particular Great Lakes areas, sometimes because of a preset goal, as when responding to mass recruiting by the lumber or mining industries of Michigan and Minnesota, other times by the linear nature of the work opportunity available, as in the case of the Irish who built the canals and railroads, generally from east to west.

The calendar of these tidal waves links them generally to the dates of identifiable European problems or Great Lakes opportunities. The Irish potato crop failures of 1818, the 1830s, and 1845, for example, brought the mighty Gaels, indentured to their ship captains for their passage and married to the dream of taking home money. The collapse of a European rebellion in 1848 brought the "forty-eighters" from Germany. Sometimes trouble in Europe and opportunity in America coincided to bring shiploads of strangers, as in the case of the cold, cropfailing 1830s in Europe, which occurred as the Great Lakes were beginning an era of vast internal improvements—turnpikes, canals, and railroads.

Some waves were so crisply traceable in timing, nationality, and destination as to be actually organized, complete with advance agents seeking out townsites, unraveling in part the favorite "great melting pot" concept of America. Europeans coming to Great Lakes America, in fact, took some pains not to melt. A look at the map reveals successful early efforts to retain proud European heritages: Holland, Rhinelander, New Berlin, La Porte, New Dublin, Shannon, New Lisbon, Pulaski, Scandinavia, Cromwell, and Metz.

T
HE IRISH WERE the advance guard. They came without their women and with light baggage into the ports of Halifax, Boston, and New York. The Irishman often hoped to return home with money in his pocket, but he seldom did. From the moment of his arrival, a chain of events began to ensnarl him. He was met at the dock by an authoritative type, called a runner, who appeared to be a friend. In one sense he was, but he was also a captor and a broker in people. The runner would often buy up the indenture paper, paying off the vessel master in cash for the Irishman's fare. In effect, then, the runner owned the man who stood on the dock, and he proceeded to take good

The mid-nineteenth century saw the greatest migration in human history as the hungry, the dissident, and the adventuresome left Europe for the vast beckoning tracts of Great Lakes country.

179

Canada offered free land to settlers who would defend it, and she attracted many. Immigrants, like these pictured on a Montreal quay, would push inland to take up farms and build a nation.

care of his new investment. He first found him room and board in a run-down rooming house where he had a standing arrangement. In addition to his trans-Atlantic indebtedness, the new Irishman now owed for his room and board.

The runner now hurried to "sell" his flock of new Irishmen to contractors working the Erie Canal across upper New York State—he needed to empty the rooms before the next boat. His bargaining position varied. During a severe shortage of Irishmen resulting from a particularly severe disease season on the canal, he could do well.

While some other nationalities arriving on these shores would have a much better reception, none ultimately would do better in America than the Irish. Other nationalities would cleave to their own kind and stay together in villages and cities, while the Irishman would wander and mix. He would become American quickly. It is true that he would leave an occasional New Dublin or Little Ireland in his wake along the canal rights-of-way, at the place where he persuaded a handful of friends to quit the canal

and take up land, but for the most part the Irishman kept moving westward—across the Erie Canal. Pay improved to $3 a month by the time the Ohio and Erie Canal south across Ohio needed him; and by the time he was ready to start digging the Maumee and Erie across western Ohio, pay had increased to $18 a month, largely because of the cholera attack in 1832. Then he dug the Wabash into Indiana. When that was finished he began digging the Illinois canals. By the time the railroads were planned, the Irish were already a trained work force. This construction took waves of tough, flat-muscled Irishmen farther across the heart of Great Lakes America.

The canals and railbeds the Irish built would transport other nationals into the Midwest. They would come in better style because of the Irish, but the Irishman had a head start at working his way up in America.

Scandinavians came early. Economics was not the only wind driving shiploads of Europeans. The concept of America as the land of the free is no naive fairy tale. Harlan Hatcher's book, *The Great Lakes*, details one episode which,

Through this portal, the New York Immigration Depot, came such steady traffic from Europe that by the end of the nineteenth century immigrants outnumbered native American citizens four to one.

with variations, was repeated time and again in the huge migration.

In 1840 a clipper in Port of Gävle, Sweden, was loading iron for New York. Having a little extra space, she offered to take a few one-way passengers for $26 each if they brought their own bedding.

Young Gustav Unonius, government employee at Uppsala, was unhappy with his native stratified society and talked of America in the classic sense, "Every workman there has the same right of citizenship as the nobles." Unonius took his bride and her maid to Gävle and boarded the clipper. A cousin and two young university friends went with him.

In New York they inquired about the great West. New Yorkers had no answers, but a Swede from Illinois, about to return there, told them Illinois was what the world was meant to be. It was enough for Gustav. He and his friends went up the Hudson to Albany and across the Erie Canal to Buffalo. On the trip they met a man returning to Wisconsin who told them that that was the best place for

immigrants. Crossing Lake Erie, they met a man from Milwaukee who confirmed that advice. The six Swedes talked it over and decided to get off the boat at Milwaukee.

They chose a place thirty miles west at Pine Lake. Thrilled with their location, they wrote home about it. Other university students, former army officers, and fallen nobles followed them, creating the first real Swedish colony in Wisconsin. In the late 1840s nearly every vessel arriving at the port of Milwaukee brought Norwegians and Swedes. The tremendous growth of Great Lakes population in the middle nineteenth century is such a worn statement that it hardly registers until one looks at the figures: this one port of Milwaukee, for example, leaped from a population of twenty-one thousand in 1850 to forty-six thousand in 1851.

From the seaport of Gävle, which sent Unonius to America, three ships sailed in 1849 with 250 Swedes. Soon the American Emigrant Aid and Homestead Company started publishing news of regularly scheduled sailings from Scandinavia to New York by five ships flaunting

Immigrant ships from Scandinavia offered employment agencies, money changers, and language teachers.

The trip west from New York was usually an arduous combination of rail and water transport.

American Indian names. The *Ottawa* brought 630 Swedes to New York in fifteen days nearly every trip. The ship operated an on-board bank that converted riksdalers to dollars, as well as a land office and employment office.

In Norway and Sweden the wonders of Great Lakes America were the talk of the young. About the time the dream seemed too good to be true, a Swede would return on a first-class ticket. Yes, it was true; you could buy land for $1.50 an acre in the Great Lakes region, a horse for $40.00, and a cow for $10.00. Yes, it was true; there was no militaristic government, and public officials were servants of the people, not rulers. Religious freedom was also important to the Swedes.

The Lake Superior Copper Mining Companies sent a delegate to Sweden in 1864 to enlist ten thousand miners, offering to lend ocean fare. Swedes came under contract to the copper mines for $250 a year. They also cut lumber in Wisconsin pineries, sailed Great Lakes ships, and wheelbarrowed wheat and iron ore. They saved their money for down payments on farms that they chopped out of the Wisconsin forest, and in a generation some of their sons were attending Gustavus Adolphus College and St. Olaf College. Their grandsons practiced law and medicine in Milwaukee, St. Paul, Madison, and Duluth.

Over one-fifth of the populations of Norway and Sweden came to America between 1877 and 1898. By 1900 a quarter million Swedes were in Minnesota; 200,000 in Illinois; 50,000 in Michigan; 48,000 in Wisconsin. The Great Lakes West was the new Scandinavia.

While the Swedes tended to merge into the general populace, the Norwegians held aloof. Cleng Peerson brought fifty Norwegians from Stavanger, Norway to the Fox River, founding Norway, Illinois. Before he died, he had established thirty settlements. Today small theaters in Norwegian towns still perform in the Norwegian language. Chicago and Milwaukee have Norwegian newspapers. Little Norway, near Madison, is still a town of blue casement windows and grass roofs.

Germans had been traveling to the Great Lakes region steadily since the early 1800s. There were growing concentrations in Cleveland, Fort Wayne, Chicago, and Peoria. But two distinct waves followed the unsuccessful revolutions in 1830 and 1848.

After years of simmering, the Revolution of 1848 opened with a demonstration on February 22 in Paris and sparked uprisings in Berlin, Vienna, and Baden. The revolutionists, fighting coercive state religion and militarism, included many educated, sophisticated, liberal-thinking men —journalists, lawyers, teachers.

A revolution is always hazardous to the health, but losing one can be fatal. Five thousand Germans emigrated to America in the three years after 1848. They were largely a gifted population of former revolutionary leaders and sympathizers.

In great numbers they chose Wisconsin, where low-cost land was available. Inland from the Milwaukee boat landing, wagons of German families moved west looking for natural clearings in the oak cover. The new country did not need many lawyers, teachers, or writers, so Germans first went to farming. The backhaul for ships bringing immigrants was grain. Four years after a German went into the woods, a wagonload of wheat or barley would come back out for transshipment east at the port of Milwaukee, which became a little Berlin. As a direct result of German settlement, the city and environs became a high-skill machine-tool builder.

Michigan coveted German immigrants enough to publish a guidebook to Michigan in the German language,

The Dutch, like other national groups, have left their names and their stamp upon the land.
In Michigan there are still communities that could be mistaken for old Holland.

183

sending E. N. Thompson into Germany during the revolution to distribute the books. Germans came in three more massive waves in the 1850s, 1870s, and 1880s.

While the Germans were great machinists, musicians, and farmers, the greatest German-American reputations may have been made by Herr Pabst, Herr Schmitt, and Herr Schlitz.

On a trip around the Great Lakes, it is easy to find the German towns—New Berlin, Germantown, Dheinsburg, and New Ulm.

W HILE IRISH, SCANDINAVIANS, AND GERMANS came in especially well-defined and large waves, many other

nations sent their adventurous, their oppressed, or their poor. Entire Swiss villages sometimes emigrated. New Glarus, Wisconsin, was settled by five hundred people from Glarus, Switzerland. The Swiss government paid for the emigrants' transportation and land to relieve conditions at home.

The Dutch came especially for the timbering, bringing their wooden shoes to Grand Rapids, Michigan. When the timber was gone, they bought cutover land and planted tulips and celery. Dutch influence is also evident on the map—such places as Holland and Zeeland, Michigan, and Hollandale, Minnesota.

Polish people settled in most Great Lakes areas, but certain cities were favorites, such as Cleveland, Flint,

Immigrants to the Great Lakes country did not necessarily "melt"; some retained their cultural identity, as did this Wisconsin clan shown celebrating Norwegian Day about 1895. (Note the flag.)

DANIEL S. BRODY

Even today Norwegian Day and other nationalistic holidays are celebrated, initiating a new generation, American-born, into the ethnic customs and costumes of their grandparents.

Hamtramck, and Buffalo. Generally, Poles first came for the timbering, then moved into mining.

From 1850 to 1870 the Danes came. These were the first large-scale Great Lakes dairymen. They settled in several states, but like the Norwegians, the Danes preferred Wisconsin, which they made into the nation's dairy.

When Russia took over Finland from the Swedes in 1809, she treated the Finns well for several decades, then began to exploit them. Finns then moved heavily into the Marquette Iron Range in the Upper Michigan Peninsula, before spreading west as new ranges were opened—the Menominee, Gogebic, Vermilion, Mesabi. Thousands who tired of the mines moved into dairying in Minnesota and Wisconsin, taking with them their hardworking drive and tingling sauna baths.

In previous chapters we have seen other specialized

waves of immigration: Welsh for mining, Slovenes and Rumanians for steelmaking, Scots for the marine trade, and Canada's tremendous call for Europeans to come and people its vast Great Lakes lands.

Besides the obvious fact that these waves from Europe built the physical improvements in Great Lakes America —the canals, rails, and lumber—what of the character of the region? While the waves of foreigners appeared to season America with distinctive languages, costumes, and customs, the immigrants in a way made America more American. Hungrily they seized at face value the democratic rules of religious and political freedom designed by the colonial statesmen. They valued them and exercised them more intensely than did the originators.

Many of these Great Lakes settlers had come just to be part of the world's huge new idea—America.

CHAPTER 15

TILLING THE FERTILE EARTH

*From farms to orchards to dairies—how intrepid pioneers
wrested a living from the land*

To all whom these presents shall come, Greetings:

*Know ye that in consideration of Military Services per-
formed by:*

JONATHAN WOODBRIDGE, PRIVATE

*as a member of the Continental Establishment in the Great
Rebellion, there is granted to said veteran in lieu of monies:*

100 acres

in the United States Military Bounty Lands.

G. Washington

MILLIONS OF ACRES worth of these bounty-land warrants were issued to veterans of the Revolution so
they might claim lands in the "Territory North
and West of the Ohio River." However, Jonathan Woodbridge was not entitled to go into the territory and simply
measure out his own hundred acres. Legally, he had to
wait until the government surveyed it into neat squares—
and that was the hitch. Many special interests delayed the
survey. Some of the newer states claimed that this land belonged to them, not to the republic; England, on several
treaty technicalities, was not really vacating her Great
Lakes posts; and the bankrupt young United States government was less eager to "give" the land to her veterans
than to sell huge tracts of it to large cash-customer land
jobbers.

When surveying finally did begin, Tecumseh and other
chiefs restated the Indian belief that it is not right for individuals to *own* land. Since no one listened, surveying parties
disappeared in the forest, requiring replacements.

Veterans—or, after many delays, their sons—were usually forced to turn over their bounty-land warrants at
heavy discount to land jobbers, who later redeemed them
with the government for full face value.

Therefore, Jonathan Woodbridge and thousands like
him read the advertisements in eastern journals:

"One million acres of Ohio Country
now open to sale and settlement.
Equal to any part of the federal
territory in point of quality of soil
and excellence of climate. Veterans'
bounty-land warrants accepted at
one third."

The advertisements stated that horses, cattle, and hogs
could find abundant forage, and that cotton could flourish
along with all grains and vegetables. The ads did not
mention whether the farmer could flourish.

Once the settler had fought his way through the com-
plexities of gaining title, he was in a race against a four-
year payment period to get his farm producing. Therefore, the first cabin he threw up was not picturesque, only
quick. If he was fortunate enough to have a hollowed
sycamore tree, he used that, and hurried to his first staggering task—clearing. The earlier and therefore more
easterly settlers had no natural clearings in the solid canopy of oak, beach, maple, and walnut. To open a field-
sized hole in this canopy with an ax was shoulder-wracking
work. The farmer-settler hoped to start clearing in winter

*Once cleared, the virgin earth of Great Lakes country, nourished
by millennia of forest humus, yielded a bountiful harvest.*

Breaking new ground to tillage was shoulder-wracking work. After trees were cleared and burned, the plow had to be forced through a thick root mat.

so he could get some seed in by spring. Thomas Blaine, an unusually strong settler in Ohio, began his clearing on March 18. By May 22, working night and day, he had cleared "what I judge to be four and a half acres." That was more than most farmers accomplished.

The first planting did not look like a field. Enormous logs lay helter-skelter; the farmer planted around them. Even if he had had time to burn the logs and the slash, shoulder-high stumps filled his clearing.

The ground itself was an untillable root mat, in which a man chopped holes with an ax to plant his seed. And his crop, until he had sweetened the soil with a few years of ashes, was meager and stunted.

The settler's first goal was mere self-sufficiency; his next goal was salable surplus, for he had three more land payments to make. However, except for the most stubborn of men, the young farmer usually began to realize that in his lifetime his dreams for the farm would probably not be realized. Still, there was hope for future generations; as Thomas Blaine wrote to people back east, "The stumps and roots will be rotted by the time the boys start."

The settler's first commercial crops were usually corn, then wheat. He had trouble marketing them, however, because there were at first no cities nearby requiring these products. So, many farmers took on some livestock and thus converted part of the grain to pork and beef.

There were also some small cash crops to be found in the woods. The aromatic root of the ginseng plant was in huge demand by eastern pharmacists, and it could be shipped economically. In 1815 wood ashes were salable at $120 per ton for the manufacture of soap, glass, and bleached cloth, but a ton was a lot of ashes. The settler could also earn some cash in the fur business. Many a farmer met his fourth land payment this way.

WHEN THAT HURDLE WAS CROSSED, a man could no longer put off his woman's justifiable demand for a *real* house. She had chosen the spot long since and had saved a piece of real glass for the window, perhaps given to her by a neighbor who gave up the fight and went back east. The new cabin had a puncheon floor and squared timbers, notch-and-dowel joined; and it was clean and maple scented.

The soil was "tamed" after four years of corn and wood ashes so that wheat would prosper. But deep plowing was still not possible through woody roots. Even the shallow harrow, if it had wooden teeth, did poorly. The farmer's first plow quickly wore out, and he had to make another. He hewed the curved mold board from a log selected for a grain that best resisted the wear of the soil. Onto this he nailed worn hoe blades or horseshoes. For handles for

HISTORICAL PICTURES SERVICE

Tree stumps took a whole generation to rot, so to assure a harvest the second year on the land, wheat was planted right around them.

his makeshift plow he sought crooked white ash roots.

The southerner, up from Virginia, plowed this new land best. He let the plow go where it wanted, slewing away from roots, finding the easiest going. The Puritan-Yankee —with his philosophy of punishment, determination, and straight rows—had a harder time.

The settler's most important farm implements were his growing boys, his ox, and his horse. The draft animals he brought with him from the East often died of overwork soon after arrival. When he bought new animals, the original cabin often became their stable.

As soon as he could afford them, the farmer acquired some hogs, both for the table and for market. Hogs accommodated his need for speed; they multiplied twenty times faster than cattle and could walk a hundred miles to market without losing too much weight. The farmer also found use for a few sheep when the family's eastern clothes were worn out. One of his urgent needs was finding salt deposits for his animals and for use in curing and preserving food.

After twenty years the main house had likely been expanded, seventy acres cleared, a large barn built, and yields increased. The settler could see that by clearing another thirty acres, he could make real money. His work-aged arms were not quite up to it now, but the oldest boy was strong and may have brought home a wife. They

BETTMANN ARCHIVE

Johnny Appleseed traveled the wilderness planting apple trees for the benefit of future settlers.

Many farmers despaired of working the thick, sticky Illinois soil until John Deere designed and built a thin-bladed steel plow that shed the muck and opened up the prairie.

could add a wing to the house and clear sixty acres more.

As settlement pressed west, men came out from under the forest cover into a large opening—the prairie. They lost their fear of open land "that won't grow trees," for this was rich, black soil on the Illinois prairie. However, breaking the sod of interlocking grass roots as thick as a man's finger and fifteen inches deep required five to ten yoke of oxen. The ground was often so wet that the plow had to be cleaned every few rods. The oxen's hooves sucked mud and the animals tired easily. Once broken, the sod quickly sprouted more grass; it required years of plowing to make a field.

But this soil, containing the humus of the centuries, yielded richly. Again, corn was the first crop. Planted when the maple leaves were as big as squirrels' ears, it would give one hundred bushels to an acre on twelve-foot stalks. Unfortunately, weeds were equally aggressive in the rich soil. A man could "take hold of the wild cucumber

vines at one corner and shake all the corn in the field."

Some farmers kept the land in sod. Rich native grasses made good pasture. Not so impressive were the early cattle, described in an 1840 issue of *Western Farmer* as "small, short bodied, thin and coarse haired, steep-rumped, slab-sided, having little aptitude to fatten, or to lay the fat on the right place."

ALONGSIDE THE GREAT LAKES farmer was a heroine. Living the first few years in a dirt-floor hut, permanently scented with cooking smoke, a pioneer farm woman's only real relief from a gray, work-tempered life was her kitchen garden. Vining plants—squash, cucumbers, beans, and hops—were planted on the west fence. Beds of vegetables—potatoes, turnips, cabbages, parsnips, and melons—were planted in the center of the enclosure. There was always a small area devoted to herbs—anise,

Chicago, transportation gateway to the agricultural midwest, became the nation's meat capital;
the Union Stockyards, where animals were sold by the acre, was unique in the world.

basil, catnip, horehound, horseradish, mint, wintergreen, sage, witch hazel, and tansy. On the borders were raspberry, currant, and gooseberry bushes.

Today, along a highway anywhere in the Great Lakes region, one may come upon a bunch of orange day lilies. In back of them one may see an old scrub rose or a grapevine tangled in the remains of a fence. At one time there was a house there. It may have burned or rotted into the soil, but certain it is that this was the home of a pioneer family, for none of these plants are native. When the first residents arrived, the women brought these hardy plants with them in boxes and pots.

To a pioneer farm woman, the treasured part of the garden was fruit. The finest treat for someone who had been three years west of the Alleghenies was an apple. Hence, one of the folk heroes of the Great Lakes region is John Chapman, better known as Johnny Appleseed. Though truth and legend about Johnny Appleseed are

intertwined, we do know that in 1800 John Chapman left his farm orchard outside Pittsburgh and headed northwest, intent on "making the wilderness fruitful." His equipment was a bag of apple seeds, a bag of meal, a lump of salt, a Bible, a hatchet, hoe, rake, flint, and steel. Before long he became a familiar figure—though a strange one—moving through pioneer settlements, planting apple trees. Never armed, he was perfectly safe among the Indians.

Chapman gathered his seeds at cider presses in winter. In the spring he resumed visiting new settlements or lonely cabins, giving out seeds and teaching the proper care of trees, budding, and grafting. Sometimes he found a small clearing and started an orchard so that future settlers would find orchards waiting.

Then, as today, a man with such motives is often assumed to be crazy, and Chapman was called that. As populations increased, however, his precious nurseries were carefully tended. In Michigan he left seeds with missionary priests and warned them to mulch and wrap the trunks in winter. In Indiana, court records appraise his nurseries near Fort Wayne at fifteen thousand trees.

In the spring of 1847 Chapman died at the house of William Worth in the Maumee Valley, and Gen. Sam Houston rose on the floor of the U.S. Senate to eulogize him: "This old man was one of the most useful citizens of the world."

Many Canadian settlers had orchards. One of them, John McIntosh, an early settler in Dundas County, transplanted a number of wild apple trees in 1796. He carefully pruned them until they bore, and then selected the most promising for further propagation. Finally, he narrowed the field down to one. He called it the McIntosh Red, and it has become one of the world's finest apples.

In New York, the orchards and nurseries started by David Thomas at Aurora on the eastern shore of Cayuga Lake in 1805 turned western New York State into orchard country.

Michigan, too, still retains its early lead in orchards. When Cadillac founded Detroit in 1701, he brought with him from Quebec a gardener whose duty was to lay out orchards. Among the horticultural wonders remaining from this period are giant pear trees—without known name or lineage. Examples of these venerable trees survive in Monroe and in Waterworks Park, Detroit, where of an original group of twelve representing the apostles, only Judas survives.

In 1824, before he became governor, the pioneer commercial orchardist, William Woodbridge set out two thousand imported apple and pear trees in Michigan; and in 1847 I. E. Ilgenfritz, a stocky New York German and a superb grower, started a nursery in the valley of the Raisin River near Detroit, introducing a number of superior fruit varieties.

DESPITE ALL OTHER PROBLEMS, the farmer's greatest hurdle in the pioneering stage was transportation. He could not get his crops to market. By the early 1830s, however, the Erie Canal and the Ohio and Erie were operating. Each decade thereafter saw the canal network expand another whole state westward, along with a parallel turnpike-building wave. By 1836 Indians were scowling as steel rails invaded the forests. Great Lakes waters were busy with schooners and a few sidewheelers, which

connected to railheads. Most farmers could reach one of these routes to eastern markets.

In 1839 Ohio was the principal wheat state, with New York and Pennsylvania close seconds. These three states produced more than half the total crop grown on the American continent. But twenty years later Illinois, Indiana, and Wisconsin took the lead. In 1860, seven wheat-producing counties in Wisconsin and Illinois, each with yields above a million bushels, exceeded the entire output of New York.

Grain schooners were carrying wheat to Buffalo for eastern markets. The completion of the Soo canal at Sault Ste. Marie admitted Minnesota and the Great Plains to this great traffic. Today a single bulk vessel can carry a half million bushels of wheat, the harvest from twenty-five thousand acres in Minnesota.

When the transportation network matured, a clear crop pattern evolved. The corn-hog agriculture stretched mainly across western Ohio, Indiana and part of Illinois. Wheat also gilded these areas and parts of Wisconsin and Minnesota, and all of Canada. The orchardists were strongest in New York and Michigan—with small-acreage general farming mixed into all these areas.

THEN, IN 1870, blossomed a huge latecomer: Wisconsin began to specialize in dairying, becoming the world leader, with Minnesota not far behind. While it is true that Wisconsin's lush grasslands among the eight thousand lakes were ideal for this pursuit, dairying did not spring up spontaneously. Unlike some products, Wisconsin dairying blossomed with a strong, calculated push from designing men. Importation of fine cattle was a deliberate move by a state concerned about its early dependency upon lead and iron mining. The German, Swiss, and Finnish Americans had a liking for cattle, which helped immensely.

One pioneering phase of dairying in Wisconsin that did start early suddenly boomed. Those five hundred settlers who were sent to New Glarus, Wisconsin, from Glarus, Switzerland, had developed a village specialty—fine cheese. With the rise of dairying in Wisconsin, their Swiss process for cheese making was suddenly important to the state, which today produces half the cheese made in the United States and exports heavily to Europe.

Eight-and-a-half million acres pasture dairy cattle in Wisconsin today, producing some 14 percent of the United

Thirty years ago Peter Hanson pioneered in scientific plowing and planting to get the most from his fertile Wisconsin soil. Today the family farm near Cashton is operated by his son William.

States' milk output and 19 percent of the butter. A third of Wisconsin's milk goes into cheese, and the rest into ice cream, powdered and evaporated milk, and a host of surprising products, such as paint.

GREAT LAKES AMERICA began in the classic agrarian frontier pattern, which then built the cities. Corn from the hot, flat counties of Ohio, Indiana, and Illinois built the cathedrallike county-seat grain elevators, the railroads that connected them, the banks and churches across the street, and the land-grant colleges down the road. Wheat built the armada of schooners and the port cities that loaded and unloaded them. The farmers' need for ever bigger tooling built the sprawling Great Lakes farm-implement industry in the cities.

Today one can drive across nearly any east-west road in northern Ohio, Indiana, or Illinois and read the agri-cultural saga in some of the classic farmhouses that still remain in the original families. They read best from back to front: In the rear the original cabin can sometimes be seen, still in use for tool storage, and logs nearly concealed under cement facing and rambling roses. At the front is the big house, New England or Virginia colonial or aging red brick with white steamboat-gothic lacework, built by the first son, perhaps. Between those extremes one sees several connecting structures of different vintages and mixtures —brick for good times, asphalt shingle for depressions, concrete block for the tool-repair shed. The third daughter-in-law may have demanded an aluminum-siding ranch-type addition unashamedly jutting out perpendicular to the axis of buildings, looking as incongruous with the older structures as the aircraft crop duster overhead. Yet, strangely, the effect is not garish; the whole house is a dignified record of work, survival, productivity, and worth in Great Lakes America.

CHAPTER 16

HARVESTING LUMBER AND ORE

Cutting the vast timberlands and opening the iron ranges —
the dawn of inland industry on a rugged frontier

AN UNBROKEN FOREST once stretched north of the lakes two thousand miles from Nova Scotia to Lake of the Woods, and south of the lakes nearly unbroken to western Ohio before reaching broad grasslands. But a growing United States hungered for lumber. The speed with which vast regions of the Great Lakes country were stripped in a huge lumber commerce is remarkable in world history and was made possible by the lakes' role as a massive flume from forest to market.

By 1840 fifty vessels were engaged in the lumber trade; by 1885, seven hundred clippers and steamers. Another torrent of lumber went down the Mississippi. Steamers even began towing multiple lumber barges. One tow in 1872 was a wonder to mariners. Captain R. Valentine, master of the *Antelope*, towed eight large lumber barges in a mile-long procession—as large a navy as Perry commanded at Put-in-Bay—bringing 6 million feet of timber out of Saginaw, Michigan, into Buffalo. In addition to such tows, the companies used rafts of several types, with literally acres of floating logs in a single tow.

In the Saginaw Valley of Michigan alone at its 1880 peak, sixty large sawmills scented the air above the twin industry capitals, Bay City and Saginaw.

A lumber camp grown into a lumber town was like no other type of settlement. The air vibrated with snarling saws that forced conversation to a shout. The fragrance was strong, especially on hot or rainy days. The whole town was originally unpainted wood. The roads were corduroy logs, the sidewalks duckboards, the houses squared timbers. Along the Huron shore the very ground was a heavily-piled carpet of sawdust and shavings.

Miles of lumber ramparts lay seasoning along the shores of the Saginaw and up the Shiawassee, Cass, Flint, and Tittabawassee rivers. Each river sent down a flood of timber until you could nearly walk across Saginaw Bay. Between the sawmills and shipyards grew high walls of finished board: pine, oak, maple, some hickory, cherry, and black walnut—house boards, ship timbers, furniture walnut, lath, shingles, and barrel staves.

There were eight hundred logging camps and twenty-five thousand loggers in the Michigan woods. In spring this red-sash brigade of largely French Canadians came out of the woods in Mackinaws and tassled hats to spend a winter's pay in Saginaw and Bay City. There were plenty of people ready to accept that money. Potter Street in Saginaw, between Washington and Third, jumped with thirty-two saloons—on *one* side of the street. When April winds thawed the ice, a huge navy sailed out of Saginaw Bay, trying to reduce the towering board feet that lined the banks. Lumber came into Detroit, Toledo, Cleveland, Buffalo, and Toronto, as the growing nations used 350 cubic feet of lumber for each man, woman, and child every year.

While Saginaw was still booming, lumber king David Ward, former surveyor and timber looker, personally walked the Saginaw forests and saw them thinning. He moved up the Huron shore to Cheboygan, logged it until the crowd came, then moved around the peninsula into Lake Michigan to Charlevoix, Manistee, and Ludington. Others leapfrogged across Lake Michigan to Wisconsin

Pickmen, shovelmen, drillers, and shooters pose for a rare shot in the pit
of the mighty Tower-Sudan iron mine in Minnesota, 1890.

MINNESOTA HISTORICAL SOCIETY

Lumbering moved west along the lakes with incredible speed. By 1899 the saws had reached Minnesota, and this camp in Wrenshall was busily shipping timbers down the Mississippi.

and Michigan's Upper Peninsula. Muskegon on Michigan's west coast was the lumber center for awhile in the 1880s, producing eighty-five millionaires and sailing fleets that could haul a billion board feet a year. Its saloons, gambling houses, and red-lighted hotels were the most deluxe in the lumber kingdom. Most of Muskegon's lumber went to build Chicago and the prairie cities nearby.

As the snarl of the saws faded around Saginaw, Alpena, and Muskegon, it crescendoed westward—Menominee, Escanaba, Manistique, Ashland, Superior, and finally to Duluth.

IMPORTANT THOUGH TIMBER WAS, iron was to form the character of the region. In the Monongahela Valley near Pittsburgh, ironmongers could still pick up kidney ore on top of the ground in 1800 to make bar iron and iron pots; but it was disappearing.

To the west, in Ohio's Mahoning Valley, Daniel Heaton blew in the first furnace in the Northwest Territory on Yellow Creek near Youngstown. After that, furnaces reddened the night sky over clearings in the valley at Niles, Poland, Youngstown, Struthers, and down the Cuyahoga Valley to Cleveland. But the production of seven tons of iron required an acre of trees for charcoal, and soon a furnace was standing in the clear, ten miles from fuel and a hundred miles from ore. That is why the Great Lakes iron story took a long leap in 1844.

On September 15, in Michigan's Upper Peninsula, William Ives called out to his surveying partner, "Come and see a variation that will beat them all!"

Ives was compass man with a party of remarkable men moving south from Teal Lake, surveying the Michigan peninsular frontier for the government. Others in the party were William A. Burt, United States deputy surveyor; Douglass Houghton, brilliant young scientist-geologist;

Many a bountiful Minnesota farm began as a dream in a lumbering bunkhouse, where Scandinavian immigrants would put in five seasons of timbering to earn a down payment for land.

and his brother, Jacob, barometer man for the party.

Suddenly the compass needle was intoxicated. It was Jacob Houghton who left the written field note of that morning that would start an army of ambitious men west and annex this cold, lonesome land to the nation: "So soon as we reached the hills to the south of the lakes, the compass man began to notice the fluctuation and the variation of the magnetic needle. We were, of course, using [also] the Solar Compass of which Mr. Burt was the inventor, but I shall never forget the excitement of the old gentleman [age 52] when viewing the changes of the variation . . . the needle not actually traversing alike to any two places. He kept changing the position to take observations, all the time saying, 'How could they ever survey this country without my compass?'" What had disoriented the magnetic needle was iron.

Rumors about the Teal Lake iron deposit traveled east to Detroit, Cleveland, Buffalo, and Boston. The one nota-

tion that was ignored by more than nine hundred enterprising men was this: "*The lure of quick and abundant wealth will prove the ruin of adventurers. . . . I caution those who would engage in this business . . . without patient industry and capital . . . will most certainly end in disappointment and ruin.*"

Houghton knew that this north country, which killed him a year later, was brutally cold and lonely. Over 900 exploration permits were granted to 104 companies, but as Houghton had warned, they were driven back by cold, hunger, and the smashed hopes of men who could not find, recognize, or bring out the iron ore.

Philo M. Everett, however, took a party of four into the Upper Peninsula from Jackson, Michigan, by way of the Sault Ste. Marie. He met there Tipo-Keso ("Full Moon"), niece of Chief Margi-Gesick (*Madjigigig*). She directed Everett to a mystic mountain, where lightning flickered around rock outcroppings. The party climbed a fifteen-mile slope of hard maple to the Chippewa camp above

Teal Lake. The next day Chief Margi-Gesick took them up to the hill that drew dancing lightning. He refused to go close but pointed to a large pine. Under its roots Everett's colleagues chopped loose a sizable boulder of iron ore that today is displayed in the Smithsonian Institution. At the place to be called *Negaunee* (Ojibway for "the first"), Everett carried in a forge and bellows, cut maple for fuel, and began to make iron in the wilderness.

While the Jackson Mining Company was struggling to make three tons of iron a day, Robert J. Graveraet trekked onto the Upper Peninsula with a small party grubstaked by Massachusetts men. Many would call him the most remarkable of the giants who entered the Upper Peninsula. . Even the men following him up the rocky slopes could hardly believe he existed. The ax helve lashed across the top of his pack barely exceeded his shoulderspan, and on either end of it hung a backpack he had lifted from his stragglers. Above the shoulders rode a handsome, laughing head that men would follow through blizzards and payless months of rock chopping.

He lifted the pack off the back of a slim sixteen-year-old member of his party and carried it four miles until they stopped for noon rations. When the trek resumed, he reached for the lad's pack again. The exhausted boy, already devoted to Graveraet, snatched it back, saying, "I'll carry my own, sir." The boy was Peter White, who, pushed into constantly accelerating responsibility by Graveraet, would someday carry Graveraet's load.

The first shipment of Lake Superior iron ore sailed away. The quality of ore was admired, but its type unfamiliar; no more was wanted. Graveraet decided to smelt first, then ship.

The result was shattering. His Marquette Iron Company made good enough iron, but it cost them $200 per ton delivered at Pittsburgh, where the market was then $80. The most valuable product of that venture was the development of Peter White.

Dedicated to Graveraet's dream of a great Upper Peninsula mining industry, the slim boy outgrew his hero a thousandfold. Working outward in widening circles from Marquette, he developed Michigan mining as a personal crusade. The great power he had was neither capital nor mining knowledge; rather, he saw to it that those who understood iron got what they needed: stores, postal service, legislation, and especially a canal bypassing the rapids in St. Mary's River.

Stories of Michigan's general mineral wealth intrigued Cleveland men, and especially a young lawyer descended from the Cotton Mather family of New England. From reports on the Jackson and Marquette operations, Samuel L. Mather felt that iron could not successfully be smelted in that killing country. The ore should be brought down to Cleveland to meet the coal brought up from southern Ohio or Kentucky via the Ohio and Erie Canal. The resulting iron would then be a short wagon haul from its market. That idea was to establish a giant three-way commerce in the Midwest.

A handful of men formed the Cleveland Iron Mining Company with Mather as secretary. This company sent a group of men from Cleveland up to the Marquette Iron Range to hack ore out of Cleveland Mountain. The winter came in hard, causing some to retreat—these men had already experienced a couple of Upper Peninsula winters. The Cleveland men also had to win a land claim dispute with the Marquette Company. They burned each other's claim cabins down and ran off each other's guards while getting out the ore.

Nevertheless, Cleveland Iron Company men had piled up a thousand tons of ore by the time the snow was hard enough for Peter White to sledge it eighteen miles to Lake Superior. When the ice went out, they floated six barrels of ore to the Sault, mule-hauled it around the rapids, then floated it to Cleveland. But the going price of $8 a ton hardly paid for the hay the mules had eaten.

The man who was least discouraged was the company secretary, Samuel L. Mather. He kept the Cleveland men digging out a thousand tons a year, groping toward an epic triangular pattern of Kentucky coal–Michigan ore–Cleveland iron furnaces.

The next few years on the Marquette Iron Range were unrelenting hardship. The job of importing everything into the cold country proved staggering. Downbound or upbound, vessels had to be unloaded at Sault Ste. Marie, the goods portaged through town and around the rapids, or the entire vessel dragged out of the water and towed around the rapids on rollers. The need for a canal at the Soo was clear, but the federal government consistently refused help.

In 1852, however, a square-jawed twenty-four-year-old scale salesman for the Fairbanks Company of Vermont, Charles Harvey, was in the region. Recovering from typhoid, Harvey watched the ships being towed through St.

Mary's main street. He wrote to his company, asking if they would want to build the needed canal. A land grant was available as payment; though the lands were valued at less than $2 the acre, he was sure the canal would make them worth a fortune. By 1853, Charles Harvey had imported a thousand men to build a canal that would become the turning point of the Northwest's destiny.

In August 1855, the brig *Columbia* under Captain Judson Wells locked down the Soo carrying 132 bulk tons of Marquette ore bound for the Cuyahoga River in Cleveland, consigned to Hewitt and Tuttle for resale. The next year 7,000 tons came down; Hewitt and Tuttle sold most of it. They had to put on another clerk, a bright sixteen-year-old with a hard-to-spell last name—a John D. something. The boy asked good questions about the business, but Tuttle started him off with some advice: "Don't you ever again accept a job without asking what your wages will be." They settled on $3.50 per week.

In 1857 this John D. was promoted to bookkeeper at $500 a year. Later he asked Hewitt for $800 a year. The firm offered $700. In 1859 John resigned, borrowed $1,000 from his father at 10 percent interest, took a partner, and nailed up a sign:

Clarke & Rockefeller

Grain, Hay, Meat . . . . miscellaneous

That "miscellaneous" later came to wag the dog, in fact the nation. Petroleum—it turned out to mean. However, he had also seen enough of Tuttle's operation to learn something about iron ore and iron shipping, which would become important to the region later.

T HE YOUNG MEN who eventually developed the iron resource tended to be jacks of several trades. A classmate of Rockefeller's, Mark Hanna, who had gone on to Western Reserve College in Hudson, Ohio, had his higher education cut off abruptly in 1858 for passing out racy programs for the student oratory evening; so he went to work in a wholesale grocery business, shipping groceries up to the Lake Superior mines and learning the lakes' shipping economics in the process.

James Pickands came out of the Civil War an unemployed colonel. He knew very little about the iron-mining business so prominent in Cleveland gossip, but he knew miners would use a lot of picks, shovels, axes, harness, lanterns, and rope. So he and his brother Henry sailed

north to the Marquette Range to open a hardware store.

Once there they received help from another young man of legendary energy, Jay C. Morse. Short, stocky, dark, mustached, and in constant motion, Morse had a hand in several phases of the ore business, including suddenly a partnership in the Pickands' hardware store in Marquette. Morse found the customers; the Pickands boys found the goods.

In addition to importing mining hardware, James Pickands soon was shipping pig iron south and bringing coal north. Since he was paying freight rates in both directions, he bought into a vessel. That vessel grew into the Pickands–Mather Fleet.

The Pickands brothers were somewhat tied to the store, but Jay Morse, as agent for Cleveland Mining Company, was moving constantly from Ispeming to Negaunce to Marquette. Therefore, he was in a good position to pick up orders for Pickands Hardware—and to pick up iron news.

By 1870, when mines and a few iron furnaces dotted the Marquette Iron Range for forty miles east of Dead River and twenty miles inland, news came of new finds south of the Marquette. It became the Menominee Range.

T HE UNSUNG HERO of iron mining was the mule—a special short, broad breed brought up to the Lake Superior country every spring by the hundreds. These mules, colored red by iron ore, were very well treated because they served the miners well and were good company. One mule could pull a string of mine cars, stand while the dump was made, then find his way back to the mine face in the dark. Once his cars learned of low roof-framing, he ducked at the right places, stepping daintily.

As mines went deeper the hazards increased; but the longer a man was in the mines, the harder he became to injure. There was a saying that a five-year Finnish mining veteran was so tough that to kill him you had to cut off his head and hide it from him.

Men took pride in the deeper mines. A favorite story told of a man applying for work at the hoist cupola at the top of the shaft, asking for the mine captain: "He just stepped in the cage at the bottom level. Come back this time tomorrow; you'll catch him just as he comes out."

But the state of the art limited the mines' depth. Therefore, Jay C. Morse pushed two trails in from the shore of Superior to open the most exciting range thus far, the

Gogebic, running some twenty miles from what would become Wakefield, Michigan, to just west of Hurley, Wisconsin. Morse was by no means the discoverer; but if Jay Morse was coming, it was a sure sign of action. The response was like a gold rush. Ironwood, Michigan developed as the business capital of the new range; but the town of Hurley was the favorite with 58 saloons, 20 hotels, 2 dry goods stores, and a minister.

Seldom has a range been exploited so quickly. Subsidence set in early, beginning at Norrie. Underground blasting began shaking the bottles off the barroom shelves, and the log barn at the No. 3 shaft house slid into the earth with ten horses in it.

W HILE THE GOGEBIC was at peak production, a flamboyant newcomer entered this range. Mark Hanna's business, Rhodes & Company, was provisioning trappers and prospectors up in the Michigan mining country. Prospectors went broke now and again, and Mark Hanna found himself inheriting some small mine claims in lieu of cash. That gave him a backhaul of ore from his upbound shipments, so he bought into a vessel.

To balance the tonnage of the two trips, he bought coal mines in southern Ohio, shipping the coal uplakes. At one point, when Hanna owned coal but could not sell his ore, he put up a blast furnace and moved into the merchant pig iron business.

In the 1880s, at the close of the great railroad-building era, there was some fear that iron supply had outrun the demand. However, Maj. William Le Baron Jenney showed architects and designers in Chicago that if they abandoned two-foot thick walls and instead put up a strong central steel frame with light walls, they could drive buildings into the clouds. Construction's iron age began.

Additionally, from the Mississippi west, the United States was becoming a tremendous cattle range. John Glidden, a farmer in DeKalb, Illinois, sharpened the ends of three-inch lengths of wire and twisted them onto fencing wire at intervals shorter than the length of a steer. They kept the cattle out of his corn; but they also started a saga of range wars and steel wars. The latter culminated in the formation of the U.S. Steel Corporation.

Issac L. Ellwood, a hardware dealer who recognized the commercial possibilities of barbed wire, purchased a half interest in Glidden's patent and hired a salesman,

Beloved mine mules gave way to steam "donkeys" like the Johnny-Bull, Jackson Pit Mine, Michigan.

John W. "Bet-a-Million" Gates, who would become steel's most flamboyant personage. Gates sold barbed wire from Illinois to Minnesota, then turned southwest. With showmanship and bravura, he sold wire in quantities that built scores of wire mills in Great Lakes country.

In twenty-seven years Gates became one of the nation's wealthiest men and set out to unite all the major wire producers into the huge American Steel and Wire Company. From that vantage point Gates envisioned merging the entire steel industry. He approached J. P. Morgan, America's number one financier. Morgan liked Gates' idea, but not Gates. ("I don't think property is safe in his hands.") When the negotiations were over, Morgan had purchased Gates' companies, forming the Federal Steel

Company. Gates was sitting outside—counting a half billion dollars.

As the nation had hungered for steel rails and barbed wire, it began now to thirst for steel nails. A sweeping demand for bicycles made manufacturers also desperate for steel tubing.

Meanwhile, Jay Morse took another horseback ride west into Minnesota country to investigate reports of a richer ore. He rounded the western point of Lake Superior, cut northeast through Indian villages along the north shore, then inland to have a look at the Vermilion Range that people were discussing.

The Vermilion had begun with a cry of "Bonanza!"— followed by a cry for help. It was eighty miles from water across formidable granite ridges and cedar swamps. The owners were building a railroad to the lake, but the project ate money and had come to near disaster with a payless payday. Jay Morse studied the ore and the development plans. His company brought cash for the back pay and finished the railroad and the dock.

On June 30, 1884, a train of cars rolled out of a pit that would become the famous Soudan Mine. Someone shoved a fir tree into the first car as a flag, beginning a mine-opening custom; and the cars rolled toward Two Harbors, a hundred Chippewas in war paint dancing alongside for the first five miles. Minnesota was in the iron business.

Jay Morse moved southwest to investigate a furor in Duluth. He found that it was caused by the seven Merritt

Amazing concentrations of nearly pure copper are found on the Keweenaw Peninsula of Upper Michigan, where early explorers reported chunks as big as a man's arm lying on the surface. This is the old Cliff Mine.

MICHIGAN STATE ARCHIVES

201

brothers (actually four brothers and three cousins). The Merritts were timber lookers. Their father had repeatedly told them, "When you're looking up at the timber, look down also at the ground." In 1890, while they were camped on a series of stony hills the Indians had named "height of land" or "giant land"—*Mesabi*—the Merritts kicked aside the foot-thick pine needles and uncovered heavy red dirt. It was not hard and chunky like the iron ore they were familiar with, but powdered and fluffy. However, they caused fifty pounds of this powdery hematite to be tested in Duluth, and it assayed 64 percent iron!

The impetuous Merritt brothers sold land they had acquired as fees over the years and put the cash into buying some of the red hills and leasing others. They named the

first mine Mountain Iron, mortgaged themselves to their swaggering mustaches, and called in the railroad builders while they went looking for more capital.

However, these tall woodsmen did not impress investors and were soon financially desperate. They had hold of more ore than anyone had ever owned, but they had no money with which to mine it or repay their loans. They traveled as far east as Pittsburgh to see the greatest steel man, Andrew Carnegie. He replied that ore was the worst part of the steel business.

Meanwhile, the brothers discovered a still greater deposit, Mesabi Mountain. Speculation in Duluth went wild. But the boots of the Merritts continued to trudge across banking and steelmaking thresholds all around the

Open pit iron mining on the Mesabi Range, already down several levels when this picture was taken in 1900, would go down many more when the United States twice became the arsenal of the free world.

This roll operator in the "pulpit" is making a structural iron I-beam. Starting with a billet, he maneuvers it back and forth between shaping rollers, which he screws down tighter after several passes.

Great Lakes while their railroad construction deepened their debt $10,000 per day.

IN 1893 NATIONAL FINANCIAL DISASTER struck and brought onstage the former clerk in Hewitt & Tuttle's office, John D. He had long since put together the Standard Oil Company, headquartered in New York. Recently he had been besieged with reports of the hazardous position of the Merritts and its disastrous effect on the whole economy. Rockefeller remained basically uninterested in the ore and steel business, but trusted friends advised him of the soundness of Mesabi ore. Others felt he should buy in so the railroad could be completed to prevent catastrophic financial damage to the thousands of businessmen involved. Rockefeller said he would watch for a while.

He adamantly resisted the pressure until one of his trusted advisers, Frederick T. Gates wired him of that disastrous payday, with railroad workers demanding their time at gunpoint and creditors threatening to foreclose.

"Must have some money at once [if you want to] save Merritt boys' collateral, which means control of best properties. . . . Complete collapse of Merritt-Wetmore syndicate, and Merritts personally and Duluth, Mesabi, and Northern R.R. now mere question of days."

In a very complex transaction, Rockefeller began to supply emergency funds to the Merritts, and ultimately, the largest known ore deposit in the world belonged to an oil man. Suddenly the steel giants—Carnegie, Frick, Morgan, and Gates—were alarmed. Would Rockefeller build a steel mill to utilize all that iron ore? If he could do it at the price advantage he had, he would be formidable competition.

The Mesabi was quickly outshipping all other ranges combined. The crude oil wars had taught Rockefeller one severe lesson—control your transportation. That meant Rockefeller would become interested in ships, precipitating sweeping changes in the Great Lakes picture.

CHAPTER 17

WAKES, LOCKS, AND TRACKS

*Transportation to link western suppliers and eastern buyers
by a network of ships, bridges, canals, and railroads*

AKING POSSIBLE THE GREAT LAKES' special core commerce of ore, coal, limestone, and wheat is the world's strangest merchant navy, operating almost secretly when one considers its immensity. Its ships are of unique design and enormous size when viewed alongside the seagoing freighters that also now operate on the lakes.

The boats move slowly, fifteen to eighteen miles per hour, yet they are in a race so urgent that crews seldom get leave even in home port. Part of the race is against the ice, which closes navigation: upper lakes' utilities need coal enough from the south to get through the winter; lower lakes' steel mills need ore enough from the north to get through the winter.

The fleet is manned by cousins, brothers in-law, fathers, and sons, largely Swedish, Norwegian, and Scottish extraction. When ice ends the season, the crews lay up the boats at any of a score of ports and go home overland to Minnesota. The captains, almost all, go to Florida.

In 1870 the trade needed a whole navy of three-masted schooners to carry the cargoes and a cavalry of mules to unload them. Although it was largely an age of owner-captained ships, some captains, like Alva Bradley, were beginning to assemble fleets.

On his own deck, a lake freighter captain was a man not readily approached. He did not want to be concerned with crew hiring nor too much trouble with cargo. His concern was the ship and seamanship. He was in an increasing navigational battle against the submerged towlines of loggers, the heavy traffic in channels and harbors, the financial battle of getting unloaded fast at crowded docks, and the competition against steamships when winds were unfavorable.

The captain, even if he had made the change from sail to steam, held aloof from the new breed of mariners boarding his ship—engineers, mechanics, oilers, firemen. Avoiding the engine room and clerk's office, a captain remained on the bridge or in a sea cabin just below, where he could see ahead. Threading the Mackinac Strait and Detroit and St. Clair rivers in heavy weather with visibility at 100 feet often kept him on that bridge thirty hours straight.

The captain lived in a rage against the lack of fog signals in the channels, the shifting bottom of Lake St. Clair, and the white hell of late fall sailing when horizons disappeared. Railings and lines grew frost four inches thick, cables pulled out of the water frozen and would not bend onto the windlass, and snowstorms hid oncoming ships, reminding a captain he was sailing over thousands of sunken wrecks.

At the turn of the century, monthly pay scales were as follows: captains and chief engineers, $105; second engineers, $70; first mates, $75; seconds, $50; cooks, $50; firemen, oilers, wheelsmen, and lookouts, $30; deckhands, $15. If the ship sailed into late November weather, the pay shot up. Today the master of an 830-footer will draw $30,000 to $50,000 per year. He is manager of a $15 million-dollar plant, which may deliver in a thirty-three-round-trip season 1½ million tons of ore and coal, exceeding the entire fleet cargo of 1879.

Although there are now a pair of thousand-footers at

*In the mid-nineteenth century a huge fleet of three-poled schooners and sloops was developed to carry grain
east from the elevators at Chicago; a few were still in service carrying iron ore as late as 1920.*

205

work, these giants are still called "boats." But the increasing size has reduced "The Fleet" (a term including all American and Canadian bulk vessels of every ownership) from thousands of vessels to about 160 at this writing.

However, in the 1870s, when the largest vessels were about 320 feet, floating 500 to 800 tons of cargo, it was not uncommon to see 160 vessels fighting for dock space in Chicago alone. Harbors were a leafless forest of masts. Once docked, the vessel masters had to fight to get unloaded. Men came aboard and shoveled ore up onto a staging, then from the staging to the deck, where a chain of wheelbarrow men took it ashore—a week's work. Mules and horses later replaced barrowmen, unloading 400 tons in three days. Steam donkey and butter tubs cut this to two days, but since the number of cargoes was increasing, the tubs were holding up America.

WATCHING THIS LABORIOUS SCENE, it seemed to Alexander Brown that what was needed was a bridge. He invented a series of movable towers with arms bridging out from the dock over the open hatches of ships. Cables conveyed a bucket from hold to shore. Larger ships could now be unloaded.

Captain Elihu Peck, a quiet, earnest shipbuilder at the mouth of the Cuyahoga, was to make a turning point in history. He designed an ugly bargelike hull, boxy in the bow, which at first offended marine eyes. He raked off all amidships gear, rigging, and housing, and stacked the pilothouse right up over the bow, the crew housing practically on the fantail. The engine and stack were also astern, so there was a sweep of uncluttered deck between with hatches on twenty-four-foot centers to match the chutes at the ore-loading ports. This was the *R. J. Hackett*. When she loaded over a thousand tons of ore at Jackson Mine in record time and came downlakes at twelve miles per hour, she suddenly looked beautiful. The special design of Great Lakes ships had been set.

The only major deviation from Captain Peck's basic design came in 1888, when Captain Alexander McDougall invented and built thirty-nine of his famous whalebacks, with rounded whaleback decks and turret-type housings.

Ensuing bigger ships required expansion of the Soo locks, which meant even larger ships could be built, which in turn required faster unloaders . . . which is the ongoing story of the Great Lakes triangle.

During the decade of the 1870s, steam propulsion moved in so heavily that when the 1880s arrived, it was pushing out sail. However, few realize what lifelong marine scholar, James P. Barry, points out: there were still schooners in the ore service in 1920. One captain, Harry Ellsmere, said he preferred sail to steam as a young man because pay was higher, due to the constant sail handling.

When steel ships first replaced wood, seamen were nervous. Bolts and rivets sprung in bad weather and plates parted. Crews could no longer make emergency repairs at sea. Wrecks and fires were common. In just two decades, 1878 to 1898, 5,999 vessels of all types wrecked in the Great Lakes; one-sixth of these went to the bottom.

In 1890 the *Manola* began to reverse that feeling, riding out some of the worst storms carrying 3,000 tons; so did the *Maritana* two years later, and in 1896 the *Sir Henry Bessemer*, which carried 6,700 tons. At the turn of the century came the *Malietoa*, a giant carrying 7,500 tons.

Just as the new Poe Lock was finished in 1896, Cleveland Cliffs built the *William G. Mather* with a 60-foot beam, followed shortly by the 426-foot-long *Cadillac*, so the lakes already needed larger locks and bigger unloaders. Alex Brown's ore bridges were holding up progress.

The improvement that came in 1898 is still one of the spectacular sights on the lakes, a genial monster called the Hulett unloader. On top of a massive traveling gantry on rails beside the ship is a giant upside-down elbow pointing into the sky. Where the hand should be is a great open claw. In the wrist is the operator, who lowers the claw and himself into the ship's hold, closes on seventeen tons of ore, and dumps it into a waiting railroad car.

In 1904, the enormous *Augustus B. Wolvin* slid off the ways, 540 feet long, with capacity for carrying 10,500 tons on midsummer marks. In July of that year, four Huletts unloaded the *Wolvin* of 7,257 gross tons in four hours. A new pace began on the Great Lakes. When the iron miners could unload ships that fast, it meant they could operate still larger ships and fleets. The stage was set for the return of John D. Rockefeller to the lakes for the modern vessel transport era.

WHEN ROCKEFELLER ACQUIRED the Merritts' Mesabi and could deliver ore to Cleveland three dollars per ton below competitors, he knew the steelmakers were getting nervous. He had learned from the oil business that

In 1888 the little 180-foot steamer S. S. Rosedale (*shown here at Fort William at the Canadian head of the lakes*) *became the first ship to carry cargo direct from Europe deep into the heart of North America.*

if you own the crude and not the transportation, you may be left high and dry. He was determined to have ships. "I was astonished," Rockefeller said later, "that the steelmakers had not seen the necessity of controlling their ore supply."

Possibly the most respected man on the lakes was Samuel Mather of Pickands Mather Company, son of Samuel L. Mather. Rockefeller asked Mather to supervise the construction of his transportation. Mather declined, stating candidly he was not interested in building a ship for a competitor.

"But if I'm going to build any," Rockefeller replied, "shouldn't you as well have the commission as someone else?"

Mather explained that he was honored by the compliment, but the commission for superintending the construction of a vessel was not that interesting financially.

"Of course, Mr. Mather; but I had in mind twenty-four."

Twenty-four!

Sam Mather thought how an order this size would unbalance the lakes, especially since these would be 475 feet long. Such an order would tie up all the yards, raising the cost of ships for all other buyers.

"I had better buy them for you, Mr. Rockefeller." In ten minutes Sam Mather took the then largest single vessel order ever placed on the lakes (it was subsequently reduced to twelve).

The Great Lakes had ten shipyards that could build this class of vessel, and they were at the time largely out of work except for desultory winter repairs. When the hull was designed, Mather sent one set of plans and specifications to eight shipyards and two sets to two yards, writing that he was interested in purchasing "one or two ships if bids are attractive enough at this time."

Each yard wanted the contract for "the one or two vessels." Each, therefore, secured tight-belted bids from subcontractors and submitted to Mather lean bids. After studying them carefully, Mather asked each shipbuilder to come separately to his office in the Western Reserve Building on a particular Wednesday to talk over his bid. On the appointed day, each builder walked out of Mather's office and smiled smugly at his competitors in the waiting room, sure that he alone was the winning bidder. Later they discovered that each had been bidding only against himself.

Rockefeller called his new monsters the Bessemer Fleet, and added some existing vessels to it. Steel producers instantly saw what this great fleet did to the steel business. Controlling the finest Bessemer ore deposit in the nation and the least costly to mine, and being able to transport all of it in the most modern and economical hulls, Rockefeller could undersell anyone. He could select the steel mill customers he would supply and at what price; or he could build his own mill and undersell the industry.

Rockefeller's fleet carried Carnegie's ore on contract. Carnegie's partner, Henry W. Oliver, and his chief operating executive, Frick, warned Carnegie about his dangerously dependent position, but the tough little Scotsman again spurned ore and shipping, "*Ore will prove to be the least profitable and most troublesome aspect of the steel business.*" His associates argued, so to teach them a lesson, Carnegie sent an ultimatum to Rockefeller to drop his carrying rates by half, adding, "Better accept."

In response, Rockefeller headquarters in New York sent out messages to all Bessemer agents and captains, and suddenly from Conneaut to Duluth boats carrying Carnegie ore lost way and dropped anchor, with wisps of smoke rising straight up from motionless stacks. Within days Carnegie mills were starving. The Scotsman gave in and paid the full rate.

In 1901 the two fractious giants, Rockefeller and J. P. Morgan, entered one of the most famous negotiations in history. Judge Elbert H. Gary, Morgan's righthand man,

The first thousand-foot ore boat on the lakes—the Stewart J. Cort, *by curious pleasurecrafters.*

explained to Morgan that it was imperative for U.S. Steel to acquire Rockefeller's Mesabi ore and Bessemer Fleet. But the two tycoons did not get along.

"So how are we to get them?" Morgan asked Gary.

"You're to talk to Mr. Rockefeller."

"I would not even think of it."

"Why not?"

"*I don't like the man!*"

However petulant, Morgan was also a realist. Knowing what was at stake, he sent an intermediary to invite Rockefeller to come to his office at Number One Wall Street. Rockefeller declined.

The lion of American finance had a roar that whitened the faces of his staff. After a few weeks when Judge Gary

owned by Bethlehem Steel—is welcomed upbound in the Detroit River

had gotten the banker quieted down, Morgan agreed to send another invitation. Rockefeller did not come but sent his son, John D., Jr., not yet thirty. Ushered into the great Morgan presence, he was ignored for several minutes while the great J. P. conferred with his partner, Charles Steele. Finally Morgan looked over at young Rockefeller, "Well?" And he loosed the bellow which had rattled two generations of American businessmen, "*What's your price?*"

Young Rockefeller delayed long enough to remain organized. "Mr. Morgan, I think there must be some mistake. I did not come to sell. I understood you wished to buy."

Morgan sat down, and negotiations began which trans-

ferred the Rockefeller Mesabi to U.S. Steel for $80 million in stock, and control of the Bessemer Fleet for $8.5 million (less than the cost of one ore boat today).

Rockefeller was out of the lakes. He had demonstrated, however, the effectiveness of the large-fleet pattern. The lesson was not lost on the trade.

U.S. Steel now put into its Pittsburgh Steamship Company the enormous Bessemer Fleet, the whole being referred to on the waterfront as the Steel Trust Fleet, and to this day a Pittsburgh Steam vessel is a "corporation boat."

Today the fleet, on the American side, embraces eleven-vessel company fleets thrashing the Great Lakes—a lifeline of bulk raw materials for the workshops of Great Lakes America.

D EVELOPING CONCOMITANTLY and in parallel with the bulk fleet were two overland transportation modes. The Great Lakes had a tremendous transportation potential, but to connect the interior to them required a vast network of canals and railroads. Against noisy opposition, New York's shrewd Governor DeWitt Clinton refused to rescind his order that the digging of the Erie Canal begin in the middle, at Rome, New York, and proceed both east and west—toward Albany and Buffalo—simultaneously.

One of his least severe newspaper critics wrote, "Not enough that the governor has bludgeoned through [the legislature] a fantastic multimillion-dollar folly . . . digging a 660-mile canal from Albany through solid rock and swamp to lift boats 571 feet in the air to Lake Erie, he now commences the fool project in the *middle* where it will be of no service to either the Albany or the Lake Erie terminal until totally finished, which may take a hundred years."

The criticism was so valid that the governor had to answer some of his reluctant political supporters: "If we start in the center and work toward both terminals, thousands of citizens and businesses at both ends will soon begin pressuring us to hasten the work. . . . If we begin at either end, we will have only the support of the few people in the immediate vicinity of construction. The people at the opposite terminal will withdraw from the project even the slight support they have reluctantly given. The canal will die. As construction moves in two directions from the center, however, we will enlist increasing support from legislators who can see the canal construction coming closer to their constituents."

Clinton knew that passage of the canal enabling act, after a quarter century of attempts, had been so narrowly won that it had as many political enemies as friends, and few men actually believed massive benefits would result from what was then the largest engineering project in the history of the world.

Clinton knew further that construction in the soft dirt near Rome would be easy. He could show quick results with completed short sections that could be put into service. Later when the contractors would hit the hard limestone hills near Little Falls and the Montezuma swamps, Clinton expected tremendous obstacles and public outcry.

The intended beneficiary of the great canal did not understand its merit. The average 160-acre inland settler west of the Appalachians was cut off in the forest grubbing out a poor existence in a dirt-floor house in western New York, Pennsylvania, or Ohio. The intermittent but enduring postrevolutionary depression worsened his life, turning his locally issued paper currency and scrip to water, so he could not meet land payments. Everything had two prices—hard money or paper.

Only a handful of leaders understood that the one hope for the western settler was low-cost transportation to the East. A barrel of wheat flour in eastern Ohio would bring one wildcat dollar, if you could find a buyer. Set that same barrel down on the New York dock, and it would fetch

$8.50 in good government currency. The trick was getting it there. Overland hauling cost $5 per hundredweight per hundred miles. By water the price could be a dollar a barrel per hundred/hundred.

Nevertheless, selling the required multimillion-dollar canal to early legislators who were wondering how to pay off their own $500 mortgages was nearly impossible. Therefore, even his opponents understood the towering achievement when on October 26, 1825, Governor De-Witt Clinton, who had dedicated years to this end, stepped onto the new oak planks of the canalboat *Seneca Chief* in Buffalo. A ceremonial cannon was fired, the horses surged into their collars on the towpath, and the boat moved east. All along the canal way cannon crews, hearing the shot just west of them, fired, sending the signal eastward that a boat was starting from Buffalo for New York City. The cannon relay progressed east to Albany, then down the Hudson River, the last shot reaching New York City in one hour and twenty minutes. When the *Seneca Chief* reached New York City, Governor Clinton ceremoniously poured two casks of Lake Erie water into the Atlantic Ocean.

Large public improvements generally require many years to enhance the economy. In this case, however, the results were immediate. Western pork, whiskey, wheat, and corn flowed east over this flat, slack-water route to

The Erie Canal was probably the most influential single factor in developing western Great Lakes country.

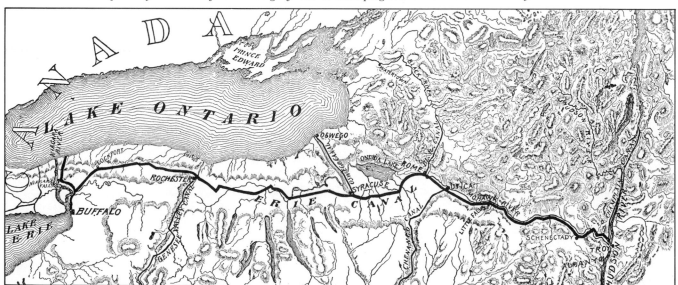

Most public improvements affect the economy slowly, but the Erie Canal brought an immediate and dramatic upsurge; western farmers could now reach eastern markets, and manufacturers could afford to ship their products west.

meet New York money. On the backhaul over the same route came manufactured goods, some to supply frontier towns along the canal, some to be transferred to schooners at Buffalo and shipped on to the infant ports of Erie, Cleveland, Sandusky, and Detroit.

Instantly land values along the canal leaped. Warehouses appeared at each port, and beside the warehouse a tavern and a port town—Lockport, Gasport, Middleport, Fairport, Brockport, Port Byron, Spencerport, Weedsport. When the canal work began Rochester had 330 people. By 1840, because of the canal, it had become a wheat-shipping and milling port with 40,000 people. By 1846 canals would be handling half as much business as all other modes of transportation in the States combined.

Meanwhile, a road-building boom quickly set in as inland towns fought to get their goods to the banks of the canal, and a boat-building boom set in as operators rushed to get boats into this profitable traffic.

New York City, which had opposed the canal fearing it would siphon away trade, suddenly became recipient of goods from the vast hinterland reached by the canal and its western extension, Lakes Erie and Huron. The canal became the heart of the economy of New York and beyond, stepping up the development of Ohio, Indiana, Illinois, Michigan, and Wisconsin, giving them a market and good eastern currency.

IN THE WEST the depression beginning in 1818 had devastated the inland frontier. Corn was priced at twenty-five cents a bushel—if you could find a buyer. A horse in Cincinnati would sell for five dollars, and a used wagon for only twenty.

For fifteen years Ohio leaders had been trying to connect Lake Erie and the Ohio River with a canal, getting little acceptance from the legislature. A lawyer-legislator from Cleveland with a heavy sense of duty, Alfred Kelley, a bachelor governor from Cincinnati, Ethan Allen Brown, and a gracious southerner, Micajah Williams, were the heart of a very small group who renewed the attempt to persuade the legislature that a canal from Lake Erie to the Ohio River would lift Ohioans out of bankruptcy by letting them get produce to New York via the Erie Canal or to New Orleans via the Ohio River. The estimated bill was a staggering $6 million at a time when state taxes brought only $133,000 a year into the treasury.

The tale of the struggle to get such a bold plan approved is a book in itself, but the proponents, assisted greatly by DeWitt Clinton, finally succeeded in passing very tentative enabling legislation. To get it, planners had ultimately had to propose two parallel canals so that every legislator's constituents would be close to one of them. And to pick up legislative support these canals had to zigzag around even though that routed them through expensive digging and aqueduct building. The excruciating difficulty of canal construction under such conditions makes these works heroic. The Ohio canal system right-of-way, finally totalling 960 miles, was divided into hundreds of construction sections, some difficult ones being as short as a half mile. When bids were let, veteran contractors from the Erie Canal moved onto the Ohio and Erie, bringing their crews with them.

These men worked under two plans. Some earned $3 a month plus board and two gills of whiskey per day, plus a dollar a day extra for those who would work knee-deep in water. Others, marked in the contractor's book with a *D*, were indentured until their ocean fare was paid—"working off the dead horse," they called it.

On each section an advance crew moved down the right-of-way, slashing the trees off waist high. The diggers moved in with picks and shovels, filling the wheelbarrows of a crew who ran in a constant circle from the digging face to the berm through the long fourteen-hour workdays. The canal was forty feet wide and four feet deep, and required a fall of two inches per mile in order to produce a gentle current.

Digging in virgin and marshy ground produced canal fever, a miasmic malarial disease. Alternate chills and fever melted the backbones of strong men and killed them by the thousands. Crosses grew by the sides of the canal at a rate of six per mile, opening berths for fresh Irish immigrants.

Wages improved as canals competed for workmen at the peak of the era. Blacksmiths earned $11 per month, carpenters, $21; men with teams, $40. When cholera swept through the canal crews in 1832, regular labor wages jumped to $18 per month. Construction of the locks employed the highest-paid craftsmen, the masons. Weak cement made from burnt limestone depended for its holding power upon stones in the lock walls being a closely matched fit. Iron hardware for the massive lock gates had to be custom made.

Alfred Kelley, himself almost constantly ill as he inspected completed sections before approving contractors' payments, walked the right-of-way, poking an iron rod deep into the towpath to make sure that the contractor had not used timber and brush instead of the required dirt and stone fill.

The canal needed to be a flat track of water. This meant the canal crews had to blast through rocky hills, build causeways over streams that crossed the right-of-way, and dig through marshes in which the banks repeatedly caved in. If the right-of-way crossed a lake, a floating towpath of logs had to be built across the water for the tow horses.

Canal construction was a war. Many a contractor would ride to the state-approved bank to draw his pay for the section, only to find that the contract inspector had put a stop order on his pay for some deficiency. Correcting the deficiency at a great loss, the contractor might then ride to the bank, collect his money and too often keep right on riding, leaving his Irish crew stranded without pay.

Some contractors would take the good government dollars, convert them to many times that amount in wildcat money, and use this to pay off crews who did not understand the currency.

This gave rise to the formation of a kind of union called the White Boys. After payless paydays several contractors found the dikes broken between their canal beds and the parallel river. When a contractor built a reputation for short-paying or mistreating his men, a group of Irish White Boys from an adjoining section would pay him a visit in the night, and many a contractor became an integral part of the towpath. One contractor was found emblocked in cement lock walls with only his hand protruding. Another was dragged behind an ox over the stone rip-rapping.

The eastern canal—the Ohio and Erie—was completed in 1827. The resultant economic uplift was even swifter than that along the Erie Canal. The fifth boat to come north to Lake Erie from the heartland, the *Western Star*, hauled twenty-five-cent corn, which upon arrival at Cleveland brought a dollar a bushel. All other commodities leaped in proportion. Although the final cost of the Ohio canal system exceeded $9 million, Ohio entered a boom that sparked a canal-building flurry across Indiana and Illinois, one of the most important being the Michigan Canal linking Lake Michigan (at Chicago) to the whole Mississippi.

The canalboats, blunt-bowed and straight-sided, became works of art, ranging from crude vessels to ornate passenger packets pulled, not by mules, but by a span of four horses, with relief horses quartered on deck. Canalboats carried farm produce east and brought back settlers, who tended to locate along the canal. This part of Great Lakes country became a canal-based society.

CANALS SET MUCH of the pattern and motivation and method for the railroads; and like the canals, the railroads' first mission was connecting natural waterways.

James Kilbourne, a prominent Ohio engineer and landholder, had tried to get the Ohio and Erie Canal route drawn to bisect the state—and his own extensive lands—terminating at Sandusky on Lake Erie. Failing this, he pushed for a railroad. All towns disappointed at not being on a canal or a feeder route now became avid railroad supporters.

In 1836, Ohio built its first railroad, the Erie & Kalamazoo, from Toledo to Adrian, Michigan, using horse-drawn cars at first. The second was the Mad River & Lake Erie, spanning sixteen miles between Sandusky and Bellevue. The next was the famous Little Miami, fourteen miles of track out of Cincinnati, designed to connect ultimately to the Mad River & Lake Erie at Springfield.

The rail boom moved fast. The state of Ohio alone chartered nineteen railroads between 1830 and 1833, and seventy-seven by 1840. Other Great Lakes states joined the boom with the same vigor.

Railroad-building crescendoed in the 1840s and 1850s. Competing lines, built too close together, started ruinous price wars, which hurt the stockholding public. Additionally, many roads were built so locally that they served neither the stockholders nor the public as dramatically as the canals. To overcome this localism, a group of promoters asked longer-sighted Alfred Kelley to build a railroad from Cleveland to Columbus to Cincinnati—the CC & C. This was a beginning of more effective railroad service.

A geneology of the origins, adoptions, and mergers of railroads is a thick catalog, but the Michigan Central Railroad was typical of many beginnings. Farmers loaned their tools and often their labor and money to help grade the tracks across their land. They cheered and waved the little firebrands that puffed past their farms—until the first cow met the iron head on. It happened everywhere, but in Michigan the state fathers who sponsored the Michigan Central did not want to antagonize the people. Therefore, the road paid triple value on cattle casualties. It did not take farmers long to discover the best-paying market for their beef. They encouraged their older stock to graze their way between the rails. By 1846 the state was happy to sell its 150 miles of railroad, which had cost more than $3.5 million, to a group of Massachusetts men for half that.

The new owners of the Michigan Central had bought an unwanted but thriving beef business as well. They cut their payments for cattle to a realistic appraisal. When the farmers objected, the railroad fenced the tracks. From that moment, the Michigan Central had to fight its way to the Lake Michigan shore over greased rails, broken switches, and chain shot in the night.

Chicago and Milwaukee had obtained charters to build railroads to the Mississippi and were competing to be the first completed, but after ten years the roads were not yet built. Railroad talk still dominated both towns, but money was lacking. One of the foremost citizens of Milwaukee was a persistent mover of men named Byron Kilbourne, who had preached and petitioned for a railroad to connect Milwaukee with the Mississippi. In 1848, when he became mayor, his voice became louder: "Boston enterprise compelled New York to build her Erie Railroad. Will not Chicago enterprise incite Milwaukee to build the Mississippi Railroad? Unless she is content to see the business of the finest region of the country wrested from her grasp, we must do it without delay . . . or Chicago *will*."

The Milwaukee & Mississippi Railroad sold its stock for harness, oats, and timber. Farmers joined the work crews to grade the way, but the men of Wisconsin could not beat William Butler Odgen of Chicago.

Will Ogden had jogged on horseback through ten

counties between the bustling port of Chicago and the tiny town of Galena on the Mississippi. His mission was to sell stock to the farmers, businessmen, and bankers of Illinois, who feared a railroad from Milwaukee might ruin their waterway trade on the Mississippi. More than a salesman, Ogden was the newly elected president of the Galena & Chicago Union Railroad.

During the summer and fall of 1846 and into the spring of the following year, Ogden commanded the attention of farmers and bankers alike. He could speak both languages authoritatively. The Galena & Chicago Union began building out of Chicago under Odgen's firm hand. He sent his chief engineer, John Van Nortwick, to try to buy an engine from the successful Michigan Central, which had now reached New Buffalo on Lake Michigan. Paymaster Mahan of the powerful Michigan Central seemed to enjoy the spectacle of a chief engineer without a locomotive: "Yes, we've got some light engines. How many do you want?"

Van Nortwick gagged. "We're just a farm-to-market road. One will be enough."

A small engine, the *Pioneer*, was loaded onto a lake steamer at New Buffalo and bounced across the lake to become the first locomotive in the Windy City. It was a great day for Illinois, Chicago, and Will Ogden when the *Pioneer* and one freight car were jacked onto the tracks in October 1848. Ogden briskly shook hands with members of the cheering crowd, sold another $20,000 worth of stock while he was at it, and signaled the engineer to roll. At the end of the *Pioneer's* first run to Oak Ridge, a farmer rested his horses at the crossing and stared at the dignitaries crowding the cab. One yelled, "Where you headed?"

"Newberry and Dole," the farmer answered.

"How would you like your wheat to be the first into Chicago by rail?"

Thus, the first train to Chicago brought a payload of wheat from the west.

In 1851, President Millard Fillmore and four members of his cabinet boarded the passenger cars of the New York & Erie Railroad with governors and ex-governors, mayors, senators, bankers, merchants, and industrial leaders of the entire eastern seaboard. As they chugged and celebrated their way across the meadows and mountains between New York and the Erie shores, Secretary of State Daniel Webster, his magnificent voice mellowed by good New England rum, sat in a rocking chair lashed to a flatcar in order to "better view and enjoy the fine country."

On May 15 the excursionists passed through an arch over the tracks inscribed "Finis," and the U.S.S. *Michigan*, floating placidly in the waters of Lake Erie, saluted with twenty-one guns. It was the beginning of an all-rail route along the Great Lakes.

The immigrants of the early 1850s depended heavily upon the lake waters to carry them west. Young Daniel Drew, the future robber baron of the Erie Railroad, was busy making his fortune with a steamship, *People's Line*, connecting two small railroads and a Lake Champlain sidewheeler for a north-south through line from New York to Montreal. Now his boats met passengers at Buffalo to carry them to the rails of Detroit and Chicago.

Most railroads connecting with the Great Lakes shores soon owned their own ships. The practical solution was deep-hulled boats to ferry entire trains between ports.

The grand era of rail building in the 1850s accelerated the waves of immigrants moving west. During the summer of 1853, the westbound settlers spilled over tiny rail depots and steamship offices of Chicago and Milwaukee, setting up temporary sleeping quarters on floors and sidewalks, amid chests, carpetbags, and cages of chickens. In one day nine thousand immigrants changed trains in Chicago.

Actually, the railroads generated much of the immigration; Great Lakes railroads become town builders. The Illinois Central, for example, was given the usual huge grant of alternate sections of land along its right-of-way from Chicago (and Galena) to Cairo on the Mississippi. This right-of-way was then the longest railroad in the world, counting its branches (built from 1852 to 1856); it passed through some five hundred miles of prairie.

What would it haul? The Illinois Central had to plant some shippers along this route to create its own customers. As the crews laid the rails south from Chicago, they built a siding every ten miles, threw up a square station in the empty prairie, and tacked up a printed plat for the future town, complete with street names. A man felt at home in nearly any early town in the West. In these treeless communities (designed by eastern financiers), Mulberry Street was always on the east boundary, Ash on the west; Hickory, Walnut, Chestnut, Oak, and Locust ran between. North-south streets had numbers. There sat the town— untreed, unpeopled, and unsold. Now the company be-

By advertising low prices for land, the Illinois Central lured farmers to come west, plant grain, and eventually become customers for the new railroad.

gan saturation advertising in eastern newspapers, magazines, and pamphlets. Walter Havighurst, for his book *The Heartland*, studied this campaign closely:

ILLINOIS CENTRAL RAILROAD CO.
OFFERS FOR SALE
SUPERIOR FARM LANDS
AT $8 TO $12 PER ACRE
NOT SURPASSED BY ANY IN THE WORLD

Pamphlets distributed widely in the East outlined in detail how a man could take on 160 acres and step by step build his fortune. Each year the pamphlets became more flamboyant. An 1856 pamphlet featured a testimonial by a minister who related a profit of $2,305 in his first year on 400 acres, earned practically on the side because his main job was preaching eighty miles away from his farm. The pamphlet also related the story of a full-time farmer who had begun with a $200 purchase and worked it up to one year's sales of $44,000.

Railroad pamphlets reached all the way to Europe and were printed in several languages. The pamphlets might not pass a truth-in-advertising test today, but thousands of hardworking men and women bought the idea, moved to a siding in the prairie, built a sod hut, and turned the matted soil to build farmsteads. Later they moved into a wooden house somewhere between Mulberry and Ash, and planted some trees to make the town as valid as the thousand bushels of wheat they shipped north to Chicago. They raised churches and grain elevators and children.

While the locomotive engineers knew a Mulberry Street existed in every town from Cairo to Chicago, the residents considered their particular town very special. And the railroad whistle screaming through the night was important to them—assurance that the lifeline to Chicago wheat docks was still there, connecting to a line of Great Lakes wheat schooners sailing for Buffalo, Rochester, Oswego, and Montreal.

There would follow years of complex railroad extensions, mergers, oil rebates, iron ore, and coal roads, robber baronism, deceit, corruption, and mismanagement; but when it was all said and done, thousands of new towns would parallel the railbeds, housing new thousands between Mulberry and Ash.

215

Part Five
THE GREAT LAKES TODAY

As Great Lakes communities rush on toward the twenty-first century, they are realizing more and more that they are a highly water-dependent region. To fill the practical needs of industry, agriculture, transportation, and municipal services for a steadily growing population, yet keep water sources clean enough for wholesome recreation, fish and wildlife, and millions of kitchen faucets—that is the challenge that has mobilized the best creative efforts of this watery heart of the continent.

Ferry to Toronto's seven Lake Ontario islands.

CHAPTER 18

THE ST. LAWRENCE SEAWAY

The dream and the reality of constructing a deep-keel outlet to the sea, from the earliest explorers to modern engineers

"THE FINAL ALL-CLEAR SIGNAL goes from me to Dr. Holden at 0800. He'll push the button. I want an all-clear call from each of your sections by 0730. Nobody within a quarter mile of the stakes."

"That's more than the project code reads."

"This river won't read."

Sun-leathered field engineer Del E. W. Smythe had no fear of explosives, high-iron construction, or top brass. But water was something else. And this would be more water than most engineers ever tried to control. He was ten hours away from the instant when Dr. Otto Holden would fire thirty tons of explosives, blowing the cofferdam upstream and releasing a twenty-foot tidal wave through the dry lake bed to slam up against the new power dam twenty-five miles downstream at Cornwall-Massena. It would create the new Lake St. Lawrence, completing what was then man's most audacious hydraulic project: deep-keel navigation to the sea—the St. Lawrence Seaway.

Smythe went through the entire list of contractors, subcontractors, consultants, architects, and utilities involved. Were these people all out from in front of the 310,000 cubic feet per second of water that would be unleashed?

"Sir, Dr. Emerson's archaeologists. He asks for just five more hours."

"No. Out!"

"They found another layer, sir. Indian pottery. Said it would be lost forever under the water."

"*Pot*-tery?"

"Yes, sir. With designs like some found in Siberia. Said it would help prove the link between Asia and—"

Smythe put up the flat of his hand. "Three hours—period! Pottery or not!"

Thousands of people were arriving to watch the great wave break loose. Smythe asked for more police. Crossing his mind occasionally was the thought that some children might make a pilgrimage back into the cut for a last look at the site of their previous homes and towns. Many children had difficulty understanding.

But there was worse on Smythe's mind. All calculations had been tested on the model. When the dam was blown, the waters of the Great Lakes *should* fill the new Lake St. Lawrence—only—and then stop. But veteran engineers had come to a mystical respect for the rampaging St. Lawrence, which had defeated man's best efforts at control and deep-water navigation. The river had startled them frequently during construction, spinning their cofferdams like revolving doors, rolling twenty-ton boulders out of dikes, melting mountains of sand.

They calculated that the blowout would only gently lower Lake Ontario an inch and raise Montreal harbor two and one-half inches, but they wondered some nights: would it wash out the planned shoreline, find soft spots to make channels of its own, skirt the dam, overflow it, drain Ontario too fast and ground vessels upstream (or downstream), blast vessels loose from moorings at Montreal, and deluge shore villages? Tomorrow they would know.

Four years before, the world really had not known what the St. Lawrence Seaway was. The citizens of Iroquois, Canada, and several other towns learned about the seaway when they heard repeatedly that their towns would

The St. Lambert Lock at Montreal is only one link in the long chain of locks and canals by which the St. Lawrence Seaway opened Great Lakes navigation to the sea.

White men began early to circumvent the St. Lawrence rapids. The first canal—seven feet wide, forty feet long, and two and one-half feet deep—was built at Coteau du Lac in 1781.

have to be moved; then plans were cancelled. They had shrugged it off. This one would also fail. *"C'est ça."*

Navigationally ice-locked during the white months and rapids-blocked during the green, the potentially greatest inland waterway in the world frustrated commerce for four hundred years. Boulder-churning rapids denied deep-keel traffic to the sea.

The proposed twenty-seven-foot-deep seaway would cut shipping costs $22.50 per ton from midcontinent to Europe by reducing the number of tolls. Far beyond that, the big savings would be the nonstop trip to the sea, cutting out the unloading and reloading into smaller vessels to bypass rapids, then reloading into ocean vessels.

To make this St. Lawrence outlet to the sea navigable would require deep slack-water canals around the rapids, with stairstep locks from Thousand Islands down to Montreal. Add to that a few more locks and canals and deepened ports uplakes, and one could float thirty thousand tons from Duluth to the ocean.

While the Americans working on the project generally felt that they were pioneering, all Canadians are historians; therefore, Del Smythe knew that he was actually working on an old, old dream.

Capt. Jacques Cartier, steering for China in the spring of 1534, was blocked by Lachine rapids. In 1689 a great engineering-minded cleric, Dollier de Casson, began digging a foot-and-a-half canal around Lachine rapids. But the Iroquois's mystic reverence for the mighty St. Lawrence tolerated no man-made interference with it. Casson's men had two thousand yards hacked out of stone when one August night a war party fell on the workers and butchered them.

Canal work stopped until 1700, when the Sulpician priests hired contractor Gideon de Cathlogne to complete the project. But money ran out, and Lachine rapids remained boss for seventy-five more years.

The American Revolution spurred the first sustained drive to make the St. Lawrence into a seaway. Canadian

As early as 1829 the 325 foot plunge of Niagara was skirted by the Welland Canal, which joined Lakes Erie and Ontario; it required forty locks.

colonists had made the pivotal decision to reject the American colonies' invitation to send delegates to Philadelphia, so the rebelling American colonies, fearing an ally of the king next door, attacked across the St. Lawrence and seized Montreal, the capital of the North American fur trade.

The following spring the English successfully counterattacked, but the event convinced Quebec Governor-in-Chief Frederick Haldimand that in the event of war with the colonies, Canada would not be able to move her troops or supply them unless she could navigate around the St. Lawrence rapids on her own side. Haldimand's first move detailed the Royal Engineers to build a linkage of small canals to bypass the most hazardous Lachine rapids in the twelve miles joining Lake St. Francis to Lake St. Louis, wide places in the St. Lawrence. He began with Coteau rapids, which bar the upstream progress from Montreal into Lake St. Francis and where he had seen eighty-four men killed. This Coteau Canal was nine hundred feet long, seven feet wide, and two and a half feet deep, and had

three locks, each under forty feet long, built of stone masonry by Cornish miners. While dangerous, Cedar rapids was nevertheless navigable by flat-bottomed boats.

The third white-water stairway was Split Rock rapids. Here a series of three small canals was built, the Faucille, the Trou du Moulin, and the Split Rock. These were completed in 1783 and were almost immediately inadequate. A revolution in trade goods was floating into Montreal. Fur from the north and upper lakes was augmented by wheat, flour, and timber. The canoe was waning on the upper St. Lawrence in favor of bateaux, scows, and Durham boats. The Durham was a shallow-draft scow, but it had a keel and centerboard that needed water underneath.

It required the War of 1812 to spark real action against the rapids. Long convoys of barges heading west with military goods for British forts on the upper St. Lawrence and Great Lakes clogged the meager canal system and were delayed by the rapids. The British naval shipbuilding base at Kingston suffered serious supply delay, threatening British Canadian defense.

221

Absence of deep canals carried still another threat—an economic one. United States leaders were already considering an incredible canal that would reach from Lake Erie at Buffalo east to Albany and the Hudson River, on which cargoes could float south to the port of New York and thence to Europe—while Canadian cargoes would be blocked by rapids, cutting Montreal and Quebec out of the trade.

Lower Canada built a new Lachine Canal, completed in 1825. For the first time some of the river's worst rapids could be bypassed by vessels big enough to carry a good payload. In that same year, however, New York State completed its spectacular Erie Canal from Lake Erie to the Hudson and New York City. The St. Lawrence cities did not cheer.

In 1833, when the Erie Canal was floating many times the St. Lawrence tonnage in wheat and flour, the competitive Upper Canada legislature voted $280,000 to improve four distinct series of rapids between Montreal and Prescott, and for vessels not of three-foot draft, but of nine feet. This was the first really coordinated master plan hinting at an eventual St. Lawrence Seaway.

But always there was formidable Niagara blocking navigation. As early as 1824 a daring promoter, William Hamilton Merritt, began a fantastic project upstream at the unconquerable navigation barrier. He was a good engineer, a fair businessman, and a superb salesman. Merritt formed the Welland Canal Company, based on an audacious plan: a nine-mile canal of forty locks, each 100 feet long and 8 feet deep, to skirt Niagara and drop vessels 326 feet from Lake Erie to the Welland River below the falls.

Although the Canadas loaned $250,000 and stock was sold, Merritt's costs drastically outran his plan by 1825. Niagara dolomite devoured drill bits, men, and money. Finally, Upper Canada rescued the company, and on November 30, 1829, two brigantines of seven-and-a-half-foot draft walked up the forty locks—St. Lawrence navigation had reached from the Atlantic to Lake Erie.

By 1850 the tiny Canadian population had completed the unbelievable—a full set of canals and locks enabling at least nine-foot navigation all the way from Montreal up the St. Lawrence, around Niagara, across Lake Erie, up the Detroit River, across Lake St. Clair, and on into Lake Huron.

The last remaining obstacle was the rapids at Sault Ste. Marie. As we saw earlier, this also required a salesman,

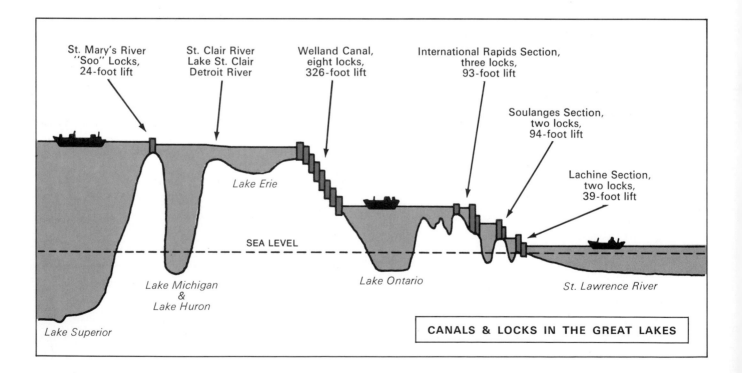

CANALS & LOCKS IN THE GREAT LAKES

American William Fairbanks, who built the Soo canal (St. Mary's Falls Canal) at Sault Ste. Marie. In 1856 nine-foot navigation was open from the Atlantic to Duluth.

All hands had barely finished congratulating themselves on nine-foot navigation when new vessels required fourteen feet. When Canada's provinces confederated in 1867, the new federal government deepened the St. Lawrence canals to fourteen feet. This program required a quarter century, and the canals were used for sixty years.

When the ice thawed in 1901, men talked vehemently of bringing deep-draft ocean ships into mid-America. The big iron-ore, coal, and limestone shippers were not interested in seeing foreign-flag vessels bring in Europe's competing steel products. But they wanted outbound wheat to reach the ocean without reloading twice. A cry rose for twenty feet of water on the St. Lawrence route.

The governments of Canada and the United States appointed an International Waterway Commission to study the feasibility of this project. A favorable report was made quickly, but came up hard against a formidable coalition. Coal and oil companies feared competition from the hydroelectric potential of the St. Lawrence. East Coast and Gulf Coast ports wailed that a deep-water channel to the heart of the continent would leave them ghost ports. Eastern business feared that the seaway would shift the financial-industrial center of gravity westward. Railroaders felt that seaway competition would bankrupt them. Together these forces defeated the joint U.S.–Canadian seaway proposals under Coolidge, and again under Hoover and Roosevelt.

In the 1950s, the U.S. antiseaway lobby was as virulent as ever, but it was suddenly outflanked by Canada. The House of Commons decided to go it alone. The result was immediate. Suddenly there was concern that Canada would have all the electric power to itself. Also there was a postwar shortage of direct shipping ore from the upper lakes and new interest in Labrador ore. Faced with a possible all-Canadian seaway, America switched to favor U.S.–Canada seaway plans.

FOR THE HYDROELECTRIC PROJECT, 18,000 U.S. acres between Waddington and Massena, and 20,000 Canadian acres between Iroquois and Cornwall had to be flooded. These included eighteen cemeteries, ten villages, and the homes of eight thousand people.

Giant house-moving machines transported each house so gently that china was left in cupboards. A glass of water was placed on the kitchen table so the owner could judge if his house had had a smooth move. As the house moved inland, its favorite shrubs followed in the next transport. Moreover, if its owners wanted it to again stand next door to its century-old neighbor, that too was arranged.

As bulldozers moved onto the largest North American engineering project ever undertaken by men, a feat of precision scheduling challenged the presumptuous engineers. On the International rapids section alone, for example, the new hydroelectric dams would inundate Canada's existing fourteen-foot canal system. The engineers must time operations so that the old fourteen-foot traffic could continue during the construction years. When the new locks were ready, traffic must be able to switch over immediately upon inundation of the old canals.

Tampering with a powerful river lined with millions of homes and scores of cities requires a precise sequence of operations. A three-inch error in water level could turn a town into an island by mistake or, conversely, ground a hundred ships. Twelve huge scale models were made to predict downstream pressures and effects.

Fleets of graders, scrapers, bulldozers, earthmovers and draglines clanked in, manned by an army of operators.

Hydroelectrically, the mission on the stretch called the International rapids section was to change the gradual eighty-five-foot drop of International rapids into a steep drop at a single point. The St. Lawrence River would be dammed to turn it into a twenty-five-mile lake; then it would be plunged eighty-five feet over turbine blades at Cornwall at a rate of 110 million gallons per minute.

To build this seaway section with its canals, locks, dams, two electric generating stations, dikes, and embankments, 100 million cubic yards of dirt would have to be moved, a third of them from under water. Four million yards of concrete would be poured; 20,000 tons of structural iron would be raised; and 20,000 tons of gates and hoists would be built. To give an idea of its size—Long Sault Dam called for thirty vertical-lift sluice gates, as wide and high as houses, to be raised and lowered by traveling crane hoists of 275-ton capacity. Twenty miles of dikes would be constructed.

Cofferdams were built at both ends of the twenty-five-mile valley to hold the river out so that contractors could work mostly in the dry. Tunnels were driven under the old fourteen-foot canal so earthmovers could get to the new work site without interrupting vessel traffic.

Regulating the outflow from Lake Ontario would be the new Iroquois Dam, which had two 350-ton traveling cranes to open and close its 32 gates. For ships to bypass these two dams required new locks, the Eisenhower and the Snell.

Looking at the feverish activity in the great cut, the curious public could see no outline of what was being built. It looked instead like a confused battleground as different contractors and subcontractors simultaneously built the power dams, powerhouses, control dams, levees, canals, locks, and dikes. But men like Del Smythe in the engineering building viewed the confusion and saw blueprints turning to concrete.

In the middle of operations, on the American side of the cut alone, the working fleet in 1957 was composed of 135 shovels and draglines, 400 crawler tractors, 730 trucks, 8 dredges and 14,000 men—watched by a half million fascinated visitors.

One day in July Dr. Norman Emerson of the University of Toronto hurried out to Sheek Island in the middle of the battleground. Word had reached him that a bulldozer had turned up an unusual arrowhead. At the site, his crew unearthed knives, drills, pipes, and adzes that were thirty-five-hundred years old, matching designs retrieved in Siberia. The power commission sent Dr. Emerson their best bulldozer operator, who surprised the scientists by shaving precise three-inch layers for them.

SIMULTANEOUSLY, CONSTRUCTION was under way on four other sections of the seaway. It was important that all five sections be finished together so that vessels could travel the whole length. They were all progressing rather evenly; however, east of Mercier Bridge on the Lachine section, land expropriation had not been completed. When the Canadian Seaway Authority came to buy Caughnawaga, a small Indian village in the path of the canal, they encountered the superintendent general of Indian affairs, whose special appraiser put a value on these lands higher than that generally paid but in line with Canadian policy toward Indians. The Indians, under the guidance of the superintendent, took the government price to court. As bulldozers worked their way toward the village, the courtroom haggling stretched out, and more and more construction diesels shut down. The matter was settled satisfactorily for all the Indians except six braves,

The Welland Canal as it looks today—a vital segment in the complex St. Lawrence Seaway, which moves a total of more than 50 million tons of shipping annually.

Drivers approaching the Eisenhower Lock may get a start as they see a ship crossing the road, for auto highway builders have had to adapt to the flat-water "highways" needed by ships.

who refused to leave their dwellings even at that price.

The Seaway Authority had enough problems without the encouragement of published cartoons showing their eviction of six attractive Indians; nor could they well afford the precedent of paying six holdouts more than they had paid others. But by this time fleets of expensive machinery had ground to a halt at the borders of Caughnawaga village, their operators standing by.

The Seaway Authority assessed its alternatives, went to the Exchequer Court, and paid a bonus settlement to the six who had stood their ground. As the six Indians loaded their carts, the construction diesels cranked up.

On the eighteen-mile Beauharnois section, the canal bed and power station sites, called the Soulanges, had to be excavated almost totally through rock so hard that drill bits had to be resharpened after ten feet of drilling. Power shovel operators wore out shovel teeth on each shift. Bulldozer blades lasted only one day. Crawler tractor pads had to be replaced every three weeks, and drillers did well to average four feet per hour.

Back on the International section, tourists driving by in June 1958 thought the natives were seeing a mirage. On the dry shore of a dry lake, the future power pool of Lake St. Lawrence, was moored a line of new rowboats. They

awaited an instant lake. Workmen were mounting a new sign—"Long Sault Marina."

The climactic moment for flooding the dry lake—and completing the St. Lawrence Seaway—was at hand. Del Smythe was receiving reports throughout the night. All ships above the works and below as far as Montreal were anchored or berthed. All contractor gear was out of the cut. All inspectors were out except for two trucks racing south with sweeping spotlights, checking.

"What about those pottery diggers?"

"Who?"

"Those arrowhead guys."

"They'll be out in fifteen minutes."

At 0800, Dr. Otto Holden, Ontario Hydro's chief engineer, pressed a button. Two clouds of dirt rose from the cofferdam, throwing boulders a thousand feet into the sky. The St. Lawrence broke through two gaps and boiled northeast in a wall of water, which an hour later smashed against the Cornwall power dam.

Three days later, on July 3, 1958, about a hundred ships that had accumulated above and below the new lake began churning through the locks. The Great Lakes were officially classified by Congress as the fourth U.S. coastline. The seven seas were now eight.

CHAPTER 19

MEGALOPOLIS ON THE SHORE

Lakeside cluster-cities—expanded versions of the company town radiating from the hubs of the booming industries

ERHAPS IT IS TRUE of all other cities, but the Great Lakes cities especially seemed to rise on the most hostile ground, but at the most strategic points. Infant Chicago's garlic-scented swamp was judged so uninhabitable that bankers refused a development loan, but it was situated at the junction of the prairie and the water, and on the river that linked the Mississippi and Great Lakes watersheds. Cleveland's miasmic flats repelled settlers for decades, but it connected the lakes to the Ohio River by canal. Akron had neither soil nor minerals but existed on the portage over the divide between the Great Lakes and the Ohio River, near the confluence of two great canals. Driving snows buried Buffalo, but the town connected Lake Erie and the West to the Erie Canal and the East. Quebec clung to an untillable rock, but she guarded the Great Lakes' front gate.

These places also have another pronounced characteristic. Except for the very old cities and the very new, a Great Lakes metropolis tends to be an exciting extension of the company town. Still too close to their own calluses to appreciate their own Americana, Great Lakes chambers of commerce are more likely to direct photographers to their new high-rise skylines, marinas, and museums. Yet the visitor often favors the old work-related monuments, which stand out to him more distinctly and speak to him more convincingly of the people. Who could miss the gray, realistic flavor of the steel megalopolis: Lorain–Cleveland–Youngstown–Pittsburgh? Hugh McCreery, visiting from England for only a day, commented, "I see. This is your Manchester."

These steel cities grew up under a layer of reassuring smoke and a respect for the twenty-four-hour clock. For the common benefit the metallurgical furnaces were not allowed to cool. Gray was the best color in house paint for complementing soot, and clear skies were a sign of bad times. Today—when steel is highly valued and the smoke is gone—the old gray habit remains.

Detroit has spawned a ring of automotive satellite cities along the Great Lakes: Flint, Cleveland, and Windsor for total auto production; Akron for tires; Dayton for batteries; Toledo for windshields and spark plugs; Cleveland, Youngstown, Pittsburgh, and Chicago for automotive sheet steel.

Nearly as distinct are the other product-founded cities. Milwaukee, drawing grain from a vast prairie hinterland, became a miller and brewer, as had Buffalo before it. The shoreline of Lower Peninsula Michigan was timber country, and many coastal cities were lumber camps. Even with the timber gone, Grand Rapids, the furniture city, is a place where one's neighbor can display a polished walnut box of woodworking tools that belonged to his grandfather or great-grandfather.

Rochester, known for cameras and office machines, has a pronounced personality, a city of earnest German craftsmen, frowning on the frivolous. A Detroit housewife will use her dishwasher as a storage cupboard and explain that she is "avoiding double handling"—a verse from the automaker's bible.

On the northwest and southeast shores of Lake Superior are the iron-mining towns of the Vermilion,

In raising vast cluster-cities like Chicago, modern man has wrought greater change on the shores of the Great Lakes than any force since the glaciers.

Though the land south of Lake Michigan was legally Indian country in 1803, the Greenville Treaty gave the U.S. six square miles "at the mouth of the Chikago," where Fort Dearborn was built.

Mesabi, Menominee, and Gogebic iron ranges. Duluth is the largest, oldest, and most diversified, yet it could represent them all. Despite the fifty miles of docks, an airline passenger looking down on Duluth would be hard put to know that he was looking at America's second biggest shipping port by tonnage. (When the lake is high, a single 830-foot ship will carry 28,000 tons of ore.) The city has been a port since the fur buccaneers, brothers-in-law Radisson and Groseilliers, came into this V at the head of the lakes, set up a fur-trading post, and shipped prodigious sixty-canoe loads to Montreal in 1660. They moved on, but Daniel Greysolon, Sieur Dulhut, operated here long enough to leave his name (or rather, a corruption of it). Fur shipping continued longer here than elsewhere. With the extinction of the beaver, Duluth shifted to lumber and iron ore.

Today, the city is spectacular, not in the conventional sense, but as a classic, chronic boomtown, with the com-

pany-town ramparts still visible just a few feet under the snow. Modern supper clubs and motels have blossomed recently to give it a gold-coast patina of lighted plastic, but it is new gold. The old gold may be found behind subdued red clapboard with white steamboat woodwork. No advertising lights invite the public into the Gitchie Gamie Club, where successions of fur, timber, and iron entrepreneurs quietly play for one-dollar chips and multimillion-dollar contracts. The town buildings walk down to the water from a six-hundred-foot frozen escarpment, a previous shoreline of Lake Superior, now a thirty-mile skyline highway.

Originally the developers were from the East, and even today iron-range ownership is in Cleveland, Chicago, or Pittsburgh. Therefore, many of the place names on streets and buildings are eastern names: Jay Cooke, Charlemagne Tower, Chisholm, Hanna, Rockefeller, Mather, Humphrey, Bradley—the same names visible on the stern plates of ore boats and the doors of offices in Cleveland and Pittsburgh.

The spectacle in Duluth is the row of iron-ore docks, cavernous bins diminishing even huge vessels. When a captain ties up below, a battery of chutes (twenty-four to thirty-six of them) from the bins fold down into the open vessel hatches. When the plug is pulled, the dock gravity-feeds the ship.

Duluth has smaller, colder counterparts on Lakes Superior and Michigan—Two Harbors, Silver Bay, Port Arthur, Eagle Harbor, Copper Harbor, Marquette, Escanaba—cold weather, cold-water ports where your nostrils stick together in early November.

Lake cities run into each other in long, thin megalopolises. The western shore of Lake Michigan is one two-hundred-mile, L-shaped city: Sheboygan–Milwaukee–Racine–Kenosha–Waukegan–Winnetka–Wilmette–Evanston–Chicago–Hammond–Gary–South Bend, linked by wall-to-wall suburbs.

Sheboygan is a shipping port and furniture city with a German-Austrian flavor. As you travel south to Milwaukee along one of the most beautiful lakefronts, frozen or thawed, you cross a suburban boundary every five miles.

Milwaukee (*Mahauawaukee-Siepe*, "gathering of great councils") was always a headquarters. Its brewery and flour-milling leadership is obvious; less apparent is its leadership in engines—diesel, gasoline, outboard, motorcycle, and tractor. The city is a distinguished national machine shop for crafting fine parts and building machine tools, manned by a German heritage that characterizes the whole city, from beer gardens to symphony.

The megalopolis continues south through a score of towns, such as Racine, with America's largest Danish population, and Kenosha, home of American Motors and the town with the judgment to retain its lake frontage as a park for the people. Waukegan was the French stockade, Little Fort; later, despite an Indian treaty prohibiting it, a white settlement was built up around a general store, established there by a Chicago merchant.

South from Waukegan the traffic quickens and thickens as it approaches the massive city of Chicago, the world's largest inland port and rail, air, and truck terminal. Except for hog butchering, the colossus remains what Carl Sandburg called it: ". . . toolmaker, stacker of wheat, player with railroads and the nation's freight handler." The city's "world's largest" list assails visitors—58 col-

leges, 800 technical schools, world's largest convention and trade-show center, 2,700 churches, 486 parks, and so on.

Chicago's best face is its lakefront; its worst is probably the Calumet River. Its best character is surging energy, its worst a genial corruption inherited from Capone days—and nights.

AMAZING CHICAGO ROSE from an untenable swamp. Louis Jolliet, Father Jacques Marquette, and five French canoeists stopped in 1673 to camp on their bold shortcut back from discovering the Mississippi. They realized that a short canal from Lake Michigan to the Illinois River would complete a continuous water route from the Gulf of St. Lawrence to the Gulf of Mexico, a dream realized today in the Chicago Ship Canal.

A small, temporary Indian community grew up here around Father Pinet's mission. The British took over the swamp in 1763 and lost it to the United States by treaty in 1783; nevertheless they remained in charge until 1794. The following year the Indians ceded to the United States six square miles of marsh at the Chicago River's mouth.

In 1803 a party from Detroit took possession of Chicago, primarily to establish U.S. treaty claims, and built Fort Dearborn at a narrow bend in the river. The community that grew on the opposite bank was frightened off by a Potawatomi massacre in the War of 1812. The fort was rebuilt in 1816, and some survivors returned to the swamp. When the settlers applied for a loan to develop their town, the bank investigators from Shawneetown traveled to the Chicago swamp and declared it uninhabitable. The bank's lack of enthusiasm for the "mudhole of the prairie" was shared by most observers: "Its river is too shallow for boats, its streets too deep for wagons."

No real growth occurred until the canal-building craze reached west, making Chicago the terminus for the Michigan-Illinois Canal. Thousands of easterners migrating through to cheap western land stopped there to outfit.

In 1841 grain coming into Chicago for shipment east via lake vessels made it a boomtown. After the grain came drovers with hogs and cattle, and packing houses and tanneries grew. Railroad operations centered here along with shipping and made this a gateway city. By 1855 the Chicago boomtown was an eighteen-mile strip of grog shops and mud ruts two feet deep. Some people still felt that you could not build a city in a swamp.

Chicagoans never accepted that. In 1855 they began a heroic work, raising the city above water. Some areas were elevated twelve feet. Engineers dredged the Chicago River to get the fill dirt needed to raise the streets. Travelers on the roads were thus able to gaze into the second-floor windows of some homes. Before he began building sleeping cars, George M. Pullman became famous for assembling five thousand jackscrews and twelve hundred men in the basement of the Tremont House Hotel to raise it eight feet "without disturbing the guests or cracking a window."

In the quarter century after 1850, Chicago's population soared to a half million, outstripping its distant rivals —St. Louis, Cincinnati, and Detroit—for the role of capital of the West. The Civil War doubled grain exports, and in 1864 the mile-square stockyards were fenced in.

On October 8, 1871, the nation's most famous cow back-legged a lantern into the straw and burned down 17,455 buildings, unroofing a third of the population. John Green-leaf Whittier wrote, "The city of the west is dead." The story of the fire needs a book of its own, but the spirit of Chicago needs only the retort of Joseph Medill in his *Chicago Tribune*, "*Think what it would have cost us to demolish all those old buildings!*"

That spirit is still Chicago; it is still tearing down and rebuilding.

THE HUGE LAKE MICHIGAN megalopolis continues east through giant industrial suburbs—East Chicago; Hammond, Indiana; Gary—a short stretch of small towns to the east and you are into South Bend, Indiana.

La Salle, with thirty-two men, set out from this Indian village for the Mississippi River to explore the Southwest for France. White settlers arrived here in 1820, when Pierre Navarre set up a trading post for the American Fur Company. The most famous South Bend settlers may have been the brothers, Henry and Clement Studebaker, who arrived in 1852 to begin building farm wagons. The wagons were followed by prairie schooners, which rolled west to settle the Great Plains. Those wagons often carried the key to the Plains, a sod-breaking plow built by another famous townsman, James Oliver. The Studebaker brothers later moved into autos, and Oliver began making general farm implements and tractors. The Bendix Corporation here is a town in itself, employees' homes and the plants of four divisions forming a large complex.

As much a part of American lore as Oliver, Studebaker, and Bendix are the Fighting Irish— Notre Dame's great football dynasty.

Flint–Pontiac–Dearborn–Detroit–Windsor–Toledo is an automotive megalopolis of a hundred towns that radiate out from Cadillac Square in Detroit. Coming in over these same spokes are steel, rubber, textiles, machine tools, batteries, spark plugs, tires, chassis, glass, and salesmen. Going out is a life-giving stream of dollars for an automotive economy.

Today, under a dramatic downtown renewal that, along with a massive summer riot, leveled acres of hamburger houses, slums, burlesques, and bars, Detroit is resplendently modern. Despite the many overlays of development, the circular pattern of streets borrowed from L'Enfant's design for the nation's capital is still visible, even though population began doubling every ten years with the coming of "the machine."

The region has a nearly visible pulse, geared to the assembly-line motion of about eighteen feet per minute. And if one's job is to paint these cars or test them, finance them, insure them, or sell them—the pace is still eighteen feet per minute.

If one is butcher, baker, or candlestick maker to the men and women who build autos, one lives by the same pulse. Stores and theaters open and close to that beat. The same rhythm pulses out to many distant cities because Detroit, the world's biggest customer, reaches out for the fifteen thousand parts that go into a car. They arrive precision-scheduled to synchronize with the eighteen-foot-per-minute pace. They must not arrive late, to halt the beat, or early to clog the line. As an example of scope, Ford alone deals with some six thousand suppliers. The industry is the main support and largest single consumer of rubber, steel, flat glass, lead, and nickel.

The business style of the Motor City has changed. Originally, in the 1910s and 1920s, industry pioneers held court at the old Pontchartrain Hotel in downtown Detroit, fighting it out over parts, orders, and dealer franchises there where the old fur trading freebooters once haggled. They would lug heavy pieces of machinery into the hotel bar and proceed, with sparks flying, to demonstrate their innovation and to argue prices. They were tough mechanics who could drive a hard bargain—men like Charles Brady King, who awakened slumbering De-

In its reflection of the ultramodern in design, McGregor Center at Wayne State University is like
Detroit itself, where according to wags even antique collectors want the very latest antiques.

troit by chugging down its streets in his four-cylinder, twenty-mile-per-hour gasoline car in 1894. Henry Ford followed him in a beautifully ugly four-banger three months later. By 1899 Ransom E. Olds had gathered the capital to launch the first real plant for commercial auto manufacture.

Three years later Ford and Packard were organized. In 1908 General Motors was incorporated by W. C. Durant; and Ford introduced the Model T.

The megalopolis's new business personality would exclude its buccaneering founders. Detroit is a citadel of caution and conservatism; woodwork is dark and suits are dark. Conversation is precise and carefully weighed; flash ideas are not the method. A mistake here has a terrifying multiplier. Words here start trains, converge earth-moving machinery on new plant sites, move populations to other cities, or build new cities where there were none. Plan, survey, and test are the way of life.

Detroit's cardiac rate is high. Funerals are often held during the lunch hour, so as not to interfere with business. Stores order their inventories and house builders plan new starts according to the success of the new-model introductions. Detroit area citizens pay high rents and high taxes, but they draw high wages, too.

L ORAIN–CLEVELAND–CANTON–YOUNGSTOWN–PITTS-BURGH is a historic steel megalopolis. Why is it not located closer either to the West Virginia metallurgical coal or to the Lake Superior iron ore?

Men tried smelting in the Upper Peninsula of Michigan, but the ore froze; the timber was not as good as coal, and the pig iron had to be shipped east for sale. At the time, there was no canal at Sault Ste. Marie, so the iron was triple-handled around the rapids and reached downlakes markets priced like table silver.

There were many efforts to move the iron industry closer to the ore or the coal, but since nature stored them far apart, these efforts were unsuccessful. A small iron industry was already established in the valleys of the Cuyahoga, Mahoning, Monongahela, and Allegheny rivers long before Michigan and Superior ores were discovered and when there was still plenty of coal in the Mahoning Valley. The solution was to leave the iron works in the middle and to build long hulls to float the ore downlakes from Superior and lay rails to haul coal north from West Virginia.

Cleveland, being at the juncture of the lakes, the Ohio Canal, and the railroad, became the leader. Making steel became a vast coordination of mines, ships, trains, furnaces, and mills over a sprawling chunk of mid-America. Rather than being scattered around chaotically, the headquarters of all these operations were located in one building—or two or three—in one city. That way you could walk across the corridor to see if there would be enough hulls to float enough of your ore downlakes before the

Cleveland's central square (brightly lit area, center) was laid out by the city's Connecticut-born founders.

channels froze—to match the coal you had rolling up from West Virginia for the winter.

On one end of the megalopolis Cleveland became the nerve center; on the other end, Pittsburgh. And between high levels in the two was a love-hate web of daily business cooperation and competition—among Carnegies, Mathers, Hannas, Joneses, and Laughlins.

On less lofty levels what one experienced between the two poles was a solid steel town. Reflecting the furnaces, a rose patina glowed on the undersides of low clouds in the good years. In worn saloons under those clouds men with hexagonal steins and stained undershirts once cursed the powdery nature of the new ore coming down from the Mesabi: "Blew the top off Number Six at Carnegie. Killed six men and burned down ten houses."

Today, in Tudor-style lounges their grandsons in thirty-dollar shirts sip scotch and express similar concerns: "Two German ships unloaded coil at the Ninth Street dock. I mean *acres* of coil."

"Maybe just for stockpile?"

"Don't you believe it, baby. That's going right to Ford."

The American descendants of Europe are now competing with their homelands. These are men from the Republic Steel Company, Jones & Laughlin, U.S. Steel, Bethlehem, National, Youngstown Sheet & Tube. In this direct showdown the mills along the rivers are undergoing sweeping modernization.

The steel region has expanded to Chicago, Gary, Calumet, Erie, Buffalo, Detroit, and Windsor. In these Great Lakes Vulcan valleys have grown up steel-using and steel-support industries, diversifying the economy.

Looking out the window of the commission house where he worked at the mouth of the Cuyahoga, young John D. Rockefeller noticed an iridescent rainbow glistening on the river's surface. He pointed it out to his partner, Maurice Clark.

"Petroleum."

They discussed it and the rumor that it came out of the ground in Pennsylvania at 50¢ a barrel crude and sold for 80¢ a *gallon* refined. Clark said he had been approached by one of the many young men rushing into the refining business upstream on the Cuyahoga, wanting $250 financial backing for a tiny refinery operation. Clark explained he had discouraged the invitation, feeling that they did not have $250 to risk.

From the thirty-five-foot parapet of Cleveland's first reservoir, Sunday strollers could view their fledgling city and the Lake Erie waterfront.

"Perhaps we ought to listen to him again, Maurice. A business that can waste like that has profit." John D.'s Standard Oil Company and Cleveland became the embattled heart of a worldwide oil industry fraught with profits and financial wars.

At the junction of Lakes Erie and Ontario is another megalopolis—Toronto–Hamilton–Buffalo–Niagara–Erie–Rochester. Mrs. Frances Trollope, distinguished British authoress and critic at large, looked over America in the 1820s and gave the country a bad review. Buffalo, she wrote, looked to have been "run up in a hurry."

It was. Being the western terminal of New York's Erie Canal and the eastern terminal for Lake Erie, the city was a sudden-growth gateway, earning its living transferring cargoes for shipment between canal and lake. Wharves, warehouses, and grain elevators rose. Wanting the same role when railroads came in, Buffalo fought the standardization of track gauge, hoping that all freight would have to continue to be rehandled from wide gauge to narrow gauge at Buffalo.

The city became a great milling and cereal center, where the Quaker packed his oats. Today, it still has 27 giant grain elevators, and its 15 freight terminals handle 25,000 trains per year. The skyscape is now miles of high-voltage towers and cables distributing millions of Niagara River kilowatts. The cable network hastens the centuries as one glances down at restored old Fort Erie, the star-shaped battlement of the War of 1812, and at the monuments and markers of the mighty Iroquois who ruled here.

IN ADDITION to these quickly identifiable megalopolis formations, in a broader sense the entire length of both shores of Lake Michigan and the southern shores of Lakes Huron, Erie, and Ontario have become solidly urban. One would have to work at it to get out of sight of a utility pole or a light in this area where less than two hundred years ago Jesuit Father Monet, having eaten his sandals, starved to death near the future site of Chicago, because no one was there.

CHAPTER 20

FRESH WINDS IN CANADA

The stirring northern giant that shows new confidence and a lively nationalism in spite of divisive French-English sentiments

EVERYONE WHO LIVES THERE and everyone who visits speaks possessively. Each is the discoverer. Although a man may appear to listen patiently as others explain Canada, he knows in his heart that *he* is the one who really knows the *real* Canada.

The "New Canada" is announced every decade or so— and validly. Ever since Cartier named it New France, this dynamic nation has been reborn periodically as it discovered new parts of itself and new regions. It has many more to go. At this writing, though, the newest new Canada is the rediscovery of the *old*.

In the 1960s Canada began preparing to receive the world at the Expo '67 World's Fair. Old Montreal was scheduled for some refurbishing, with layers of patched asphalt in the streets to be replaced. Bulldozers scraping off three inches of old tar uncovered a base layer of cobblestones. The new asphalt was already ordered when an official said, "Hold on a minute." Reconsidering, they refurbished the cobblestones.

In a similar manner they abandoned other face-lifting plans and instead stripped old stone buildings of several layers of nondescript modernization—fly-specked neon tubing, anodized aluminum fascia, lighted plastic, chipped porcelain in cola red, camera yellow, and other promotional rainbows. They scraped off layers of Chicago, Detroit, Paris, and London. Underneath, they found Canada, and they liked it. When they rebuilt Montreal's downtown into what many call the most dramatic architecture in North America, they did not make it a Chicago, Paris, or London. They made it Montreal.

The same attitude pervades the other pivotal cities, which cluster around the Great Lakes: Toronto and Montreal, the seats of economic power; Ottawa, the seat of government, and Quebec, the seat of tradition and of the powerful French minority.

As Canadians scraped off layers of Yankee and European influence, they rediscovered Canada in art, music, theater, business, literature, and sports. The new nationalism was not to abjure the outside world; on the contrary, Canadians were preparing their house to receive the world, which caused them to ask, "What *is* truly Canadian?" The answers were exciting. The memorable World's Fair architectural exhibit, "Habitat," an apartment complex of seemingly randomly piled housing units, was hailed worldwide as revolutionarily new. Yet the first successful formal settlement in Canada was a cluster of dwellings called *The Habitation*, built to Samuel de Champlain's plan.

When Canada went Canadian, the results were artistically original. The sixteen miles of subway in Montreal, for example, are called the world's largest art gallery. A different architect was commissioned to design each underground station. In a competition of talent, Le Metro's walls became a breathtaking spectacle of bold art in mosaic tile and stained glass. Toronto's totally unique city hall draws artists from all over the world to photograph its two high-rise crescents cupping between them a low rotunda debating forum. These visitors also travel to Ottawa to view the spectacular new national art gallery. The distinctive and compelling carvings by Eskimos—

The changing of the guard in front of Parliament Hill, Ottawa, typifies the old-world charm that survives side by side with growth and industrialization in today's Canada.

Montreal's silhouette, a landmark for four centuries of St. Lawrence seamen, leaves little doubt why Cartier named this Indian village site "Mount Royal."

which had been largely taken for granted at souvenir stands—were recognized by global travelers as artistic expressions of unique beauty.

A highly creative documentary film and television industry developed in Toronto, and live stage performances are so much a part of new Canada's life that, in addition to regular theater, some restaurants even stage performances during lunch.

Formal art aside, Canada is also highly artistic on a daily-living basis. This is most quickly reflected in the cities' high fashion, which is striking and extreme. Montreal is Canada's design center, and the motifs grow out of the big, cold country of balsam and hemlock, snow and fur. Designs are bold in cut and color.

The Canadian, once too busy for the spectator role, has become aggressively sports-minded. The tickets for hockey games at Maple Leaf Gardens have been sold out since 1946. Season-ticket holders pass on their seats in their wills. Canadian athletes more often choose to stay with home teams rather than join those in the United States.

WHILE CANADA shows the outside world a new nationalism, new regionalisms churn within its borders. Constantly analyzing his national character in painful candor, the Canadian daily encounters some form of the question: *Le Canada peut-il résoudre son problème des deux langues?* ("Can Canada solve its language problem?")

If one is among strangers in Canadian Great Lakes country, one may have to utter a statement twice or print

Ripping asphalt from her cobblestoned streets and garish veneers from her fine old facades, Montreal is rebuilding a city of the past even as she builds a cosmopolitan city of the future.

it twice. And often it will be important which language one puts first, and how well one pronounces it.

The bilingualism of course is only a sympton of the deep, cleaving historic dichotomy. While French-speaking citizens of Ontario Province number only 6 percent of the population, one may well be dealing with a visitor from Quebec Province, where 81 percent speak French. Across Canada in general, 27 percent speak French, 60 percent English, and 13 percent other languages.

The bilingualism of Great Lakes Canada makes life difficult, expensive, and tense. But it is a fact of new Canada that affects selling a product, printing a book, running a political campaign, or governing the nation. A bilingual nation is the problem; bilingual citizens are so far the best solution. The government has launched a $150

million program to make everyone bilingual. Federal officials must speak both languages. Government signs, food labels, and official documents must be in both languages, doubling many expenses.

Although both languages were official in 1867 when Canada became independent, English ascended in usage in all provinces except Quebec. Hence, a new law was pushed through Parliament in 1969 reminding all that both languages are official.

French Canadians, however, feel that while they *must* learn both languages to get along, English Canadians really do not need to learn French and will not. The French make their point in many ways each day. One may see a STOP sign crossed out and the word ARRÊT scrawled over it. Nor do the French Canadians settle for anglicized

The much-used plaza in front of Toronto's award-winning city hall provides a setting for concerts in summer and ice-skating on the reflecting pool in winter.

French as do Parisians. Paris accepts *le hot dog*; Quebec City insists on *le chien chaud*.

French resentment of English-language dominance in official matters has fed the separatist movement, which aims to create a free sovereign nation of Quebec. The separatists' case may be pragmatically weak, but it is emotionally powerful. When Genevieve Bujold, the international film star, stood in a spotlight and quietly intoned, "I am Quebeçoise, and it is Quebec I carry within me," the crowd of nine thousand people rose to its feet ready to follow any orders. (She had the good judgment not to give any.)

"La Révolution Tranquille" the movement is called, and many trace its birth to the death in 1959 of the provincial premier, Maurice Duplessis, who ruled Quebec like a duchy for sixteen years, keeping it a tourist attraction of underdeveloped handcrafts and quaintness, and a source of low-cost labor for multinational companies.

The Quiet Revolution was started by men asking embarrassing questions. Pierre Trudeau founded the magazine *Cité Libre* to challenge Duplessis's repression. Jean-Paul Desbiens, a Catholic, wrote editorials questioning the church under a pen name, Frère Untel (Brother Anonymous).

The new Quebec premier, Jean Lesage, who succeeded Duplessis, pushed education for the French. He made a high school education, previously a privilege for the few, available to all French-speaking Canadians. Quebec then widened university admissions to accept more French youths. With broadened French education came French-speaking radio and television, and therefore greater political awareness on the part of rural-Quebec French, who added force to the vocal urban French.

Michel Tremblay wrote plays in *joual*, a dialect of the Quebec workmen comparable to cockney English. These plays, outstanding enough to be exported to English-

Situated like Montreal's Expo on a series of man-made islands, Toronto's Ontario Place offers residents and tourists nearly one hundred acres of varied entertainment.

speaking Canada, spread the Quiet Revolution. The modern communications giant is the comedian; comics Marc Faureau and Yvon Deschamps, taking ironic jabs at Canadian federalism, spread the Quiet Revolution and Quebec nationalism with devastating quotability: "It isn't that we really want to separate; we just want to be treated nicely—like foreigners."

With the support of the church, playwrights, comedians, and educators, the Quiet Revolution gained momentum. Naturally the revolution belonged to the youth—who liberalized church and school. That liberalism inevitably absorbed worldwide liberalism, which brought to conservative Quebec—the pill. This is cited here only because of its profound affect upon Quebec. Freed from the confining destiny of nine children per decade, the young women of Quebec suddenly had time to aspire to higher education, better jobs, careers, furniture, clothes, and better public officials.

Quebec, with enormous new help from its women, joined the twentieth century and North America. Its people moved quickly into better careers and professions. They arrived, however, not as shy newcomers, but as returning descendants of the discoverers of New France, newly aware of their proprietary heritage from Cartier, Champlain, La Salle, Frontenac, and a hundred other French founders. The ways to reassert that heritage were through emphasis of the French language and support of the political party, Quebeçois.

Although separatism has been simmering for two centuries, it boiled over in 1970. Many French-speaking Quebec citizens had long felt that they were paid less than English-speaking Canadians in a province economically controlled by English. Specifically protesting that condition, the separatist terror organization Front de Libération (FLO) kidnapped the British trade commissioner and murdered Pierre Laporte, the Liberal Party's labor min-

239

ister. The Ottawa government imposed martial law on Montreal.

Leader of the separatist Parti Quebeçois at this writing is René Levesque, a brilliant journalist who left the Liberal Party because of its strong support of Ottawa federalism. However, his and the Parti Quebeçois' method is not radical action but shrewd practicality. At party conventions Levesque insists upon independence by parliamentary action, not by revolution.

Robert Bourassa, recent Liberal Party candidate for reelection as Quebec premier, has been battling separatism as destructive. Despite the fact that in just over three years his programs had made new industry blossom and reduced unemployment from 15 percent to less than 6 percent, Premier Bourassa made no progress against separatist sentiment until his attack focused on currency. "Separatism would force Quebec to create a new currency, which would lose value in relation to the Canadian dollar." It was an idea that many had not considered.

Although the 1973 elections did not elect enough Quebeçois candidates even to begin to secede, the party's vigorous presence did advance French-Canadian influence. Beyond progress in education and culture, Quebec, under the momentum of its reborn self-esteem and self-reliance, has moved aggressively to improve its own economy at a faster rate than Canada's in general. Additionally, by becoming the leader of the poorer provinces, Quebec has gained a very powerful voice at Ottawa.

While Levesque will not give up his bold fight for separation and says there will be another chance as good as the 1973 election, he told his own tearful party, "I don't know when, and I don't know how."

To some the prospect of keeping Canada together is frightening. However, Prime Minister Trudeau said, "These confrontations actually prevent dissolution as provinces league together against Ottawa in various combinations to achieve various legislation."

Canada seems to be a nation of 22 million resident prime ministers and an equal number of absentee godfathers who know what is best for it. That makes it in a sense the most exciting country in the world—yet one of the hardest to govern and to hold together.

ANOTHER IMPORTANT INFLUENCE may well arrive in time to offset divisive sentiment, namely, the wave of new Canadian economic nationalism. As worldwide resource wars threaten over fish, metallurgical ores, petroleum, timber, energy, and chemicals, Canadians realize that second only to the vast Russian land mass, they have it all. They realize that they can soon be supplier to the world in many basic resources. They will choose to export many resources only as finished products, rather than as raw materials.

Canada's present ascending economy rises on hydroelectric power; the aluminum and pulp and paper industries that need tremendous kilowattage; iron ore, automotive, asbestos, banking, communications, computers, construction, fur, plastics, oil, gas, textiles, and the lesser metallurgies of copper, gold, lead, nickel, uranium, and zinc.

Nearly as electric as the question of a dominant Canadian language is the question of whether to shut off U.S. investment in these resources. "Buy Back Canada from the U.S." is the slogan under which Canada's economic nationalists have forced federal politicans to be alert against American investors. American companies already own 98 percent of the Canadian auto business and 67 percent of the mining, a condition that troubles many Canadians.

Opening Parliament in January 1973, Prime Minister Trudeau promised "strong measures to ensure further control by Canadians over our economy, measures respecting the transfer of technology abroad, measures to increase Canadian participation in control of resource projects, and measures dealing with new direct foreign investment and sale of land to foreigners."

The old relationship is hard to change, however. The same edition of the *New York Times* that carried Trudeau's speech also carried half-page advertisements inviting U.S. investment in Ontario and Quebec.

This argument, though, reveals the appealing new confidence of Canadians. Formerly aware chiefly that the United States was their best customer, today they suddenly realize and make known that *they*, with only one-tenth the population, are the United States' best customer.

Despite Canada's divisive problems and its constant and public identity search, a new giant certainly is stirring north of the Great Lakes. This news is passed along confidentially in lowered tones by those who *really* know the *real* Canada—whenever they can find a listener who has not yet heard it.

*Small foreign packet boat enters the St. Lawrence Seaway
downbound at the Thousand Islands.*

Binding together the disparate cities, states, provinces, and the forest, farm, and mining hinterlands in a complex commerce is an unusual merchant navy calling at a hundred Great Lakes ports. The historic core is the unique fleet of some two hundred enormous United States and Canadian bulkers carrying iron ore, limestone, fluorspar and taconite for the steel complex, transshipping West Virginia steam coal to the upper lakes, and floating the grain east. Sailing alongside are the smaller seagoing general cargo ships of nearly every flag. These can now penetrate 2,300 miles into the heart of America and Canada over the seaway, officially designated as the fourth United States coast.

Thus deep inland cities like Duluth, Milwaukee, Grand Rapids, Detroit, Sarnia, Windsor, and Cleveland are seaports, trading with one another and with Europe.

The Duluth railroad yards at the head of Superior connect the Great Plains to the Great Lakes.

The Great Lakes automotive manufacturing belt now spans Ohio, Indiana, Illinois, Michigan, Wisconsin, and the Ontario peninsula.

This is the world's largest open-pit iron ore operation, the Hull Rust Mine at Hibbing, Minnesota.

Steel mills like this Republic Plant at Cleveland are concentrated on Lakes Michigan and Erie.

GRANT HEILMAN

JOSEPH FIRE

THOMAS D. LOWES

The Coast Guard cutter Eastwind *(foreground) works to free an ore boat from Lake Erie ice, a frequent spring scene.*

TOM ALGIRE

Giant freighters churn upbound and downbound through the Soo locks.

JOSEPH FIRE

Chicago's great seaport is actually a complex of ports ranging from the famous Navy pier to specialized unloading berths like this one.

"Mighty Mac," the five-mile bridge crossing the Straits of Mackinac and joining Michigan's Upper and Lower peninsulas, was a hundred-year bridge-building dream, completed in 1957.

JACK ZEHRT   ROBERT PERRON

Chicago's O'Hare Field is the Great Lakes
gateway to everywhere. View from control tower.

The Moses–Saunders Power Dam is the heart
of the seaway electric power generator.

247

KEN DEQUAINE

THOMAS D. LOWES

The sugar maple is a significant part of the economy. Above, part of a 6,000-tree stand.

Old-style marketing at the orchard is a popular pastime in Ontario.

TOM ALGIRE

The Great Lakes pulpwood industry flourished at one time because of easy water transport, but the lakes eventually became overcrowded.

GRANT HEILMAN

A rich corn belt runs across the Ohio, Indiana, and Illinois central plains, encouraged by hot summer days.

World-famous Wisconsin dairying produces half the nation's cheese and 15 percent of the milk supply.

KEN DEQUAINE

*The internationally distinguished
Cleveland Art Museum is enhanced
by its beautiful flower gardens.*

*The Milwaukee River winds through Milwaukee, noted for grain milling,
brewing, machine tools, and basketball.*

*The Chicago River snakes through concrete and steel in downtown Chicago,
gateway to the Great Lakes.*

*Buffalo, strategically located at the junction of the Erie Canal
and Lakes Erie and Ontario, developed early as a transportation center.*

*Detroit, once a fortress, remains today
as the world's motor capital.*

*Toronto, Canada's boomtown, appears
to rise out of Ontario's waters.*

*Parliament Hill in Ottawa, Canada's capital city,
has captured a bit of Old World flavor.*

*The old carriage seems more in character than the parking signs
in this view of Old Montreal.*

An ice-boating regatta on Lake Monona, Wisconsin,
comes to a close at sunset.

"I'd rather be sailing" is a popular
slogan on Great Lakes weekends.

Fishing is the favorite outdoor sport,
on the lakes or along rivers and streams.

*All kinds of winter sports, especially ice skating, flourish
in Great Lakes country, where the season is long and cold.*

*Lakes and beaches abound, but there is a special joy in finding
the "old swimming hole," like this at Gooseberry Falls, Minnesota.*

CHAPTER 21

GREAT LAKES PLAYGROUND

A smorgasbord of recreational activities—sport fishing, cruising, camping, hiking, swimming, skiing on water or snow

WHEN THEY ARE FREE from their work, the people of the region take off for the water. Beyond the ninety-five thousand square miles of the Great Lakes, tens of thousands of small lakes lace the states and Canada. Michigan, for example, has over eleven thousand small lakes; Wisconsin has eight thousand; and it is estimated that Ontario has thirty-five thousand just north of Superior, and a quarter of a million lakes in the entire province.

Fishing is the most popular water attraction. The cane-pole-and-bobber crowd drowning worms off a downtown Great Lakes breakwater have special techniques for bringing in carp and recipes that make them haute cuisine. Specialist sportsmen looking for certain kinds of bass, trout, pickerel, and pike like to go north of the Great Lakes, where millions of acres of unnamed waters have seldom been broken by a spinner. Others make a lifetime search of the Great Lakes proper for a trout as big as a basset hound and a pike longer than a caster's arm.

Michigan, touched by four of the five Great Lakes and fed by thirty-six thousand miles of streams, could well represent all Great Lakes fishing. Not only are its waters highly accessible to the great population in the heartland, but its extensive breeding and stocking program—with which the Michigan Fisheries Division has especially courted the angler—is dramatically offsetting past disasters from predators and commercial overfishing.

Although nearly every fisherman has adamant preferences in catch, trends in species popularity are apparent. In recent years a dozen varieties of trout and salmon seem to have been favored and, of these, there appears to be a partiality for coho, Chinook (king) salmon, steelhead, and lake trout.

Introduced in 1966 and 1967 to counteract the losses of native game fish, these salmon have proven the strategy to be successful by thriving on the vast stocks of alewives. The coho is available to large numbers of people because it is caught within ten miles of the shore in the upper twenty to forty feet of water in summer and in fall near the mouths of spawning streams. While the coho adult averages about eight pounds, master anglers will tell of twenty pounders. The Chinook, averaging twenty-two pounds, does not jump and roll like the coho but lurks closer to the bottom.

The lake trout are Great Lakes natives now making a comeback after decimation by the sea lamprey in the early 1960s. The steelhead, commonly five to twenty pounds, is usually found in big waters but also may be sighted within a mile of shore in less than fifty-foot depths. The lake trout, which averages ten pounds, is a deep-, cold-water fish that may also be caught in inland lakes; and in the spring it may be taken in the lake-edge shallows.

The fisherman is as much hooked as these salmon and trout, because these fish offer the thrilling potential of *the big one*: Coho are reported above thirty-five pounds and over forty inches long. The Chinook has been brought in at fifty pounds.

More traditional favorite prize catches in the Great Lakes and smaller, satellite lakes are the walleye, muskellunge, and northern pike. Largemouth and smallmouth

From the days of the voyageurs' birchbarks, the canoe continues to be a favorite way to travel the lakes.

RONALD MORREIM

With five inland seas and hundreds of thousands of smaller lakes and streams,
Great Lakes country is a fresh-water fisherman's paradise.

bass are exciting sport fish and make mouth-watering camp dinners.

For the indifferent fisherman who is just out for casual action, there are some 240 species in the waters of the region. Some of the smaller lakes have only limited varieties; others are a teeming catalog. Every state publishes directories showing where to find specific game fish, including which streams have been stocked with what varieties and where they may be expected to spawn.

Ice fishing is one of the biggest sports in the region. On western Lake Erie, especially near the islands, fishing shanties made of canvas over light wooden frames dot the ice for miles. The sportsmen who are physicians place large red crosses on top of their shanties so that the Island Airline (a fleet of three Ford Trimotors) can find them and wigwag them ashore in case of emergency.

On Minnesota's Mille Lac three thousand walleye fishermen can be seen on twenty square miles of ice even at 25°

below zero. The parka-clad fisherman cuts a hole in 32-inch ice and pushes a heated canvas shanty over it. Then, bare-fingered, he puts a minnow on his hook, breaks the skim of ice that has already formed over the hole, drops in his line, and puts on his mitts. He may be wearing electrically heated socks and using a candle-heated minnow bucket. If he is watching two holes at once, he may rig a pop-up, which triggers a red flag when he gets a bite.

An observer can quickly see whose luck (skill) is best. Since the landed fish freeze board stiff almost instantly, the fisherman merely stabs them nose down into the snow, forming a picket fence around his shanty. Off the Wisconsin shore one sees men carrying 100-pound frozen sturgeon on their shoulders like logs. An average sturgeon weighs 50 pounds; unusual catches top 160 pounds.

Game wardens patrol the lakes in propeller-driven ski-mobiles with retractable wheels. Although game supervision is tightening, officials in all the Great Lakes states

More than a million pleasure boats ply the seemingly endless channels of the Great Lakes
and St. Lawrence waterways. This is the Ontario Place marina, Toronto.

and provinces actually court the sport fisherman, for he comprises a large part of their tourism, but one who is friendly to the environment.

O
N SUMMER WEEKENDS the Great Lakes and its tributaries blossom with boats. The Sunday flotilla of car-top outboards, trailered boats, inboard and outboard cabin cruisers, and sail vessels represents a dramatic subculture.

Few people beyond the shore settlements realize the scope of this waterborne way of life. Almost half the numbered pleasure boats in the United States are registered in the eight Great Lakes states. Of the 2½ million Great Lakes state registrations, it is estimated that more than 1½ million travel Great Lakes regional waters. This still leaves uncounted the legions of far-ranging fishermen without boats who carefully stow their precious outboard motors in car trunks, renting craft when they reach their favorite waters hundreds of miles from home.

Boat-industry studies on the Great Lakes indicate that nearly half the owners of outboard boats and motors use their equipment principally for water-skiing. The sport has become highly organized, with fifty-three water-ski clubs in the region. Members who hold regular jobs dur-

ing the week ski all weekend and evenings from March to November, the hearty early-spring icebreakers not even wearing wet suits. Regular tournaments are held, with such events as slalom skiing, three-story pyramids, bare-foot skiing, and more recently kite-flying, a variation of hang-gliding.

Kite-flying is still for the very bold, but it has come a long way since the 1950s, when it first got off the water. The kite is generally a delta wing measuring about thirteen feet six inches, with which the skier soars as high as fourteen hundred feet, but more often two to three hundred feet. He is aloft for just a few minutes, and his flight is spectacular to watch.

A
NOTHER BIG SPORT is cruising, traveling long distances to see new shores and waters. The Great Lakes are considered the greatest cruising system anywhere: Their deep waters are as challenging as the ocean; their storms are savage; their variety of ports is exciting, from industrial Chicago to lovely Mackinac. The marinas encountered by the traveling cruiser vary from the swank Detroit Yacht Club to a plank floating between two oil drums at Pointe du Morte, Ontario, with a phone on a post on the shore bearing the sign, "*Pour le gaz, téléphonez Pierre DuPont ici. Il*

TOM BIEBER

The midcontinental climate provides plenty of snow and ice for winter sports. Numerous ski slopes have been developed in Minnesota, Wisconsin, Michigan, lower Ontario, and upper New York.

arrivera cinq heures avec le gaz." ("For gasoline, phone Pierre DuPont from here. He will arrive in five hours with the gasoline.")

The cruising sailboat skipper and the power-cruiser skipper each thinks the other a despoiler of the lakes. The power man feels the sails clog the narrows and are hazards to navigation; the sail skipper feels that the power cruiser pollutes the air and water with noise, fumes, and a rude wake. But both enjoy the thrill of self-reliance out of sight of shore and are slaves to the age-old challenge of the sea: to plot a course and reach that destination, outwitting the weather and discovering new sights in new waters.

Many of these cabin cruisers and sailboats are large, sleeping two to six, even eight or ten. While they range from 18 to 60 feet long, most are in the 26- to 36-foot class. The large powerboats tend to be twin screws with two 300-horsepower engines, with fuel capacity for eleven to

eighteen hours of continuous operation in normal weather. They are usually radio equipped, monitoring a call-and-distress channel and switching to a working channel for transmission of ship-to-shore or ship-to-ship traffic. It is common for two or three boats to travel together on long cruises, staying in touch by radio in fog or bad weather.

The boats hold their value well; and one encounters many a highly varnished, painted, and sparkling thirty-year-old vessel in the hands of its fifth or sixth loving owner. Surprisingly, large boats are not necessarily owned by the wealthy. Owners will mortgage their lives for the boat; some sell their homes and live on their cruisers.

A most compelling aspect of Great Lakes cruising is the surprising distances one can travel and the considerable portion of the continent one can reach from these waters. From Detroit, for example, a cruiser can cross Lakes Erie and Ontario to Kingston, travel up the Rideau Canal to Ottawa, and tie up within a block of Parliament hill.

The Rideau was built by Col. John By to assure Canadians of water transport to their capital if the Americans ever denied them the St. Lawrence. Today the canal is maintained for recreational travel, a stairway of locks between lakes winding through breathtaking wilderness.

When traffic is heavy, a half dozen boats may crowd into a single lock. By hand crank, the lock tenders close the gate behind the vessels, which are in the bottom of a stone canyon. Overland tourists can look down on the boaters from the lock wall. The sluice gates open, pouring in millions of gallons to fill the lock, raising the boats twenty or thirty feet. To keep a boat from careening around in the turbulence as it rises, the crew runs the bite of a line around vertical cables on the lock walls fore and aft. The *Genoan* out of Vermilion, Ohio, skippered by NASA engineer Richard Kemp, came through equipped with a special fender for the locks and special hooks for gripping the lockwall cables. A stairway of six locks raises the boat up some of the steeper hills, and the skipper, looking astern, has the eerie sensation of climbing out of a deep valley.

From Ottawa, a cruiser can travel down the Ottawa River to Montreal, sail east or west on the St. Lawrence, or go down the Richelieu River Canal system to Lake Champlain. It can work its way down the Hudson to New York City. From New York City a cruiser can come up the Hudson as far as Albany, transfer to the New York Barge Canal, travel west across New York State, and enter Lake Erie near Buffalo. From there it can cruise all the way to the head of Lake Superior.

The same vessel leaving Detroit can instead go down the Mississippi River by first heading north and following the lakes around the Lower Peninsula of Michigan to Chicago. From there it can navigate the canal to the head of the Illinois River and down that to the Mississippi and the gulf.

Every cruiser owner plans a trip to what is called the sixth Great Lake, Georgian Bay, a giant body of water off Lake Huron that is entered between the tip of Bruce Peninsula and Manitoulin Island. Inside the bay the cruiser is in a world of ten thousand rocky islands.

From Port Severn on Georgian Bay, the cruiser can travel east through Canadian locks and lakes on the Trent–Severn Waterway—a linkage of rivers, lakes, and canals—all the way to Port Wellington on eastern Lake Ontario. This waterway, established by Canada to supply its out-

post at Mackinac when the Americans controlled the Great Lakes, is today maintained in beautiful condition for boaters, each lockmaster's station a parklike setting.

The cruiser that heads for Lake Superior travels north from Detroit via the St. Mary's River and Soo canal, along with a steady stream of iron ore ships funneling through the locks. Superior is for the adventurous; its harbors are few; its iron-ore shores can dance a vessel's compass in circles, and its thousand-foot water is cold.

The Great Lakes are dangerous, primarily because they look so safe. Because they have no tides or substantial currents and appear sheltered, the uninitiated approach them more casually than they would a similar expanse of ocean. When a storm kicks up, the friendly lake is suddenly a stranger.

From Grand Portage on Lake Superior, the Pigeon River leads to a whole watery empire upstream of literally hundreds of large and small lakes reaching toward Alaska. A dozen more inland waterways accessible from Great Lakes moorings make it impossible for boaters to wear out the adventure in a lifetime.

THE NATIONAL UPSURGE in skiing is mirrored in Great Lakes country, although the terrain is not notably mountainous. Reaching the ski slopes requires a considerable drive up into hills, where once the only intruders between snowfall and spring thaw were bears and the mail truck. Now natives stare in wonder as bumper-to-bumper cars wind up through their villages, as builders pay high prices for hillsides that once went for taxes, as Swiss-looking lodges mark the ski centers, as new ambulances scream along the narrow roads, and as city people in elastic pants ask if there is a hairdresser in the village.

The ski areas are quite well defined. The counties of Wisconsin from Kenosha to Wunderberg (just south of Sheboygan) are excellent. Skiing diminishes immediately to the north, except for a small area south of the city of Green Bay, but becomes heavy again in an area that includes several counties under the northern Wisconsin border and laps over into the Upper Peninsula of Michigan. The north shore of Superior at the western and eastern extremities is great ski country, but too far from the cities to draw weekend crowds. Michigan's Lower Peninsula probably has the largest number of ski tows, the majority of them in the western third of the peninsula, flaring out from north to west. The heaviest concentration of slopes clusters around the southeast shore of Georgian Bay. Upper New York State and the Laurentian Mountains above Montreal also draw heavily.

More and more people are hiking, camping, and backpacking in this region, making use of the spectacular trails recently built in national and state parks. Despite the high traffic, the most popular trails have not yet suffered from overcrowding.

Bruce Trail, described previously, is the best known of all, some 433 miles from Niagara Falls to the very tip of Bruce Peninsula at Tobermory. On Bruce Peninsula's counterpart, the Door Peninsula demarking Green Bay, the short Ahnapee Trail runs along the peninsula from Algoma, Wisconsin, out to Sturgeon Bay. Between these two, in the northern half of Michigan's Lower Peninsula, is a wonderfully scenic wilderness trail starting from Tawas Bay at the mouth of Saginaw Bay and running northwest through Huron National Forest up the Au Sable River to Au Sable State Forest.

Through Wisconsin thread two especially rugged trails. One is the hundred-mile Tuscobia Park Falls Trail running from Park Falls west through a vast swamp between the Chippewa and Thornapple rivers to Haugen on U.S. Route 53. The other—a favorite of hikers who are fascinated by geological phenomena—is Ice Age Glacial Trail, a short but fascinating trip through Kettle Moraine State Forest just inland of Sheboygan, Wisconsin.

There are many such pathways but the hiker who abjures the formally designated trails is not handicapped. Vast regions of the western Great Lakes have been set aside for the pleasure of the public as national, state, and provincial parks, forests, and wilderness areas. These parks and forests are woven with trails, not specifically equipped or designated for hiking, but more exciting to some mavericks for that very reason. A detailed guide to trails in the region, *Hiking Trails in the Midwest* by Daniel Sullivan, covers all the Great Lakes environs except for New York and Quebec, and contains maps, illustrations, and advice.

The camper also finds plenty of room in national and state parks, even though he presently must search harder to find it. The backpack camper has little trouble, but the heavily equipped recreational-vehicle camper, who brings everything including the sink, is increasingly limited to trailer parks, where he is losing the feel of the wild.

For both hiking and camping, the eastern lakes—Erie and Ontario—have limited facilities on the American side. Most of these are small state parks, definitely not of the wilderness variety, and often nothing more than a small, manicured area surrounding a historic site.

The large wilderness parks on the United States side are concentrated in Michigan, Wisconsin, and Minnesota. (See the box below.) The Lower Peninsula of Michigan, above a line from Bay City west to Silver Lake, is nearly three-quarters forest preserve; the Upper Peninsula is even more than that. These forests are so vast that one needs advice on where the public entrances and park areas are located.

The land around the three western Great Lakes is drained by many of the wild and scenic rivers, like the Escanaba in the Upper Peninsula, the Au Sable and Muskegon in the Lower Peninsula, and the Pine, Popple, and Wolf in Wisconsin. These regions do not have official hiking trails, but they do have trails scarcely touched since the Indians used them.

A CONCENTRATION OF WILDERNESS PARKS

MICHIGAN—UPPER PENINSULA	MICHIGAN—LOWER PENINSULA
Baraga State Forest	Hardwood State Forest
Escanaba R. State Forest	Huron Nat'l. Forest
Ford R. State Forest	Manistee Nat'l. Forest
Grand Sable State Forest	Marquette State Forest
Hiawatha Nat'l. Forest	Missaukee State Forest
Iron Range State Forest	Oscoda State Forest
Isle Royale Nat'l. Park	Thunder Bay R. State Forest
L. Superior State Forest	
Mackinac State Forest	
Manistique R. State Forest	WISCONSIN
Michigamme State Forest	Chequamegon Nat'l. Forest
Miswabic State Forest	
Munuscong State Forest	Nicolet Nat'l. Forest
Ottawa Nat'l. Forest	N. Highland State Forest
Tahquamenon R. State Forest	MINNESOTA
	Superior Nat'l. Forest

CANADA

Algonquin Provincial Park	Mississagi Provincial Park
Gatineau Provincial Park	Pukaskwa Nat'l. Park
Killarney Provincial Park	Quetico Provincial Park
L. Superior Provincial Park	Voyageurs Nat'l. Park

The northern rim of the lakes, unlike their urbanized southern shores, offers much unspoiled wilderness to explore. Isle Royale, home of this moose calf, is one such place.

The eight states bordering the lakes have four national lakeshores, and they are buying shore land for public use as well. The entire region has 20 national parks; 11 national forests; and over 675 state parks (with new ones being added annually). Much of the Great Lakes country, including deep inland, is dotted with miniparks, public beaches, picnic grounds, and camping grounds used by vacationers traveling by bike, foot, and car, and in motorized campers.

Most states have built attractive and comfortable lodges in their parks. Although these are rustic in appearance, the departments of tourism have gone to great lengths to see that their efficiency is neither rustic nor bureaucratic.

Beyond the rustic in Great Lakes recreation is some elegance. Hidden away are grand old resorts like those in the historic parts of Canada, near Niagara Falls, along the Finger Lakes of New York, in the Thousand Islands and

Lake Erie islands, and on Wisconsin's Door Peninsula and Minnesota's northwest shore. In these hidden islands of quiet, a certain formality and nostalgia prevails, encouraging historic sightseeing, tennis, golf, and, believe it or not, croquet in front of the veranda in the evenings.

Typical of the old-timers is Mackinac Island, site of rambling old Grand Hotel, and possibly the Midwest's most exclusive resort. Host to nearly every presidential family, it features and enforces relief from the "rat race." The island's most garish feature is quiet; no autos are allowed. The entire Mackinac Straits area—every island, every shore, and every channel—is historic country, still displaying relics of the Jesuit missionaries, the Indian wars, and the fur wars. The waters conceal scores of distinguished shipwrecks. Visitors to this area tour these sights by day and return in the evenings to wooden hostelries gleaming in the dusk with the slight sheen of a hundred coats of paint.

CHAPTER 22

THE CHALLENGE AND THE PROMISE

The new battlefront: an ever-growing encroachment by man and his machines on the natural world of the inland seas

CAPTAIN ED HERTZ of the *Betty K* towed his notorious cargo up to the Center Street unloading dock in the Cuyahoga River, Cleveland. He ordered his lighter made fast and yelled ashore to owner John Vincent O'Dee, "Any chance to get another lighter? One more run to the winding basin yet today?" Hertz acted as if the *Betty K*'s cargo—twelve tons of water-rotted logs, debris, and oil she had skimmed off Cleveland harbor—was the most important on the Great Lakes.

Many agree.

The nation is generally aware of the severity of the region's environmental problem. However, very few know of the vigorous counterattack in progress on all fronts.

In a newspaper office five blocks away from the *Betty K*, Betty Klaric, for whom the boat is named, types the column in which for a decade she has been scolding, praising, encouraging, and exposing Great Lakes polluter populations, cities, and industries. She is one of a large corps of professionals—engineers, executives, scientists, politicians—whose full-time job is Great Lakes environment. They are augmented by an army of informed activist laymen who are extremely effective.

It is no wonder that the Great Lakes region was hit early. About 40 million Americans and Canadians occupy the Great Lakes basin. Of these, 29 million live right along the shore, which includes three great metropoles that extend from Milwaukee to Buffalo. Fourteen percent of the United States' population is crowded into this 4 percent of its land area. The watershed drains a population density four times the national average. And people pollute.

Here America's industrial belt churns out about 60 percent of the nation's iron ore, about half the nation's steel production, a high proportion of refined petroleum, chemicals, automobiles, and paper and food products. These industries employ a quarter of the nation's manufacturing work force. And manufacturing pollutes.

Strangely enough the same watershed contains a five-state strip of the corn-hog-wheat belt. And agriculture pollutes.

What brought this concentration of people and industry, though the fact is nearly forgotten, is the very water that is now threatened. In the beginning it carried explorers in by canoe and made possible the fur trade until the beaver were gone. It made possible the vast lumbering era, floating forests to market. It still makes possible the vast iron-coal-steel complex that forms the backbone of the Great Lakes economy; and it makes possible the vast manufacturing complex that is a big user of water—but it needs clean water.

Cleaning up the environment has become the Great Lakes future.

Today Lake Superior is crystal clear with only a few localized problem areas, chiefly at the western tip, from taconite tailings. With only a half million people on her shores, and these alert, Superior's future is bright. This is extremely fortunate for the nation, because if Superior became polluted the problem would hold little hope for many generations, since Superior's flush-out time is estimated at five hundred years.

Lake Huron's water quality is excellent except for

Great Lakes America is today working hard to re-create an environment that is wholesome for all species, whether fish, wildlife, or small boys.

ROHN ENGH

Industrial wastes that pollute the Great Lakes' greatest resource, clean water, are the target of massive clean-up campaigns by nearly every metropolis in the region.

localized premature aging in Saginaw Bay and along Au Sable River, Alpena, and Harbor Beach.

Michigan, the third most threatened lake after Erie and Ontario, receives effluent from industry, municipalities, and farm runoff. Since the flushing action in Michigan is slow, its water being entrapped by twin basins and lacking the strong straight-through flow of the other lakes, it is crucial to halt its pollution buildup. Flush-out time is estimated at one hundred years. The Calumet, Indiana, area especially overburdens the lake—600,000 people and 90 industries using 3,200 million gallons a day, according to studies by the Environmental Protection Agency (EPA).

The Fox River basin, with 500,000 people and high effluent industries (paper, food processing, and livestock), discharges a choking load into Green Bay, including 2,500,000 pounds of phosphorus annually from municipal sewage treatment plants.

Lake Ontario, though surrounded by only three million people, is downstream of all the others and receives their torrential pollution outflow plus the substantial Buffalo-Niagara electric power contribution.

That Lake Erie is nationally known as the most threatened is attested in the folk wit, "You can etch copper in Detroit River, plow western Lake Erie, set fire to the Cuyahoga, and walk across Buffalo River." What is hardly known is that it is the most correctable lake because of its fast three-year flushout.

Lake Erie's shores carry a terrible weight of population

and industry, practically solid from Detroit to Buffalo and Sarnia to Port Colborne, Ontario; and it is fed by heavily industrialized rivers like the Maumee coming from Fort Wayne, the Cuyahoga from Akron, and the mighty Detroit. Daily loads of phosphorus and nitrogen from several hundred unsewered or poorly sewered municipalities are staggering; tremendous nutrient-bearing silt runs off from farms, suburbs, highway construction, and housing developments; industrial wastes (acid, phenol, oil, and other chemicals) and crankcase oil from service stations are dumped since recovery has become uneconomic.

This impact is not just from the immediate shore. Millions of Americans are living on ground that slopes to Lake Erie from as far away as Wapakoneta, Ohio, and Fort Wayne, Indiana, one hundred miles inland.

The most damaging pollutants at this writing are the ubiquitous, invisible, overenriching chemicals that foster explosive algal growth, which in turn demands dissolved oxygen from the water, depriving the rest of the aquatic community. The chief nutrients involved are phosphorus and nitrogen. The main sources of these are municipal sewage and soil runoff.

The heavy input from large-city municipal waste is obvious, but safely hidden miles behind the shoreline is another heavy contributor—the beautiful inland farmscapes, highways, and suburban lawns, all sloping to the streams. The runoff and sewage from hundreds of pretty little villages is poorly treated or totally untreated. Worse, it is invisible.

Another major source of nutrient-laden runoff is aggressive land development, especially the filling in of marshes, which destroys nature's buffer zones, food factories, and flood storage tanks.

Soil runoff flushes at least 2.5 million tons of silt into Lake Erie annually. Loss of soil in the Maumee basin (Fort Wayne–Toledo) is estimated at .4 tons per acre per year. A third of the nitrogen entering Lake Erie is estimated to come from soil runoff, the balance largely from municipal outfalls. Discharged daily to Erie is over 120,000 pounds of phosphorus. Over 70 percent of it is believed to be from municipal sewage. Industry discharges many chemicals but, with exceptions, it contributes only small amounts of the nitrogen and phosphorus leading to eutrophication in Lake Erie.

The "dying lake" is a misconcept. Lake Erie is not dead but too much *alive*. Unfortunately, scientists with tower-

ing credentials have used the "dead sea" phraseology while accepting public funds to seek data for the charge.

Actually Lake Erie fish life equals the other four lakes *combined*—yielding about 100 million pounds per year commercially. Fishery has changed drastically from the high-value trout, burbot, whitefish, and walleye, but the notion that the lakes are now principally inhabited by carplike fish is erroneous.

Always unclarified is the fact that while U.S. commercial fishing in Lake Erie has plunged, Canadian fishing is booming. Canadians are applying aggressive modern business management to the ancient vocation while U.S. father-and-son operations are still underequipped and legally disadvantaged. Also, Canadians can legally market a smaller fish than Ohio fishermen.

"Lake Erie is an open sewer" has been a widely believed statement that discourages corrective action. Who wants to throw money down a sewer? Yet Lake Erie municipalities receive drinking water through offshore intakes with very little treatment and deliver it to other towns twenty miles inland, so the lake must not be "a sewer." Delivering nearly half the fish catch of all the Great Lakes, Lake Erie must not be biologically dead. Receiving a summer recreation crowd of millions on its beaches, Lake Erie must not be bacterially lethal. In a recent July, visitors to East Harbor State Park alone registered 1.7 million people for swimming, boating, camping, and fishing. This is only one of seventy-two public beaches and hundreds of private beaches on the U.S. side of Lake Erie.

The "Wet Desert" concept? From 1937 to 1955 Stone Institute of Hydrobiology sponsored a year-round staff of Ohio State University investigators at Put-in-Bay, Lake Erie, under the direction of Thomas H. Langlois. On that staff from 1948 to 1955 was Jacob Verduin (Botany Department, University of Southern Illinois), one of the most highly respected Great Lakes ecologists. He has continued a Lake Erie research program from 1955 to the present. People echo the headlines to him, "Dying Lake"; "Wet Desert"; "Open Sewer"; "Dead Sea," asking, "Is it true?"

"No," he replies. "Lake Erie is very much alive, blessed or cursed with a superabundance of plant nutrients. The waters of Bass Island region are used extensively for recreation. The yellow perch has largely displaced the walleye, the midges have displaced the mayflies; but the abundance of life contradicts the 'wet desert' concept. Moreover, the immense numbers of summer residents and visitors who ski on and swim in these waters do not seem to suffer from epidemics of waterborne diseases."

John E. Kinney, a problem-solving sanitary engineer, advisor to Great Lakes states, cities, and industries, and three congressional standing committees, states flatly, "Only a scientifically illiterate person will call Lake Erie a dead sea."

THE TRAFFIC, urban sprawl, billboards, and thermal, air, noise, and water pollutions that go with population density are all here around the lakes. There is not space for the full catalog. But throughout the Great Lakes region, a counterattack is in full stride, with governments, industries, and citizen groups participating.

The region has already developed veteran environmental troops, an achievement that can require two decades. Those involved are beyond podium evangelism and are down to the pragmatic—the science, the arm twisting, the budgeting, the sewer digging. The action generally has advanced beyond the paper snowstorm of initial studies and pamphleteering, which also consumes a decade. Today the action is in the courts, laboratories, legislatures, and industries, where working clean-up hardware is already in place.

Action is naturally not evenly advanced, either across the region or across the environmental problem board. Lagging notably are the campaigns against overdevelopment and overconsumption of energy. However, a massive water treatment effort is in vigorous motion. Gerald Remus, knowledgeable veteran of the environmental wars, operates the Great Lakes pollution hot spot—Detroit. He is also running the largest water pollution abatement construction program in North America.

Backhoes and trenchers are tearing up southeast Michigan and will be for at least five years. The pivotal Detroit water system serves seventy-six towns for water and eighty-seven for sewage (40 percent of the Michigan population). Remus has programmed sewer and water treatment construction approaching a half billion dollars for this one area, and the dollars are committed.

Although Detroit is now the heaviest municipal polluter on the lakes, it is far ahead of every other Great Lakes city in one respect, which will shortly pay off in an im-portantly cleaner Lake Erie; namely, Detroit now *controls* what is discharged into its river from sixty-seven municipalities.

"We've been able to do it in Detroit," Remus says, "because our area leadership in industry, CIO, UAW, League of Women Voters, and civic groups—being largely automotive people—understand costs, materials movement, and engineering. They know it is going to cost more, and they got the people up for it. That's what it takes."

Remus's phone rings constantly as legislators, councilmen, and area leaders call to confer and argue. Many want exceptions to the discharge rules for their constituents. With controlled patience, Remus marshals facts for them concerning load sizes and consequences.

"A big help to us in Detroit is that our industry understands we've got to go more and more to prevention," Remus says. "Being in the business of handling materials, they all understand it's no longer practical to make a mess and then move it."

Remus believes that a dollar in prevention buys three times as much depollution as a dollar in control: "Say the city runs low on funds, for example; cuts back on street cleaning. We get a two-inch rain. All that stuff goes in my sewers. I can get it out. Point is . . . it costs us $60 per dry ton to get it out of the water, whereas it costs only $20 a ton for the city to sweep it up and dispose of it. Same thing applies to *every* pollutant. Costs us more to get it out of the water than to grab it before it gets *in*." Each day now, vastly reduced loads of phosphate, bacteria, solids, oil, phenol, iron, and oxygen-demanding materials are flowing into Lake Erie from the four-and-a-half-county Detroit service area.

While this is the largest water clean-up action in progress on the Great Lakes, the other major metropolitan areas are doing the same to a lesser degree. In Ohio, New York, and Michigan coastal cities, motorists are fighting their way to work daily through torn-up roads where new sewer trunks are going in because states have cracked down on area development until septic-tank towns tie into water treatment plants. These same motorists have at home notification of assessments averaging perhaps $1,200 per house lot and instructions to tie their houses into the new systems at their own further expense, approximately $800 per house.

Environmental Science & Technology Journal states that in five years Cleveland will have the best sewage treatment system in the United States. Meanwhile, Toledo, with one of the most pollution-abatement-minded citizenries, has already authorized construction of a new treatment plant that is the largest public work in its history. The city also reorganized its department, installing a sophisticated professional staff, the only antipollution department in Ohio to have cabinet status. This department's ability is such that neighboring municipalities enter into contracts with it for professional assistance in solving water problems. Traceable to their efforts were pronounced improvements in the effluent of large and small corporations around Toledo (among them, Kaiser Jeep, Standard Oil, Gulf Oil Corporation, Toledo Edison, National Biscuit Company, Norfolk & Western R.R. Company, U.S. Coast Guard Station, DeVilbiss, Sun Oil Company, Bay Shore Edison Plant, Chevrolet, and Continental Aviation). Toledo furnishes water service to three Lake Erie counties.

Those lakeside cities that supply water treatment to many towns now exercise an interesting and important control function by refusing new connections to satellite communities not fully sewered. The states clamp a moratorium on new development, refusing permits for additional sewers until there is a tie to a *good* treatment plant.

Around major Great Lakes cities, committees of business, political, and lay leaders have formed, like the Cleveland-Akron watershed group (called the Cuyahoga River Basin Water Quality Committee), which aims to improve water management all along the Cuyahoga.

The research drive is intense. Scientists had been crying in the wind for fifty years that there was much we did not know about Great Lakes waters: the circulation of materials, the productivity of algae, the geochemistry of sediments, the activity under ice. For a long time no one had funds for them, but today nearly every major university in the region has a sophisticated Great Lakes research laboratory.

A crash program of concentrated research has been launched by Canada, too. Not waiting to construct buildings for its Canada Center for Inland Water—presently manned by seventy scientists plus support staff—Canada linked together fifty-eight large mobile homes like dominos at Burlington Bay on Lake Ontario. The missions charged to this project are: reporting the true conditions of the lakes, hydrologically, chemically, and biologically; describing the lakes' processes and interrelationships, creating computer models to enable man to predict conse-

In the face of burgeoning housing, like this development at Madison, Wisconsin, only inventive high-rise architecture and controlled density of population can save precious open areas from being devoured.

DANIEL S. BRODY

Harvesting is necessary to control weeds that thrive
in waste-enriched waters of Lake Mendota at Madison.

DANIEL S. BRODY

quences of man-made decision regarding use and abuse of
Lake Ontario—and, by extension, of all the Great Lakes.
Fifteen million dollars and nearly every Great Lakes environmental lab were enlisted, bringing to the action a
formidable fleet of research ships, aircraft, monitoring
buoys, towers, and underwater vehicles.

In this binational attack on lake pollution, Canada has
a special effectiveness because, while U.S. water research
is fragmented among seven states, scores of bureaus, and
hundreds of institutes, Canada has launched a unified
research drive in this single unit at Burlington.

Possibly the most important joint effort was the negotiation of an executive agreement for water equality in the
Great Lakes, which was later signed by President Nixon
and Prime Minister Trudeau. It sets maximum allowable
daily phosphorus discharge from all large municipal waste
treatment plants at one milligram per liter in Lakes Erie
and Ontario, and the St. Lawrence. Standards for other
waters are under negotiation. The agreement mandates
the Great Lakes Basin Commission to determine the water

quality degradation of Huron and Superior, and to formu-
late corrective plans.

On the activist-layman front, people are putting their
money, jobs, and reputations on the line for the Great
Lakes. For example, Mrs. Evelyn Stebbins, private citizen,
has worn out two cars traveling at her own expense from
Rocky River, Ohio, to Columbus, fighting lake pollution
in legislative committees. There are several thousand
others like her. Linked by deep purpose and a long list of
phone numbers, they can alert each other quickly to a
faltering senator, a new swamp-fill for a shopping mall, a
political pressure point who must be reached—"tonight."
Jim Storer, vice-president of a broadcasting chain, at the
risk of losing advertisers, runs a daily antipollution radio
series to save the lakes. Don Gebbon of the Sierra Club
spends six nights a week to the same end.

One Great Lakes environmentalist believes in taking
individual action.

In a factory near Chicago, a foreman suddenly asked,
"Where in hell is all the smoke coming from?" Some remembered that two nights before a slight, wiry service-
man climbed the seventy-foot industrial stack, measured
the opening, climbed down, and drove away in an
authentically battered pickup. The following night he returned with a large drumhead-type device, climbed the
stack, installed the device, and climbed down. He was
long gone when the foreman next day coughed out his in-
quiry about the smoke. A search finally revealed the stack
was capped. On the cap was a familiar signature—a sketch
of the face of a fox.

The Fox, who occasionally works with a small group of
friends, has become a legend along southern Lake Michigan. He blocks polluting smokestacks, plugs outlets that
are piping pollution into lakebound creeks, and piles junk
in the front yards of big polluters, leaving his mark—the
sketch of a fox head, frontal view. He has evaded a network
of plant guards, who are on alert for him and who have
caught a certain amount of pressure from their manage-
ments. But one Illinois plant raided by the Fox seven
times finally put in an efficient effluent treatment plant.

IF WE CAN REDUCE phosphorus entering the lakes, will
they recover? One of the most esteemed Great Lakes
scientists is Jacob Verduin, now at the University of Illinois. He pinpointed Lake Erie in his reply: "Lake Erie is a

*Gathering and analysis of water samples are important parts of the sophisticated and coordinated research
under way at the Canada Centre for Inland Waters in an effort to solve environmental problems.*

very open system. The western basin is flushed out at a rate of once every 2.4 months, the entire lake every three years. If plant nutrients were brought down to a severely limiting level, the stores of phosphorus on the bottom would be transported out in significant quantities. I predict that such measures would show beneficial results within as little as two years, and that most of the phosphorus stored on the bottom would be gone in ten years."

Robert D. Reitz, Ohio EPA biologist, has been analyzing bacteria and algal content at water intakes along the Ohio shore. All intake stations except Lorain show significant improvement or remain within criteria limits [of the law] for bacteria.

"The algae data," said Reitz, "indicate that the ratio of lake aging has returned to levels of the 1940s in the Port Clinton area and to the 1920s for Cleveland Harbor."

Various Great Lakes communities approach the future differently. Some, in the older regions, are fighting a rear-guard economic action against dwindling population; others are staving off too rapid growth; and still others, in the wild and island regions, are just fighting to be left alone to watch the centuries roll down.

Since the region is fragmented into several climates, nationalities, and landscapes, the future will not be monolithic. A tale of three very different cities tells a lot about the future.

Toronto—big, rich, and busy—leads those cities retaining youthful, unashamed boosterism. Fastest-growing major city on the continent, her conversation and media bubble a love affair with Progress—rotating spindle-top restaurants, gleaming glass high-rises, and rising tonnage through a port that employs fifty thousand people. It is boomtown grown up.

While murmuring the proper catchwords about building an environment with elbowroom for the average citizen, she is striding into a six-year, $250 million lakefront project to pack a thirty-five-story complex of office building, shopping plaza, hotel, and 2,500 luxury apartments between Yonge and York streets. Simultaneously, vast expansion of its port is in progress.

CANADA CENTRE FOR INLAND WATERS

Rondeau Provincial Park on Lake Erie is one of thousands of beaches and wilderness areas now being protected by the United States and Canada for the enjoyment of present and future generations.

There are many Torontos, and that will be one type of future in the Great Lakes. Canada, as a whole has an astonishing potential for economic growth and development, exceeding that of most other industrialized nations.

Traverse City, Michigan, represents another Great Lakes future that will be typical of many cities.

Grand Traverse Bay is a beautiful shoreline, rich with natural life, notched into the upper west coast of Michigan.

The area had recovered from the lumbermen and was slumbering away enjoying the fact that it was not Gary, Indiana, when citizens awoke to discover that two future superhighways from the south were aimed right at them, a fact which soon had advance scouts from the hospitality industry driving red stakes into the delicate shoreline.

Citizens around the bay went to the University of Michigan Sea Grant Program and asked for help in keeping the future onslaught of recreational development down to a level nature could support. The Sea Grant people showed them how to get organized and said that a good opening move would be to visit the statehouse and see what else might be in the planning that could affect Grand Traverse. What they found was two more highways on the drawing boards. The state tourism bureau, they discovered, was busy promoting Grand Traverse Bay. Already a small gold coast of four new pool-to-pool resort motels had sprung up, and in winter a motorized brigade of snowmobiles growled out onto the ice among the ice fishermen. Grand Traverse Bay citizens sat down to project what *else* might be coming their way from all sources. The list, corroborated by what had already happened to neighboring areas, shocked them.

Today a sophisticated, intelligent back pressure flows from Grand Traverse Bay to the Michigan statehouse, advising them in scientific and engineering terms of the limited tolerances of the land. Traverse City's committees, comprised of engineers, lawyers, and biologists, are polite, pragmatic, knowledgeable, and alert. They are educating their state legislators in immense detail and check regularly to see what other surprise plans against Grand Traverse are generating in what other state bureaus.

The citizens have no desire to cut off tourism; they actually need it. The effort is to divert the overburden of construction that negates the very type of recreation the area offers. As stated by Barney Tokay, who does business with a regular clientele of serious fishermen, "How the hell they gonna fish through a terra cotta curtain of hotels?"

MINNESOTA EXPERIMENTAL CITY (MXC), planned for completion in 1985, is to be located 120 miles north of Minneapolis on 50,000 acres in the birch and pine forests of "big north country."

A score of the trumpeted "planned cities" across the nation have failed. However, one factor in MXC's favor—when it selects a name better than a gasoline additive—is that its planning board looked not only forward but backward, spending eight years studying the failures of previous Shangri-Las. Additionally, the planners of this $12 billion city are not insurance and petroleum company investment portfolio managers or real estate sociologists. They include such experienced innovators as Athelstan

Spilhaus, oceanographer, physicist, meteorologist; architect Buckminster Fuller, of geodesic dome fame; economist Walter Heller; and architect Neil Pinney.

Present designs for MXC call for some wind power, some garbage-generated power, computer-run driverless minibuses, and moving sidewalks. An environment to attract a mix of agriculture and industry is planned to provide 130,000 jobs for a population of 250,000, who will have a chance to live in partnership with nature in the big north country.

While MXC could run into surprises as others before it have, this city starts with a powerful difference. Where other planned cities tried to adjust the land to the people with man-made lakes, irrigation of alkali flats, or pile reinforcement of a fragile shoreline to support millions of tons of high-rises, MXC is adjusting people to the land and planning such industry as benefits the environment.

MXC will be still another type of Great Lakes future.

"GO WEST!" was the cadence of a nineteenth-century America on the move, and west is still the direction of migration. Hence a key place to look for the 1985 picture of Great Lakes country is Minnesota. To prepare for the future, Minnesota put John Borchart, a geographer, and Donald Carrall, a planner, to work with a team figuring out what Minnesota might be like in 1985. Here is what they predict: Men will continue to leave the farms, and farms will be bigger and fewer; the economic base of small towns will probably shift to manufacturing. Population will rise around the major cities but not in them, continuing a twenty-year decline of center cities. Population increases will be oriented, not to railroads and flatland, but to highways, lakes, woods, and rolling land; this applies not only to homes but also to commercial-industrial development. Minnesota will probably shift emphasis from resource exploitation to resource management, for example, monitoring waste-water discharge from mining. The fantastic Hiawatha Valley and Lake Superior North Shore highways probably will be protected against developmental encroachment.

The first region of the continent to be ravaged by successive waves of fur men, lumbermen, fishermen, farm builders, and city builders all of whom strayed from nature's rules, Great Lakes America bids fair to be the first to come home.

Overleaf: Rising out of the ancient rock of Lake Superior's western shore, Split Rock Light stands as a tireless sentinel over the cold blue waters of the inland sea.

APPENDIX

CHRONOLOGY

1000 Possible Viking exploration.

1536 Frenchman Jacques Cartier sails up St. Lawrence in search of a route to China. At foot of Mount Royal he is stopped by the rapids. Names them *La Chine* (Lachine today) and plants French flag. Claims continent for Francis I.

1608 Samuel de Champlain founds Quebec.

1615 Champlain, Father of Canada, reaches Great Lakes via French River, Georgian Bay, Lake Huron. Remains unaware of Lakes Erie and Ontario.

1622 Étienne Brûlé, eighteen-year-old Frenchman turned Indian, reaches Lake Superior.

1634 Jean Nicolet discovers Lake Michigan.

1641 Jesuit Fathers Jogues and Rambault establish missions at Sault Ste. Marie; St. Ignace; near Ashland, Wisc., and at mouth of Fox River entering Green Bay.

1669 White men discover Lake Erie.

1673 Father Jacques Marquette and Louis Jolliet discover Mississippi.

1678 Father Louis Hennepin becomes first white man to. see Niagara Falls or at least to report it.

1679 Robert Cavelier, Sieur de la Salle, and crew launch first ship to be built and sailed on the Great Lakes, the vessel *Griffin* (60 feet), a fur boat. It disappears while traveling from Green Bay to Montreal and is never found.

1701 Antoine de la Mothe Cadillac builds French fort at present Detroit. Pivotal fort in future wars.

1754 Beginning of French and Indian War, which will become part of Seven Years' War in Europe.

1759 British Gen. James Wolfe storms Quebec, defeating Gen. Louis Joseph de Montcalm. Both killed.

1763 Canada is ceded to England by France at end of Seven Years' War.

1764 Pontiac's Indian coalition is defeated by British, giving control of Great Lakes to British.

1776 American Revolution starts trek of over 40,000 Loyalist Yankees into Great Lakes Canada.

1783 Treaty of Paris concludes American Revolution; establishes U.S.–Canadian Great Lakes boundary.

1787 Constitutional Ordinance of 1787 creates U.S. Northwest Territory, from which Great Lakes states of Ohio, Michigan, Indiana, Illinois, Wisconsin and part of Minnesota will eventually be formed.

1797 North West Fur Company builds first rudimentary lock at Soo (Sault Ste. Marie).

1803 Ohio admitted to the Union.

1808 John Jacob Astor founds American Fur Company.

1812 War of 1812 begins between United States and England.

1813 Battle of Lake Erie (September 10) near Put-in-Bay. Commo. Oliver Hazard Perry defeats British Capt. Robert Barclay, becomes the war's naval hero.

1814 War of 1812 ends with Treaty of Ghent.

1816 Digging of Erie Canal begins across upper New York State, connecting Lake Erie to the Hudson River and New York City.

1816 Canadians launch *The Frontenac*, first steamship on Great Lakes.

1816 Indiana admitted to the Union.

1817 Americans launch steamer *Ontario* (220 tons) at Sackets Harbor, N.Y.

1818 Illinois admitted to the Union.

1820 Sault Ste. Marie comes under American flag.

1825 Construction is begun on Welland Canal, which will bypass Niagara Falls and link Lakes Ontario and Erie.

1825 Erie Canal opens. Freight rate from Lake Erie to New York City plunges from $100 to $4 per ton.

1829 Welland Canal opens 326-foot lift via 40 locks.

1836 Michigan admitted to the Union.

1844 Iron and copper are discovered in Upper Peninsula of Michigan.

1848 Wisconsin admitted to the Union.

1853 Construction of Soo canal starts.

1855 Soo lock opens, making feasible the Great Lakes iron ore, coal, limestone triangle, which results in region's vast steel industry.

1858 Minnesota admitted to the Union.

1865–70 Peak of commercial sailing activity on Great Lakes; 2,000 vessels listed.

1867 The British provinces north of the Great Lakes confederate as the Dominion of Canada.

1871 Chicago fire.

1872 England's Bessemer conversion process is used in United States.

1882 *Onoko*, first iron freighter on Great Lakes, is launched at Cleveland.

1899 Ransom E. Olds begins the first commercial manufacture of automobiles in Detroit.

1908 Henry Ford introduces the revolutionary Model T.

1913 "The Big Storm"; 14 ships lost or wrecked.

1915 Most catastrophic Great Lakes shipwreck; steamer *Eastland* overturns at Chicago; 815 lives lost.

1916 "Black Friday" storm on Lake Erie takes toll of ships.

1927 Prince of Wales dedicates Peace Bridge over Niagara River between Buffalo, N.Y., and Port Erie, Ontario.

1929 Ambassador Bridge between Detroit and Windsor opens.

1930 Tunnel beneath Detroit River—between Detroit and Windsor—is opened.

1939 Blue Water Bridge between Port Huron and Sarnia is dedicated.

1957 Mackinac Bridge opens, linking Upper and Lower peninsulas of Michigan.

1959 St. Lawrence Seaway opens April 25.

1967 World Fair, Expo '67, celebrates Canada's centennial.

1973 American Shipbuilding launches the M/V *Roger Blough*, first 1,000-foot ore vessel, at Lorain, Ohio.

1985 Minnesota Experimental City (MXC), 120 miles north of Minneapolis, scheduled for completion.

SUGGESTED READING

General

Blue-Water Boundary by Alida Malkus; Hastings House, 1960.

The Great Lakes by Harlan Hatcher; Oxford University Press, 1944.

Great Lakes Country by Russell McKee; Thomas Y. Crowell, 1966.

The Great Lakes Reader by Walter Havighurst; Macmillan, 1969.

History of the Great Lakes, 2 vols., by J. B. Mansfield; Freshwater Press, 1972.

Inland Seas, quarterly journal of the Great Lakes Historical Society, Vermilion, Ohio.

Lake Erie by Harlan Hatcher; American Lakes Series, Bobbs-Merrill, 1945.

Lake Huron by Fred Landon; American Lakes Series, Bobbs-Merrill, 1944.

Lake Michigan by Milo M. Quaife; American Lakes Series, Bobbs-Merrill, 1944.

Lake Ontario by Arthur Pound; American Lakes Series, Bobbs-Merrill, 1945.

Lake Superior by Grace Lee Nute; American Lakes Series, Bobbs-Merrill, 1944.

Land of the Long Horizons by Walter Havighurst; Coward-McCann, 1960.

Land of Promise by Walter Havighurst; Macmillan, 1947.

Limnos Magazine, LesStrang Publishing Corp., Ann Arbor, Mich.

Pictorial History of the Great Lakes by Harlan Hatcher and Erich A. Walter; Crown, 1963.

Also the quarterlies issued by state and province historical societies bordering the lakes.

Nature

Exploring Canada from Sea to Sea edited by Robert L. Breeden; National Geographic Society, 1971.

The Fate of the Lakes by James P. Barry; Baker Book House, 1972.

Freshwater Whales by Richard J. Wright; Kent State University Press, 1969.

The Illustrated Natural History of Canada: The Great Lakes by Robert Thomas Allen; Natural Science of Canada, 1970.

Mammals of the Great Lakes Region by William H. Burt; University of Michigan Press, 1972.

Ohio Trees (rev. ed.) by F. W. Dean and L. C. Chadwick; Ohio State University Press, 1946.

History

Canada and the French-Canadian Question by Ramsay Cook; Macmillan of Canada, 1966.

The Genessee by Henry W. Clune; Rivers of America Series, Holt, Rinehart and Winston, 1963.

The Heartland by Robert McLaughlin and the Editors of Time-Life Books; Time Inc., 1967.

The Making of the Nation by William Kilbourn; Canadian Centennial Publishing Co., 1965.

Ohio Canal Era: A Case Study of Government and the Economy by Harry N. Scheiber; Ohio University Press, 1969.

The Ohio Canals by Frank N. Wilcox; Kent State University Press, 1969.

Ohio Scenes and Citizens by Grace Goulder; World, 1964.

The Road to Confederation by Donald Creighton; Macmillan of Canada, 1964.

The St. Lawrence by Henry Beston; Rivers of America Series, Holt, Rinehart, 1942.

Stars in the Water: The Story of the Erie Canal by George E. Condon; Doubleday, 1974.

The State of Ohio, Vol. VI, edited by Carl Wittke; Ohio State Archaeological and Historical Society, 1942.

Wolfe at Quebec by Christopher Hibbert; World, 1959.

Indians

Great Lakes Indians by William J. Kubiak; Baker Book House, 1970.

Indians of Ontario; Department of Indian Affairs and Northern Development, Indian Affairs Branch, Ottawa.

Indians on the Warpath by David C. Cooke; Dodd, Mead, 1957.

Tecumseh by Carl F. Klinck; Prentice-Hall, 1961.

Ships, Shipping, and Sailors

A Century of Iron and Men by Harlan Hatcher; Bobbs-Merrill, 1950.

Complete Guide to the Great Lakes by Andrew Hepburn; American Travel Series, Doubleday, 1962.

"Cruise Guide to Georgian Bay" by Marjorie Cohn Brazer; *Lakeland Boating,* March and April, 1972.

Freighters of Fortune by Norman Beasley; Harper & Brothers, 1930.

Great Lakes Log by John Lamour; Lamour Printing Co., 1971.

Great Stories of the Great Lakes by Dwight Boyer; Dodd, Mead, 1966.

The Honorable Peter White by Ralph D. Williams; Penton Publishing Co., 1907.

The Long Ships Passing by Walter Havighurst; Macmillan, 1942.

Lore of the Lakes by Dana T. Bowen; Dana T. Bowen, 1940.

Memories of the Lakes by Dana T. Bowen; Dana T. Bowen, 1946.

Recollections of Men and Events by Joseph G. Butler, Jr.; G. P. Putnam's Sons, 1927.

Ships of the Great Lakes by James P. Barry; Howell-North, 1973.

Shipwrecks of the Lakes by Dana T. Bowen; Dana T. Bowen, 1952.

Stories of the Great Lakes by Earl Parsons; Rob-Roy Graphic Arts, 1963.

Vein of Iron by Walter Havighurst; World, 1958.

ACKNOWLEDGMENTS

I am indebted to many authors in a broad way but especially to a corps of men who have been regularly reporting the Great Lakes for a quarter century from different specialized views: Walter Havighurst, whose books rediscovered the Great Lakes region as a special entity; Harlan Hatcher; James P. Barry; Dana Bowen; and from the previous century J. B. Mansfield, who wrote the broad-gauge 1,800-page *Great Lakes*, published in 1899 and republished in 1972 by Freshwater Press, Inc.

Special thanks are also due to Pauline Griffitts Fanslow for an administrative job of retrieving materials from eight states and two provinces, and for interviewing some of the many people who contributed special knowledge. I called for assistance in special areas from my previous colleagues, notably my former partner Frank Siedel, founder of "The Ohio Story" documentary radio and film series; Everett L. Dodrill, author of *Survival*; and John James, author of *Create New Plants and Flowers*.

Julia Green, staff writer on the *Wisconsin* Magazine and former staff member of Wisconsin Historical Society, compiled lists of sources. J. Michael Higgs, chairman, Wood Utilization, ATI, Ohio State University assisted with the forests of the region. Chief photo journalist Neil D. Ruenzel of the Ninth U.S. Coast Guard District helped with several chapters. F. W. Paulson, boating editor, *Field and Stream*, contributed special assistance in the area of recreation.

Two people who made this complex project happen by day-to-day determination are editors Patricia Kollings and Donald E. Bower.

Of the numerous libraries and historical societies assisting, I am especially grateful to Janet Coe Sanborn, History Department, Cleveland Public Library, and editor of *Inland Seas*, publication of the Great Lakes Society; Daniel R. Porter, Ohio Historical Society; and John A. Packard of the Lake Carriers Association.

William Topping of the Canadian consulate in Detroit found and lent twenty-eight documentary films for research.

From individual Great Lakes states, help has come from Departments of Planning, Natural Resources, Travel, Public Information, Development, and Conservation—especially from Richard L. Ross, executive planning officer, Wisconsin; Donald P. Yaeger, natural resources planner, Minnesota; William E. Tyson, executive secretary, St. Lawrence–Eastern Ontario Commission, New York; James A. Merritt, director of planning, Jefferson County, New York; Mary H. Biondi, historian, St. Lawrence County, New York; Richard L. Lehman, Department of Natural Resources, Michigan; Henry G. Williams, Jr., Office of Planning Services, New York; Richard B. Fernbach, State Planning Board, Pennsylvania; John A. Scott, Fisheries Division, Michigan; Robert Saalfeld, Great Lakes Fishery Commission, Michigan; Kathryn West, *Lakeland Boating* Magazine, Ann Arbor, Michigan; Matt Kaufman, Boating Industry Associations, Chicago; Great Lakes Basin Commission; Sault Ste. Marie Chamber of Commerce.

Help also was generously given by the Canadian Government Travel Bureau, particularly by Art Shearer, chief, A/V Photo Services; Maisie Clark, A/V Photographic Service Department; Stephen A. McNamee, travel trade and news editor; Ross McLean, Reference and Research Unit; Consul R. Allen Kilpatrick and April West Vyas, secretary, of the Canadian consulate in Cleveland; Madeleine Brock, Ministry of Industry and Tourism, Toronto.

My regret is that I will have omitted scores of people who furnished a letter, a book, or a memory of this 95,000-square-mile region.

William Donohue Ellis

INDEX

THE GREAT LAKES REGION
Physical Features

Scale in Miles

0   50   100   150

© Jeppesen & Co., Denver, Colo. Reprinted by permission
of the H. M. Gousha Co., proprietors, San Jose, Calif.

L. Abitibi

QUEBEC

L. Timiskaming

Cabonga Reservoir

Quebec ★

L. Timagami

L. Kipawa

St. Lawrence R.

Sudbury

L. Nipissing

Ottawa R.

Montreal

CANADA

GATINEAU PARK

Hull

LARNEY
OV. PARK

Ottawa

ALGONQUIN PROV. PARK

L. Champlain

Georgian Bay

ADIRONACK
MOUNTAINS

VERMONT

Bruce Peninsula

Thousand
Islands

Kingston

L. Simcoe

Petersborough

APPALACHIAN

Oshawa

LAKE ONTARIO

Toronto ★

Mohawk R.

Mississauga

Guelph

Oakville

Rochester

Syracuse

Kitchener

Hamilton

Cambridge

St. Catherines

Brantford

Niagara Falls

Niagara Falls

Finger Lakes

NEW YORK

London

Niagara R.

Buffalo

LAKE ERIE

Erie

Cleveland

ALLEGHENY PLATEAU

Youngstown

PENNSYLVANIA

Akron

New York

Canton

Pittsburgh

Philadelphia

The body type for this book is Baskerville, set by Mackenzie & Harris, Inc., San Francisco, California. The display faces are Bernhard Modern by Paul O. Giesey/Adcrafters, Portland, Oregon; Book Jacket Italic by Hazeltine Typesetting, Oakland, California. Color separations are by International Color Systems, Portland; printing and binding by Kingsport Press, Inc., Kingsport, Tennessee.

Design by Dannelle Pfeiffer